IMAGES
of America

GRANT COUNTY

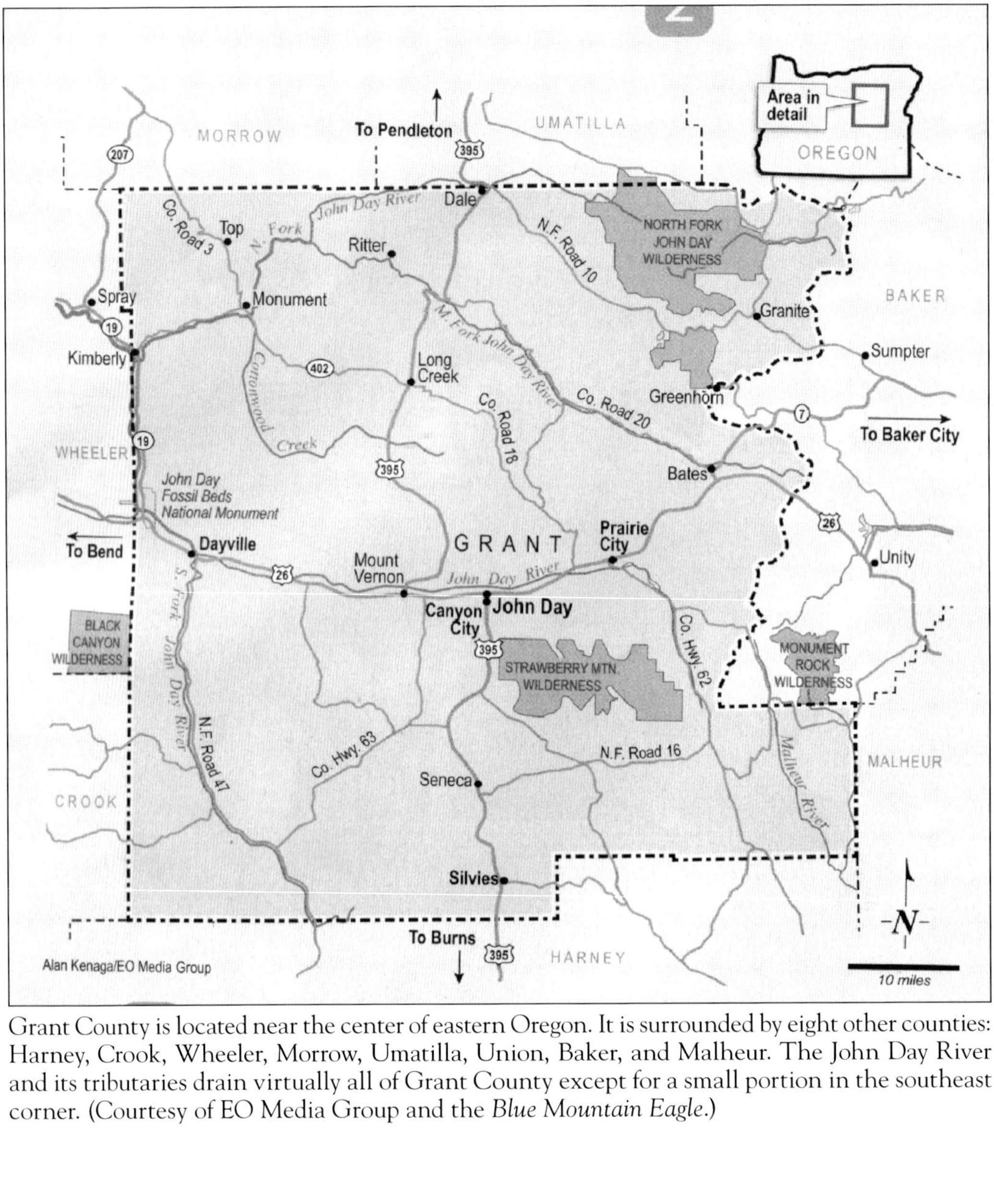

Grant County is located near the center of eastern Oregon. It is surrounded by eight other counties: Harney, Crook, Wheeler, Morrow, Umatilla, Union, Baker, and Malheur. The John Day River and its tributaries drain virtually all of Grant County except for a small portion in the southeast corner. (Courtesy of EO Media Group and the *Blue Mountain Eagle*.)

On the Cover: The cover photograph blends the old with the new. In the 1950s, the Trailways bus from Portland has just dropped off its passengers in front of Benson's Restaurant and Hotel, later Benson's Shoe Store in John Day. Others are waiting to board for the long trip to Boise, Idaho. Cattle are being driven through town to their summer range. (Courtesy of Oregon Historical Society.)

IMAGES
of America

GRANT COUNTY

George R. Miller

ARCADIA
PUBLISHING

ISBN 978-1-4671-2568-0

Published by Arcadia Publishing
Charleston, South Carolina

Printed in the United States of America

Library of Congress Control Number: 2016955655

For all general information, please contact Arcadia Publishing:
Telephone 843-853-2070
Fax 843-853-0044
E-mail sales@arcadiapublishing.com
For customer service and orders:
Toll-Free 1-888-313-2665

Visit us on the Internet at www.arcadiapublishing.com

This book is dedicated to the people of Grant County; to the farmers, ranchers, miners, lumbermen, cowboys, truck drivers, businessmen, and women; to all individuals who for over 150 years have worked hard to develop the area. They have struggled against the weather and other inconveniences, all the time seeking to improve the area they love.

Contents

Acknowledgments

Authors never work alone; at least this author doesn't. So many individuals have helped with the creation of this book that it will be difficult to mention them all. Grant County may be small, but its influence is widespread. Jayne Primrose, manager and head curator of the Grant County Historical Museum, spent many long hours searching for photographs that could be used in the book. Her services were invaluable, including use of the back room where the author worked. Two Gresham, Oregon, residents, Georgene Hansen-Witmer and Bob Smith, were both raised in Grant County. Bob worked in his father's grocery store, currently Chester's Market. Georgene, whose family connection to the area goes back nearly 150 years, provided pictures for use and reviewed all written material in the book from the introduction to the last chapter. Jack Southworth's history in the county goes back to when his great-grandfather settled in the area. He kept the author's comments valid. Mention something about Grant County to either of them and if they do not know about it, it did not happen. The curators at the Kam Wah Chung Museum, currently a state heritage site, the Grant County Ranch and Rodeo Museum, the Sumpter Valley Railway Depot/DeWitt Museum, and the John Day Fossil Beds National Monument all provided photographs and valuable information. Sean Hart, editor of the *Blue Mountain Eagle*, provided helpful hints and images. A lot of credit for this book goes to Arcadia editor Caroline Anderson. She was tough but kept the author going in the right direction. Last, but by no means least, credit goes to the author's wife, Janice. As with every book the author has written, she has proofread every word, several times. You would not be holding this book in your hands had it not been for the above individuals. My thanks go to all of them.

Unless otherwise noted, images are from Grant County Historical Museum files.

INTRODUCTION

Grant County was named after Gen. Ulysses S. Grant, the leader of the Northern armies during the Civil War. Earlier in his career, he was stationed at Fort Vancouver, located along the Columbia River where the town of Vancouver, Washington, is now. His assignment was to protect the increasing number of immigrants along the Oregon Trail. Grant County was created mainly from portions of Wasco County and a bit of Umatilla County on October 14, 1864. Although not the largest county in Oregon, it extends over 4,497 square miles, larger than some eastern states. The county ranges in elevation from less than 2,000 feet to over 9,000 feet. The climate is basically dry, with annual precipitation less than 15 inches a year to around 40 inches at the higher elevations, where around 150 inches of snow falls annually. There are no large towns with a population of over 5,000 in Grant County, but there are many small towns, some with less than 100 people. This book describes most of them and how they received their names and other interesting facts.

The cities within Grant County received their names from a variety of sources. Perhaps the most intriguing is the name John Day. In 1811, John Jacob Astor sent two expeditions, one overland and one around South America's Cape Horn, to establish a permanent settlement at the mouth of the Columbia River. A man by the name of John Day was part of the overland expedition. He probably never set foot within the county. His trip west was arduous, to say the least. He was sick and weak, and the main party abandoned him and a fellow traveler in the Hells Canyon region along the Snake River. At first assisted by friendly natives, who most likely saved their lives, they made it to the Columbia River. Here misfortune struck again. They were attacked by hostile natives, stripped of their clothing and anything to eat, and left for dead. Fortunately, they were rescued by some trappers who happened to be passing through the area. The location was near where the John Day River enters the Columbia River. The John Day River and its tributaries drain a large portion of Grant County. Hence we have the name John Day.

A few miles south of John Day is Canyon City. It was formed along a creek with steep canyon walls when gold was discovered in the area in 1862. It is currently the seat of Grant County. Now smaller than John Day, it once referred to the settlement to the north as "Lower Town."

Prairie City is located 15 miles east of John Day. As placer mining mostly destroyed a small settlement called Dixie, so named for its existence along Dixie Creek, the community was abandoned and a new town was established slightly north, where the creek enters the John Day River. The name is descriptive of areas in eastern Oregon.

On the western border of Grant County, neighboring Crook and Wheeler Counties, is Dayville. The current site is at the mouth of the South Fork of the John Day River. The name was created from the John Day River. The first post office was established on December 8, 1868, some three miles west of the current town.

The town of Silvies is in the extreme southern part of Grant County. In 1826, Peter Skene Ogden directed Antoine Sylvaille into the area to look for beaver. He found them along a stream that was named Sylvaille's River on his return. Over time the pronunciation was corrupted and it became known as Silvies River. The first post office was located along the river in Harney County. It was moved north to the southern part of Grant County in 1915.

Several towns were established in Oregon's high mountain valleys. Seneca is south of John Day. Once a thriving lumber town, the name was given in 1895 by Minnie Southworth, the first postmaster. Southworth seemed too long, so she suggested Seneca, since her sister-in-law was named Seneca Smith. Seneca has the distinction of having recorded Oregon's coldest temperature, minus 54 degrees. It shares that distinction with two other sites, Ukiah and Bates.

Long Creek, north of John Day, is in a high mountain valley. The name comes from the thought that the creek running through the town was the longest in this part of Oregon. Whether true or not, the name stuck. On June 3, 1894, a tornado swept through the eastern portions of this small town, demolishing many structures and leaving an estimated three people dead. Help was brought in from John Day to care for the injured. The author has placed the event on the adjusted Fujita scale as an F1, with winds of 73 to 112 miles per hour.

The town of Mount Vernon is west of John Day along the river. It has been said that a David Jenkins in the area owned a black stallion by the name of Mount Vernon and that is how the town received its name. During the Bannock War of 1878, the stallion was locked in a small stone building to protect him from the natives. The area is also known for the Belshaw prune developed there.

Nestled in the northwest corner of Grant County is the town of Monument. The town was named for a particular rock or mountain nearby that resembles a pulpit or rostrum.

Also in northwest Grant County is Ritter. The town is near some mineral hot springs. Joseph Ritter was a pioneer Baptist minister in the area. The springs were discovered by William Neal McDuffee, an early packer between Umatilla and the John Day mines.

Izee, west of Seneca, was named for the cattle brand IZ belonging to early resident M.N. Bonham. About 1885, Bonham homesteaded in the area. The town is located along the South Fork of the John Day River. Large quantities of bunch grass growing here did not go unnoticed by the early settlers.

In far western Grant County, Elizabeth C. Murphy suggested naming a town Kimberly. Records indicate that the Kimberly family was well known in the area. The town lies along the John Day River and is slightly more than a stone's throw from Wheeler County.

The town of Bates is found in northeast Grant County. The town was named after Paul C. Bates. He was successful in negotiating the purchase of timber lands by the Oregon Lumber Company. The train from Baker City to Prairie City would stop here for lunch.

In far northeast Grant County is the town of Granite. Originally called Granite City, it was established shortly after gold was discovered in Granite Creek in July 1862. Granite Creek was named for the granite rocks prevalent in the area.

One might think Top, in extreme northwest Grant County, received its name because of its location at the top of the county; not so. The name was suggested from one of the prominent residents, Top Reasner.

Susanville, west of Bates, was settled in 1865 due to the Elk Creek lode found in the area. It received its name from Susan Ward, one of the earliest inhabitants. The Susanville post office was closed in 1952.

There are other small towns in Grant County that have come into existence over the years because of the proximity of gold or heavy stands of timber. For the most part, they reached their peak, many with an operating post office, and then lost their identity or became ghost towns. This book explores the county, its towns, industries, and peculiarities from its early settlement to the mid-1960s.

One

The Towns and People of Grant County

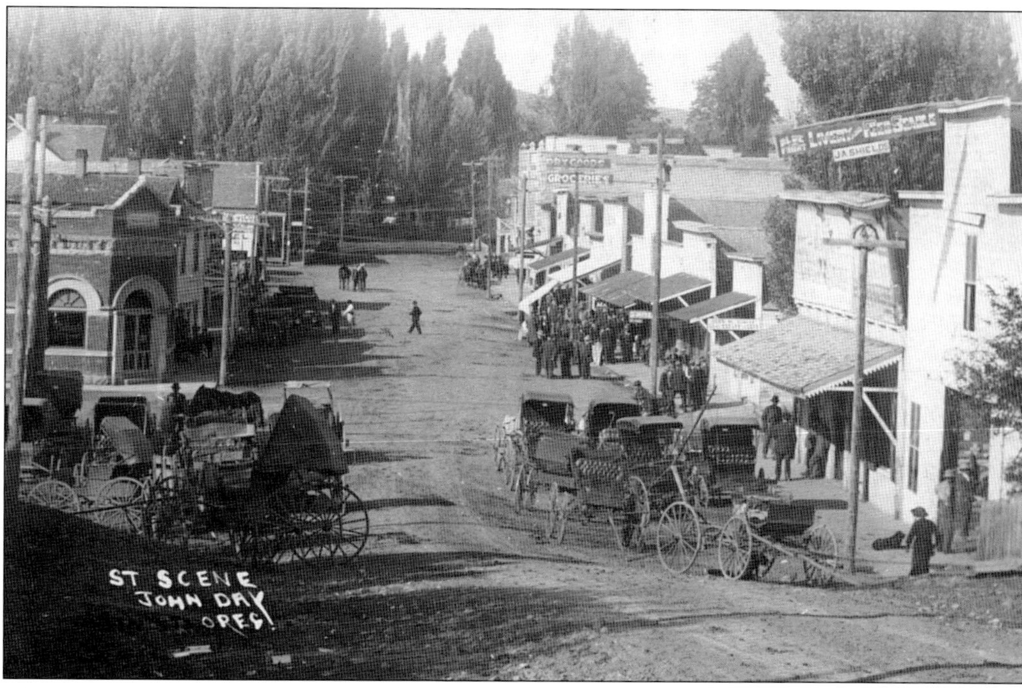

This photograph of John Day was taken around 1904 to 1910. It is looking west from the end of Main Street at the corner of Dayton Street. The image shows the Grant County Bank, Johnson and Parrish, and Blue Front Livery Stable. Today the population is around 2,000, much less than the estimated 5,000 that inhabited Canyon City to the south shortly after gold was discovered in June 1862. John Day was often referred to as "Lower Town" or "Tiger Town."

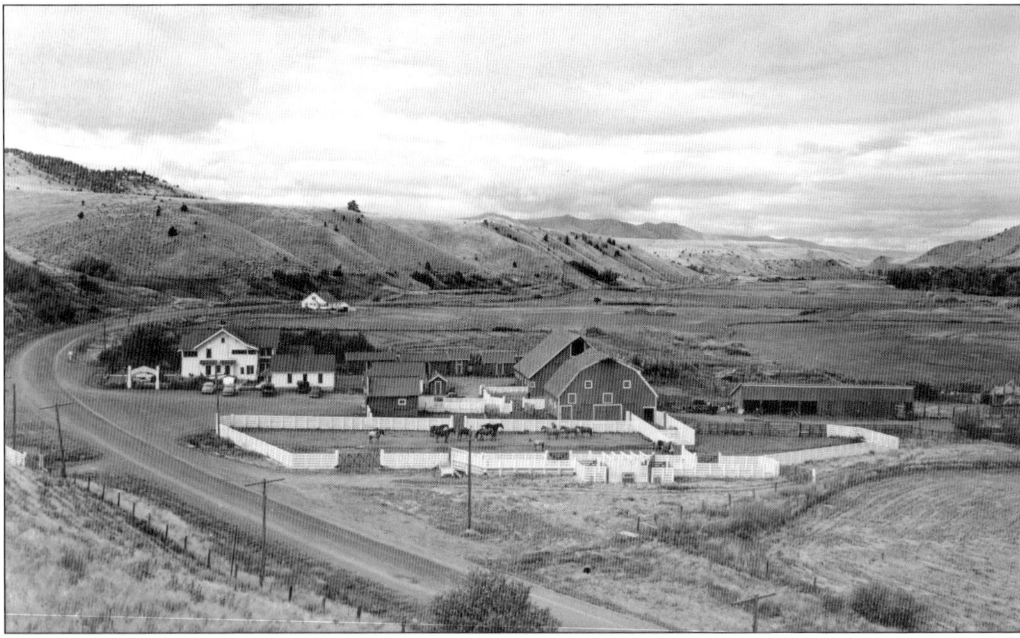

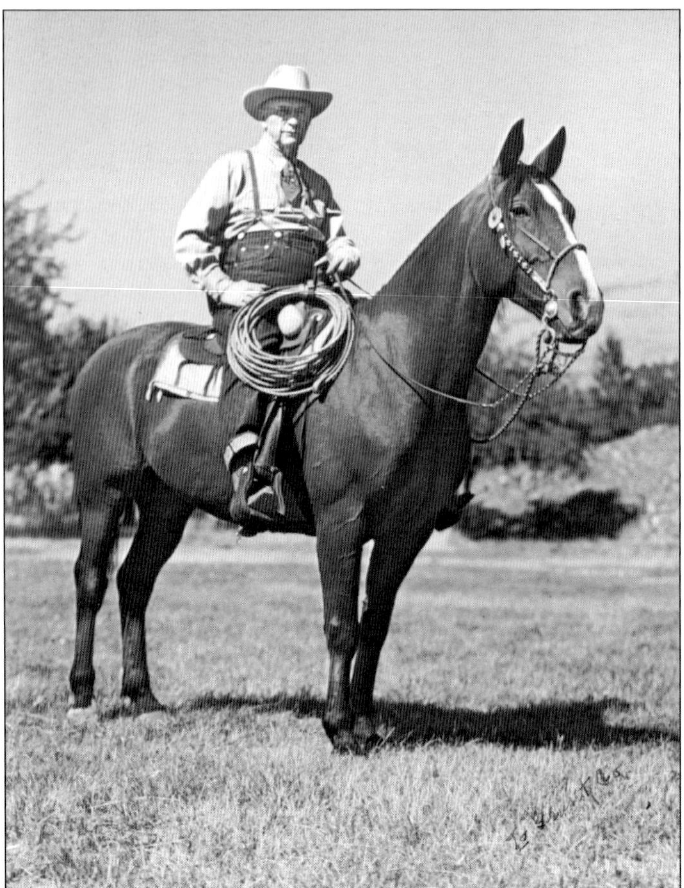

Herman Oliver is considered by many to be the best-known cattleman in Oregon. His name not only brings back memories but also innumerable favorable comments. His methods of breeding, feeding, and pasturing cattle were new and progressive, which attracted professors from Oregon State University. He also served on several state boards and committees. During the country's hard times in the 1930s, he was principal owner of the Grant County Bank, which stayed open when many other banks closed their doors. His ranch east of John Day, above, at one time stretched over 50,000 acres. He is shown at left riding his favorite horse.

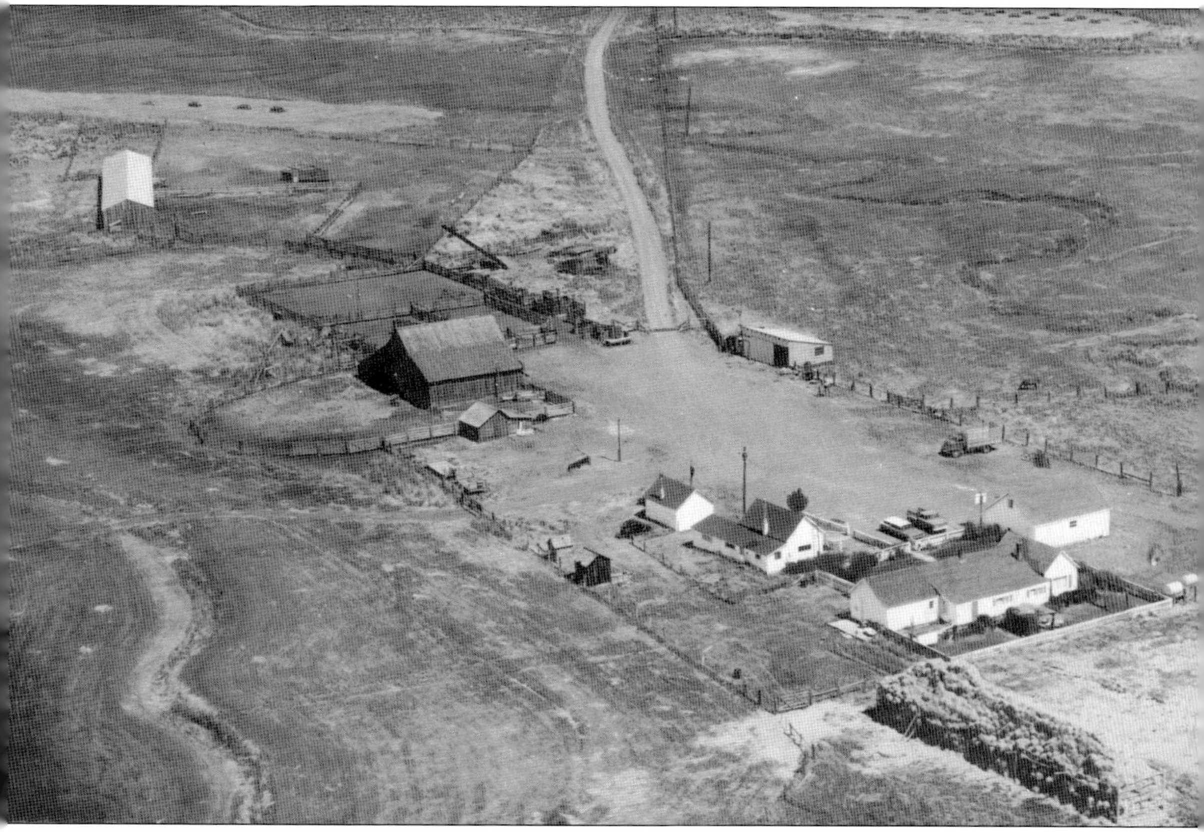

There are and have been many other well-known ranches in Grant County. The Southworth ranch near Seneca in Bear Valley is one. The Southworths go back to the early days of Grant County. The Southworth ranch was started by Jack Southworth's great-grandfather William Sawyer Southworth in 1885 as a 160-acre homestead. Today, their grazing rights encompass over 25,000 acres. The Southworths are some of the more progressive ranchers in the area. The ranch practices of preserving the environment have won them numerous awards, including Grant County Stockgrower of the Year in 2010 and Conservation Farm Award in 2009. Once, when Jack planted willows along the streams, he was scolded by his father. Those willows now provide needed shade for the streams and the inhabitants. The Southworth spread is shown above. (Courtesy of the Grant County Ranch and Rodeo Museum.)

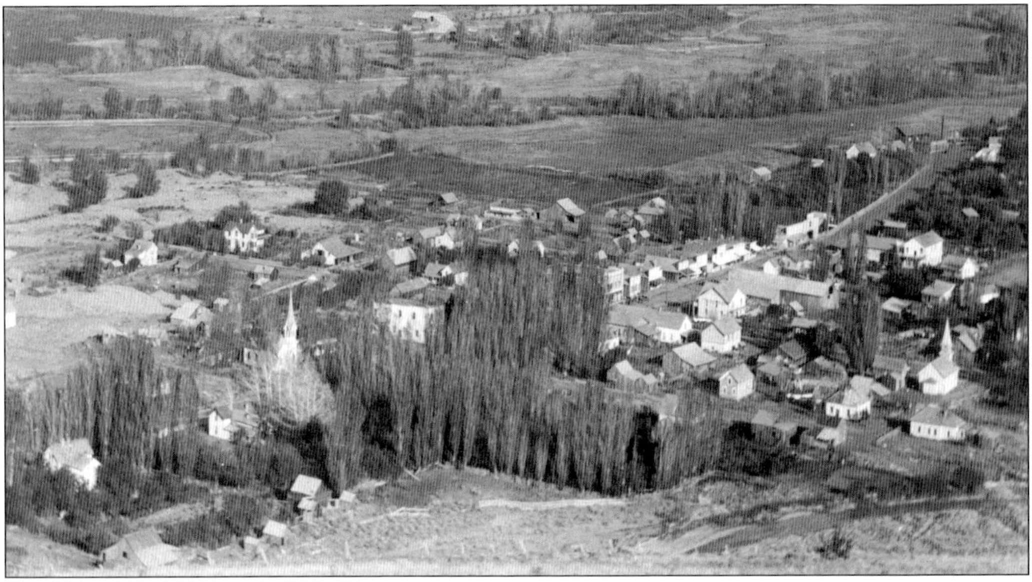

This early-1900s photograph of the John Day area was taken looking toward the northeast. It shows Highway 26 running from the upper right to the lower left. The Advent Christian Church is in the left foreground, the Methodist church is at right, the Johnson and Parrish building is in the center, and the Basford Roller Mill is at the top center.

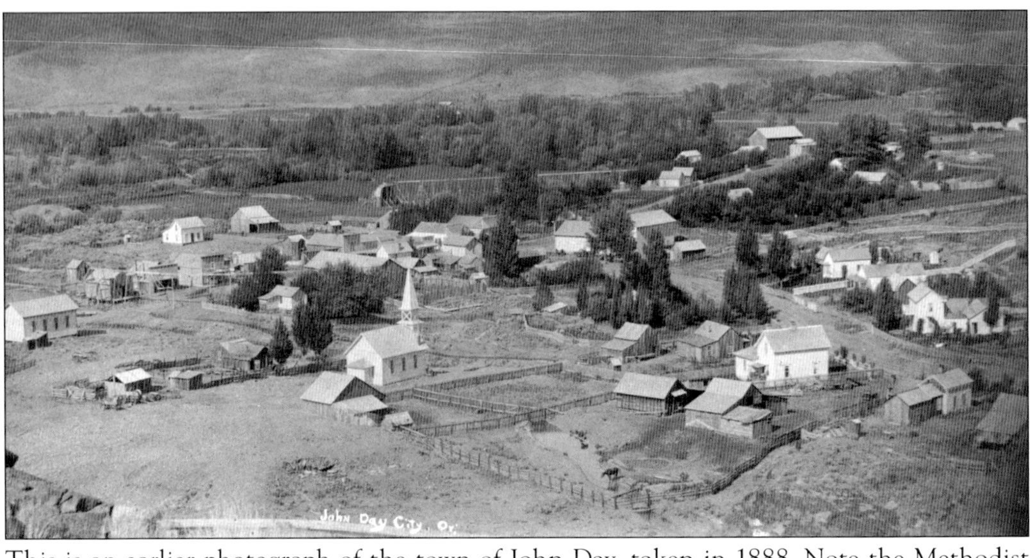

This is an earlier photograph of the town of John Day, taken in 1888. Note the Methodist church in the center of the photograph and how the town had changed in less than 20 years. The photograph was taken looking northeast, with the John Day River running through the grove of trees near the top.

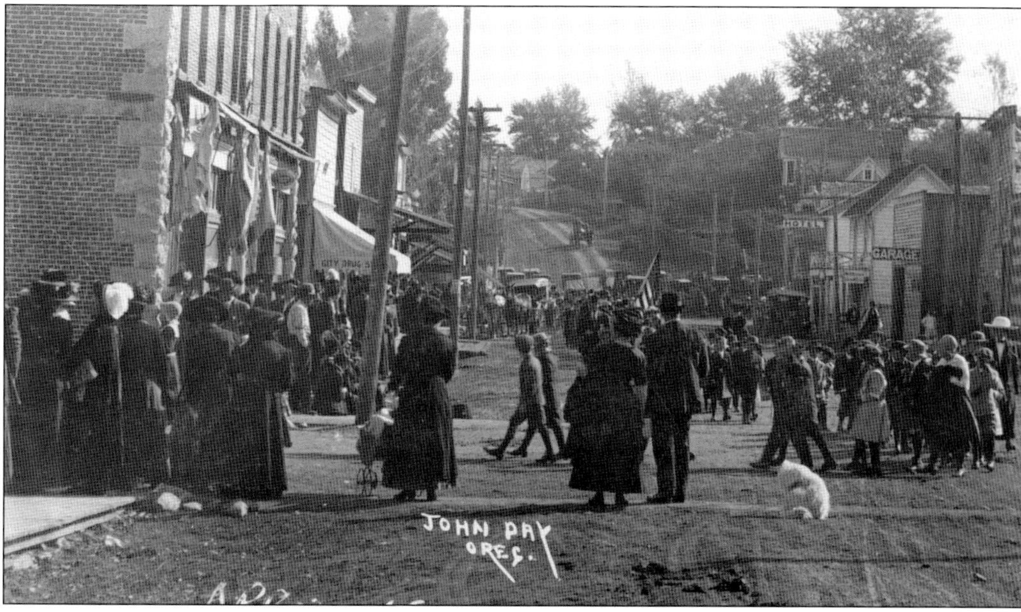

John Day is the largest city in Grant County. It is located along the John Day River and lies at the intersection of Highway 26, going east and west, and Highway 395, going north and south. This view was taken around 1910 looking east along the route of Highway 26 today. The large number of people wandering around and the flag suggest some sort of celebration, perhaps around Easter.

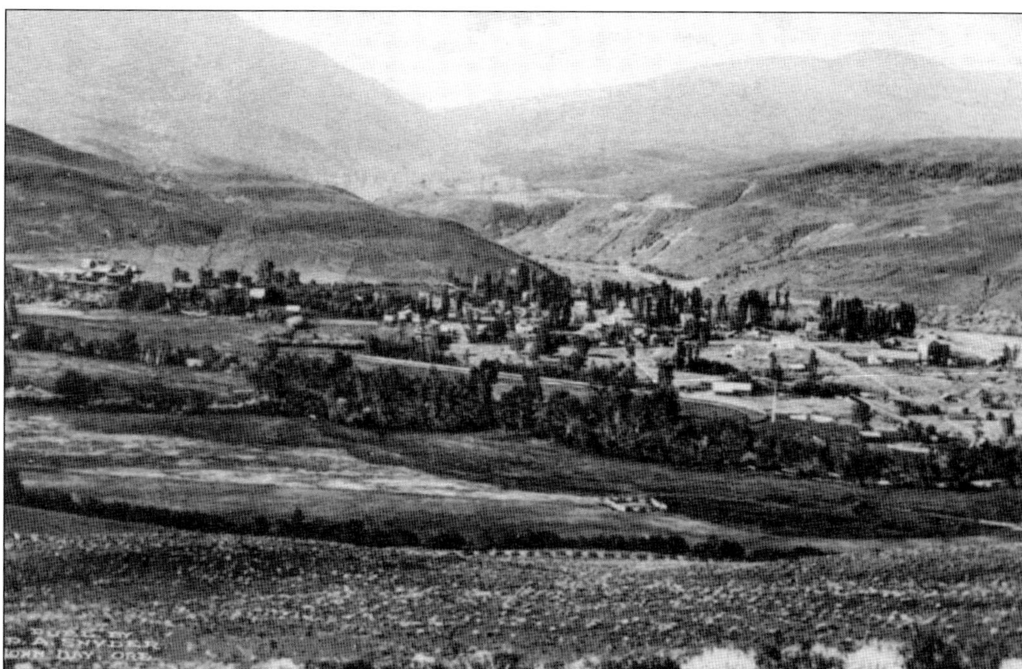

This photograph shows John Day around 1910 looking south, with Canyon Creek in the background and the John Day River in the foreground. Main Street runs east to west through the center of the photograph. On the right, it is intersected by Canyon Creek Boulevard.

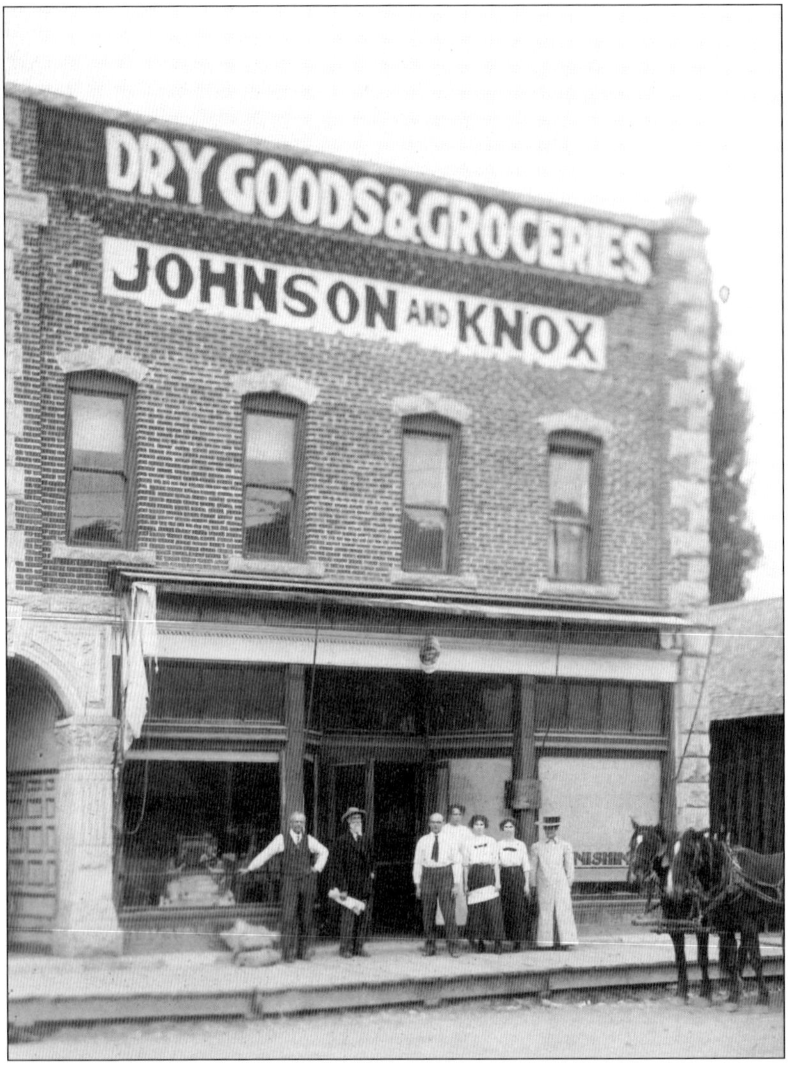

The Johnson and Knox dry goods store was a popular shopping place in the early 1900s in John Day. It was located along Main Street and served the area within 50 miles. Note below all the canned goods on the shelves and the jewelry items in the case with a display of hats on top. From left to right are E.L. Knox, Carl Tucker, and, behind the counter, Theron Knox and Louise Conner.

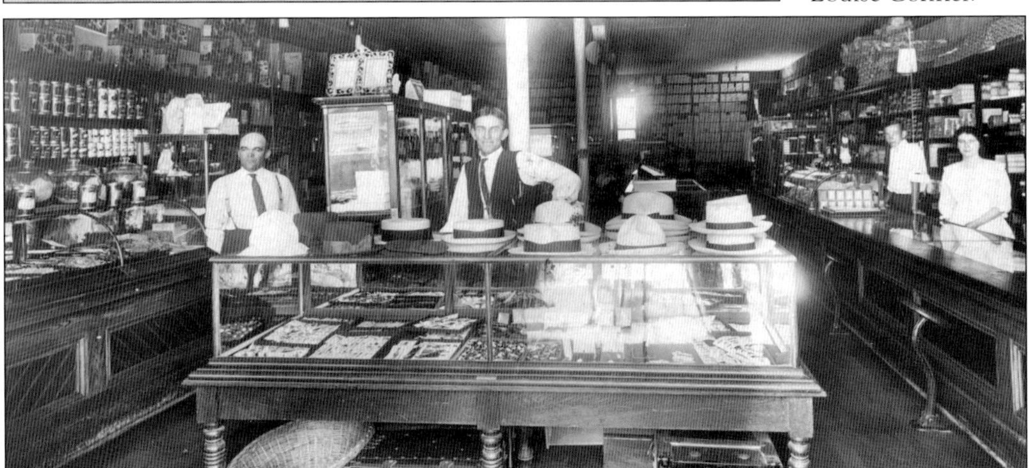

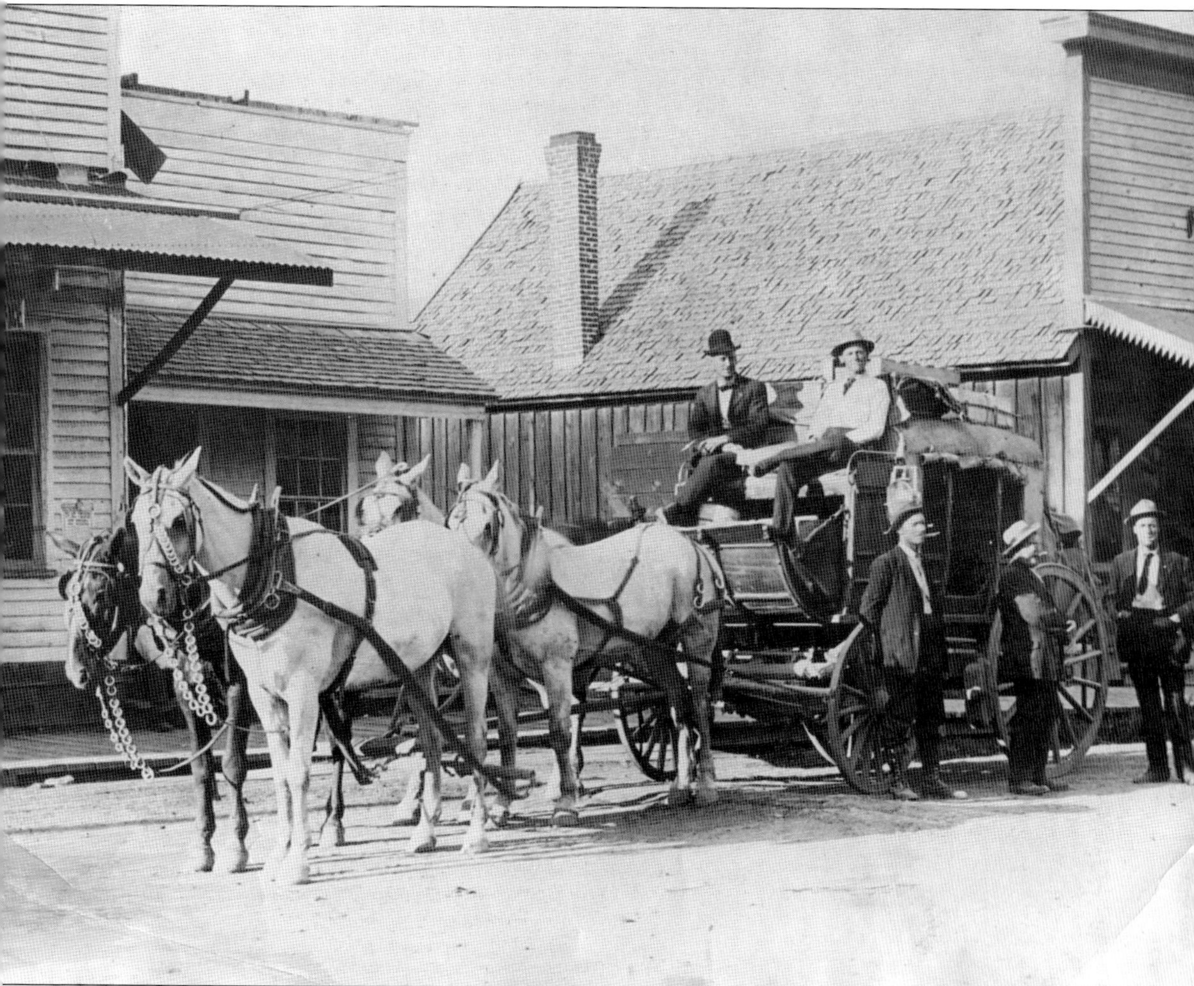

Travel in the area in the 1800s was generally by stagecoach. This c. 1880 photograph shows the stage in front of the post office in John Day. Stage lines ran from The Dalles to John Day, John Day to Baker City, and John Day to Burns. The trip from The Dalles to John Day took three days, with overnight stops generally in Antelope and Mitchell. These times and stops depended heavily on the weather. Travel was by what was called the Military Road, but to call it a "road" was perhaps a misnomer. The teams of horses, be it four or six, had to be changed often. Stops were often at farm houses. Rivers and creeks had to be forded, as there were no bridges. The driver was in charge, and riders did what he told them to do. He was accompanied by one other person, usually another man with a rifle.

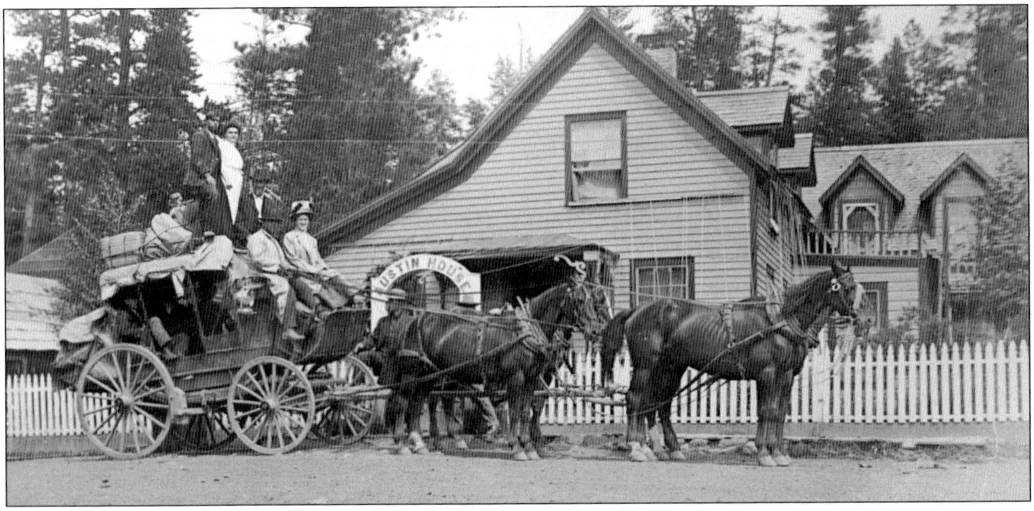

The stagecoach line to Baker City always stopped at Austin in the mountains. Whether going east or west, it had to cross two summits of over 5,000 feet. This stage, sitting in front of Austin House, will soon wind its way down the mountains to Prairie City after the travelers have been served a sumptuous feast.

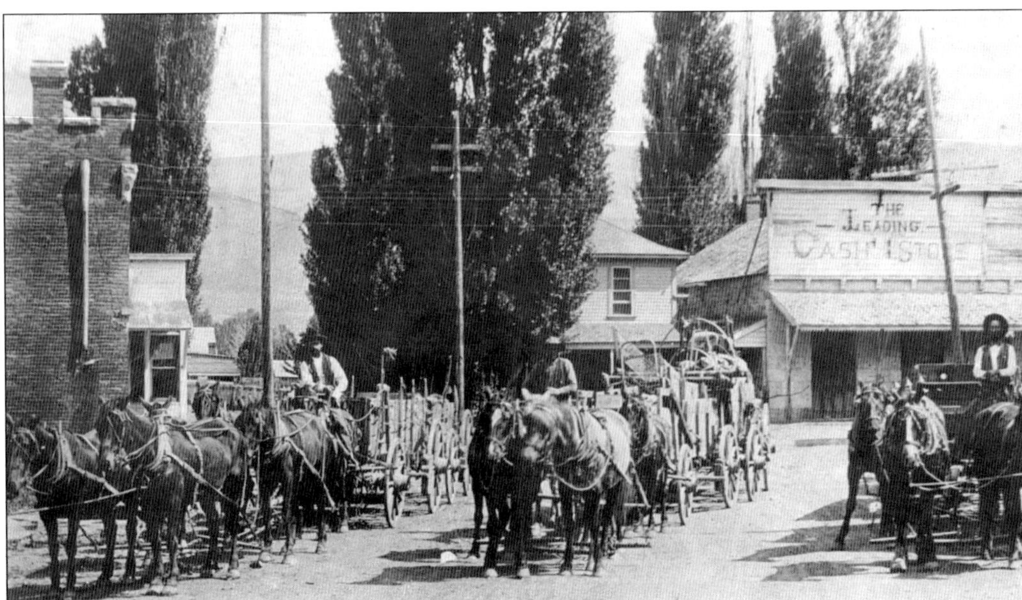

Mule and horse teams were the only means of bringing goods to the miners. They were also how any commodities left the area. The trip to and from The Dalles traveled the same route along the old Military Road. Mostly six-horse teams were used rather than four due to the large amount of goods packed on the wagons.

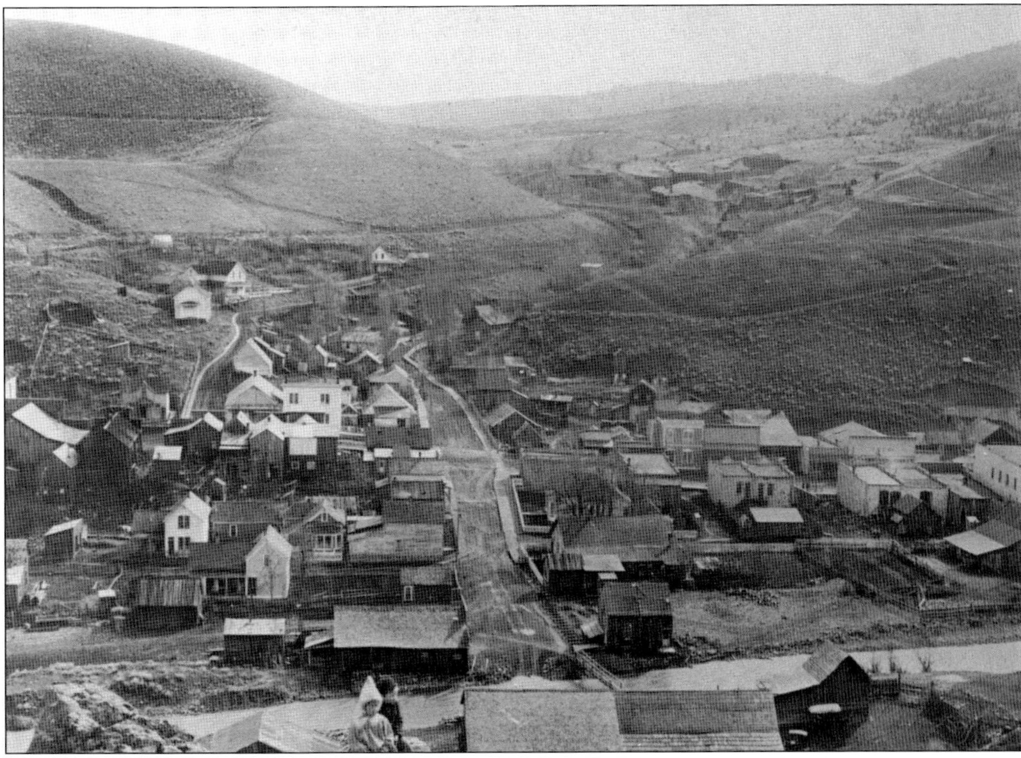

When gold was discovered in the Canyon Creek area in 1862, thousands of miners were drawn into the region. Canyon Creek drains the landscape to the south with steep canyon walls. This image, however, looks east with Canyon Creek in the foreground.

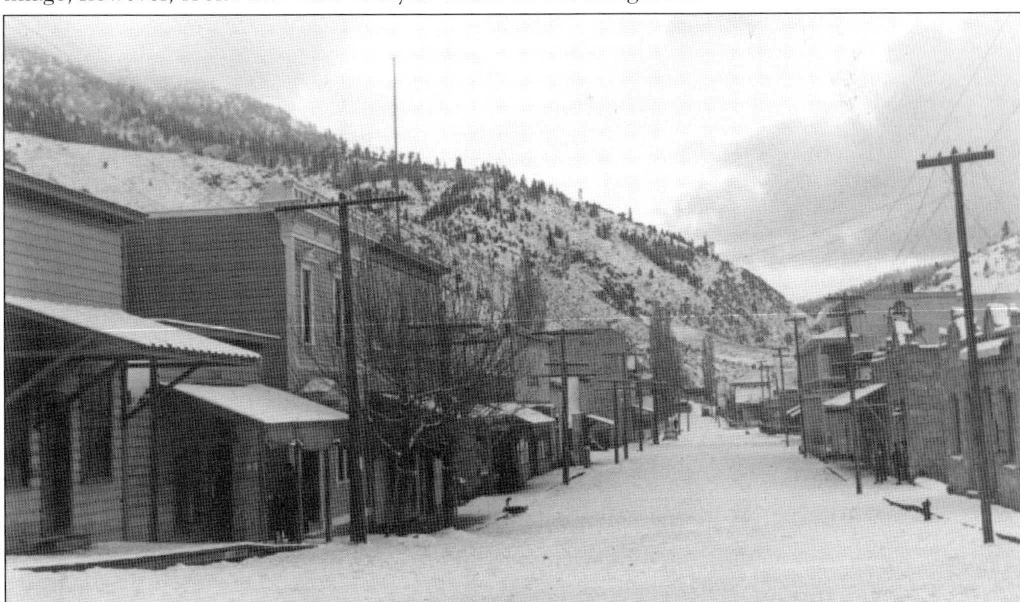

This image shows Main Street in Canyon City looking south around 1895. From late November to early March, most of the precipitation in eastern Oregon falls as snow. Amounts vary greatly from lower elevations such as Canyon City to higher elevations in the mountains to the south.

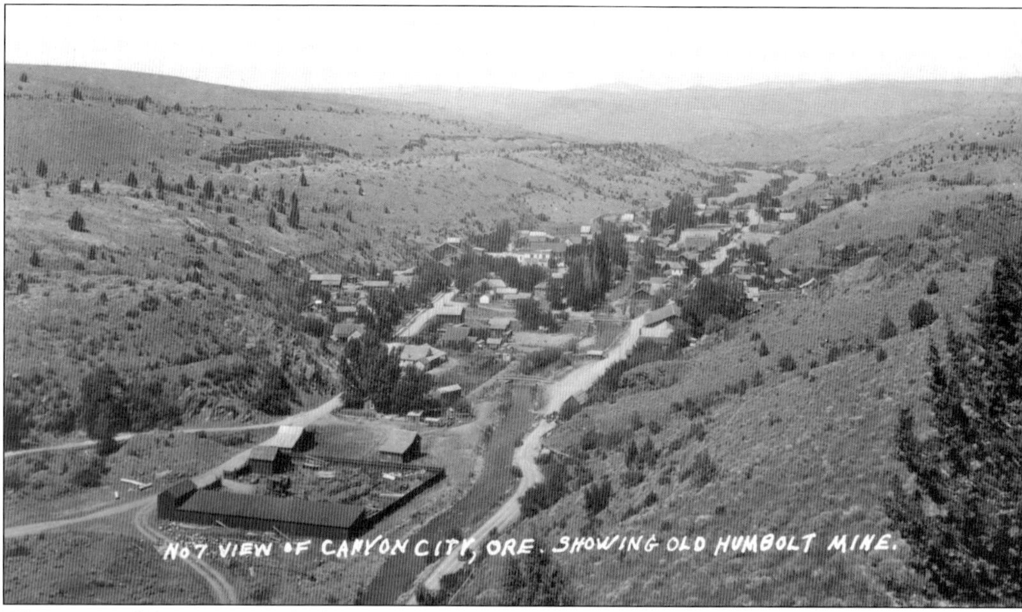

This view of Canyon City looks north and shows the old Humbolt Mine on the side of the hill to the left. Canyon Creek runs north from its headwaters in the mountains to join the John Day River at the top of the image, paralleling the road on the right. Today, an airport lies at the top of the hill to the west at the left of the image.

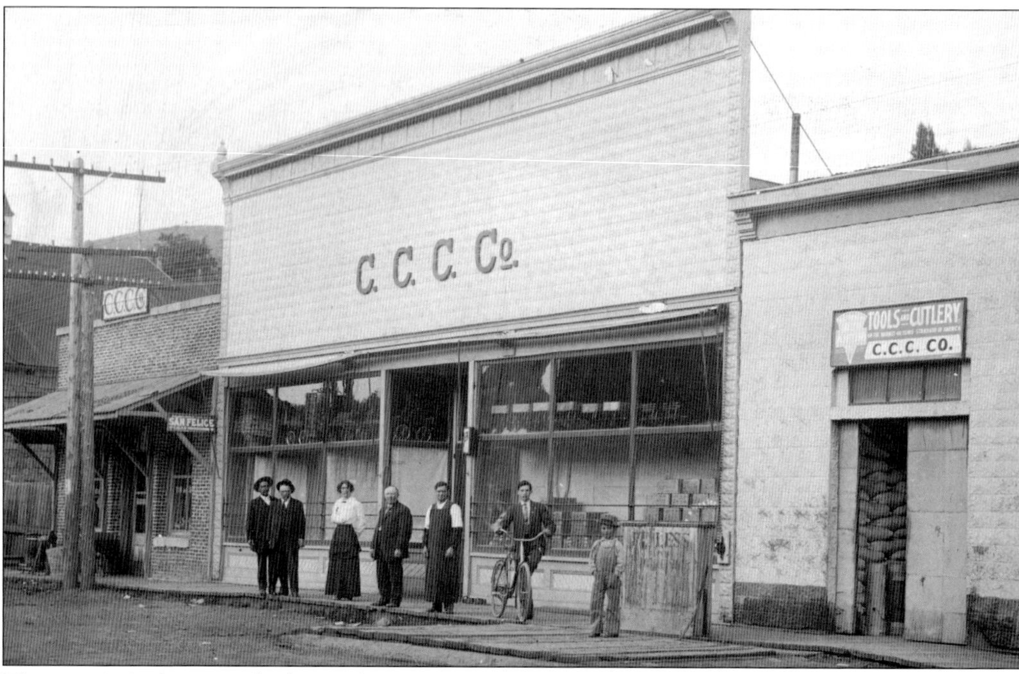

This c. 1910 photograph shows the Canyon City Commercial Company building along Main Street in Canyon City. The company sold many dry goods items, including tools and cutlery, as can be seen in the sign above the doorway at right.

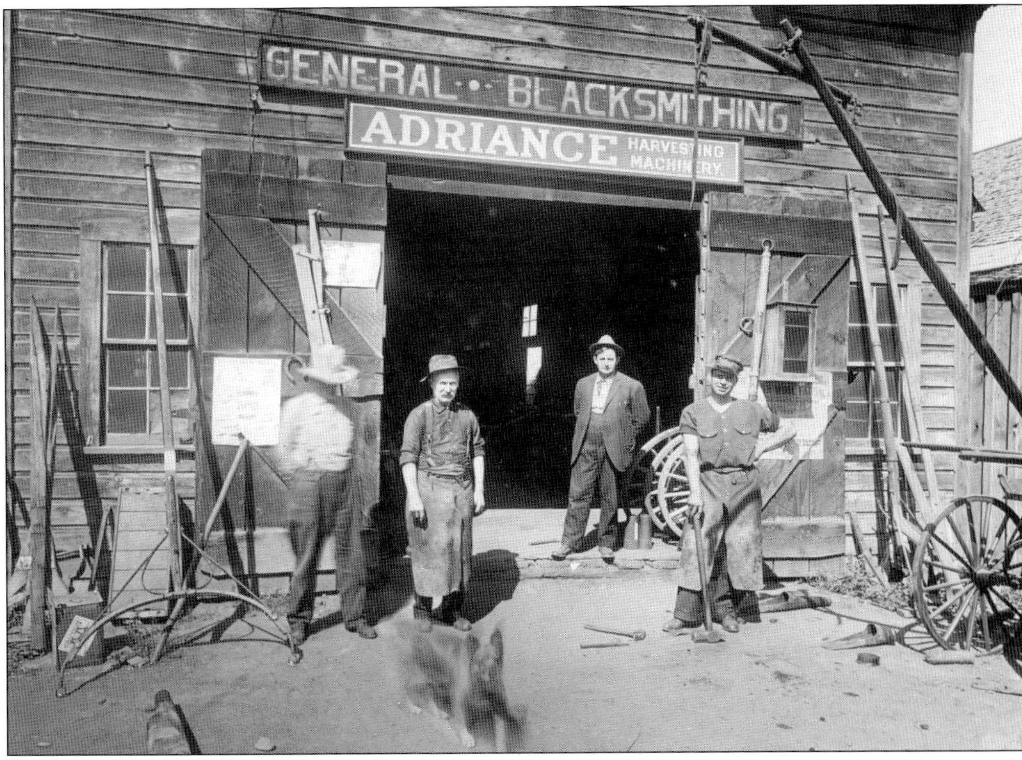

Blacksmith shops were an integral part of the West in the 1800s and early 1900s. Above is the blacksmith shop on North Washington Street in Canyon City around 1900. From left to right are Payne Folsom, Bob Hines, unidentified, and Jack Anderson. The folks below are unidentified, but note the horseshoes hanging from the ceiling and walls. A blacksmith created objects from iron or steel by forging the metal, using tools to hammer, bend, and cut it. Famous for horseshoes, they made other objects like gates, grills, railings, light fixtures, furniture, sculpture, tools, and cooking utensils. They also made weapons. Several blacksmiths are still operating in Oregon today.

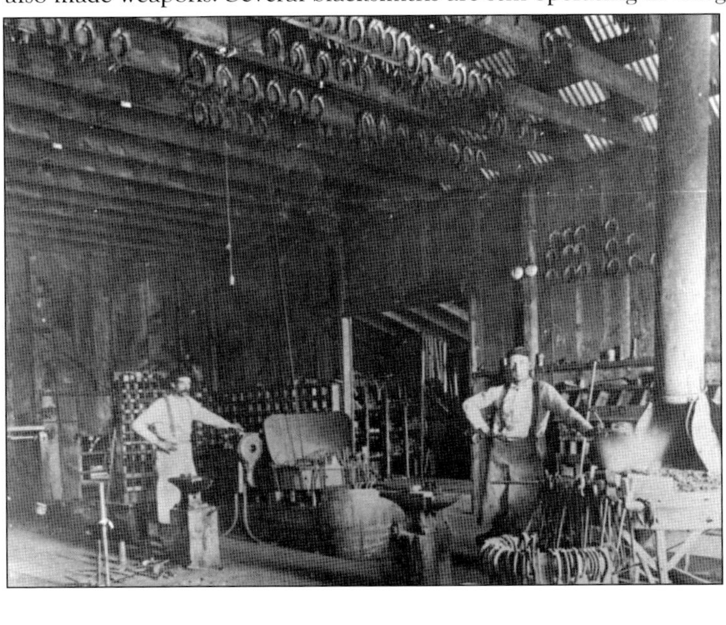

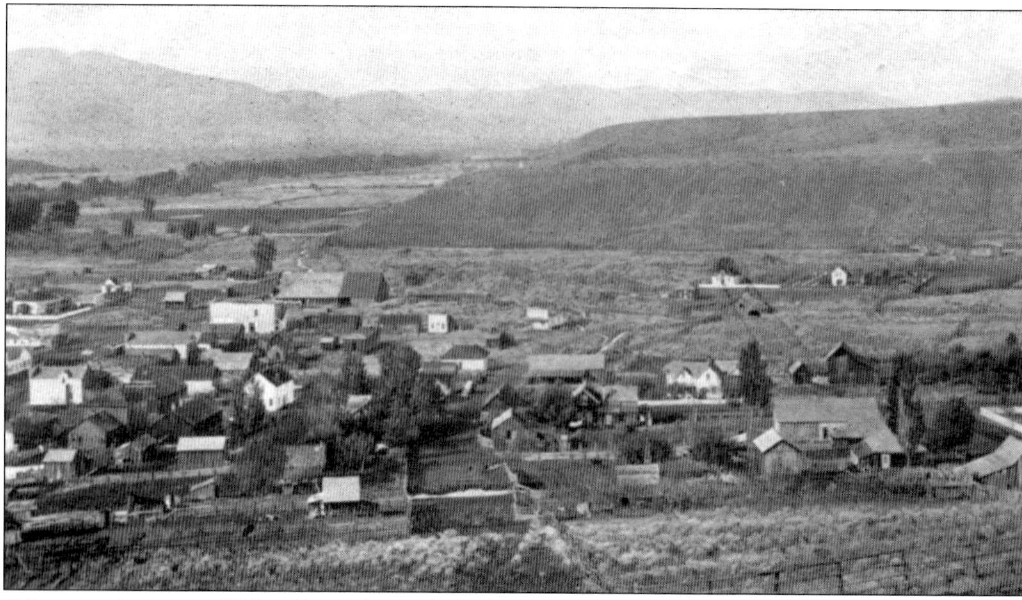

Fifteen miles east of John Day, along the John Day River, is the town of Prairie City. It was originally called Dixie from a creek that flowed south from the mountains into the John Day River. The site was three miles up the creek. The photograph was taken looking west toward John Day. The town sits on the north side of a large prairie, hence its name.

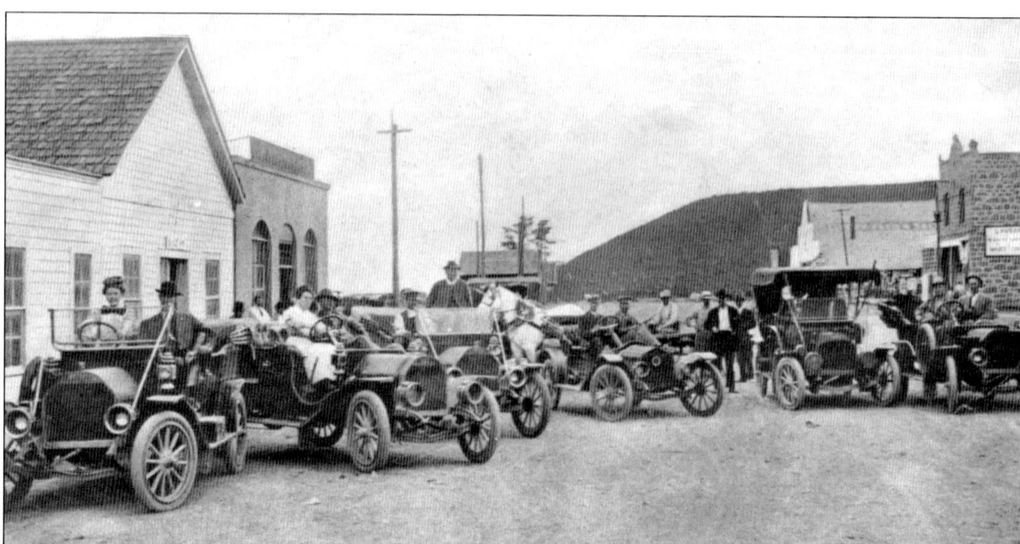

This image, taken in Prairie City shortly after 1910, shows how automobiles are beginning to take over from horses and buggies. Only one horse can be seen in the center of the picture. The reason for the gathering is unknown, but it likely drew automobiles from around the valley.

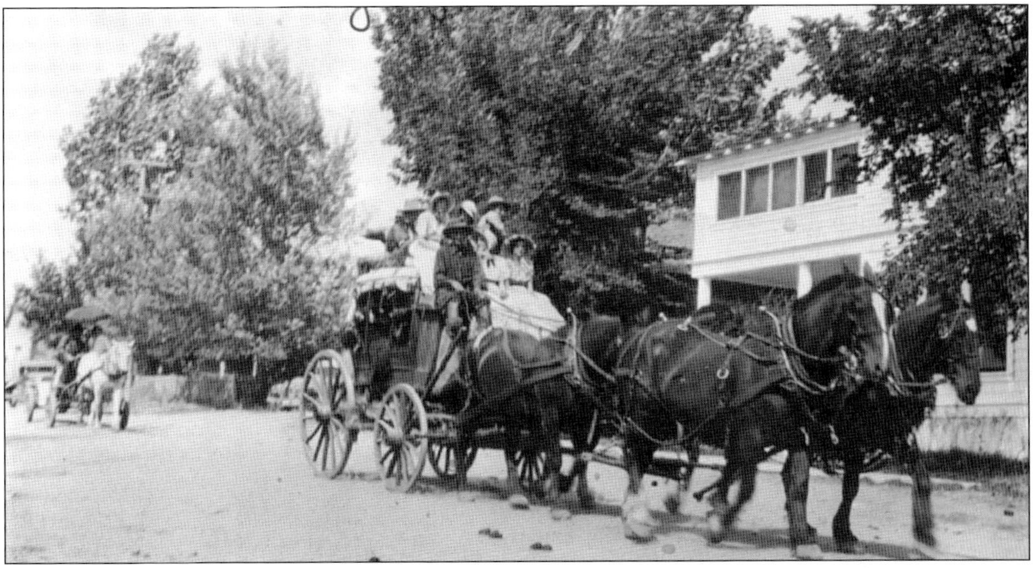

The town of Prairie City may be small, less than 1,000 people, but nevertheless it has its annual celebrations. This photograph shows the Canyon City float participating in the Prairie City Round-Up Day parade in 1932. A large area around the town was destroyed during the gold rush days by dredge mining.

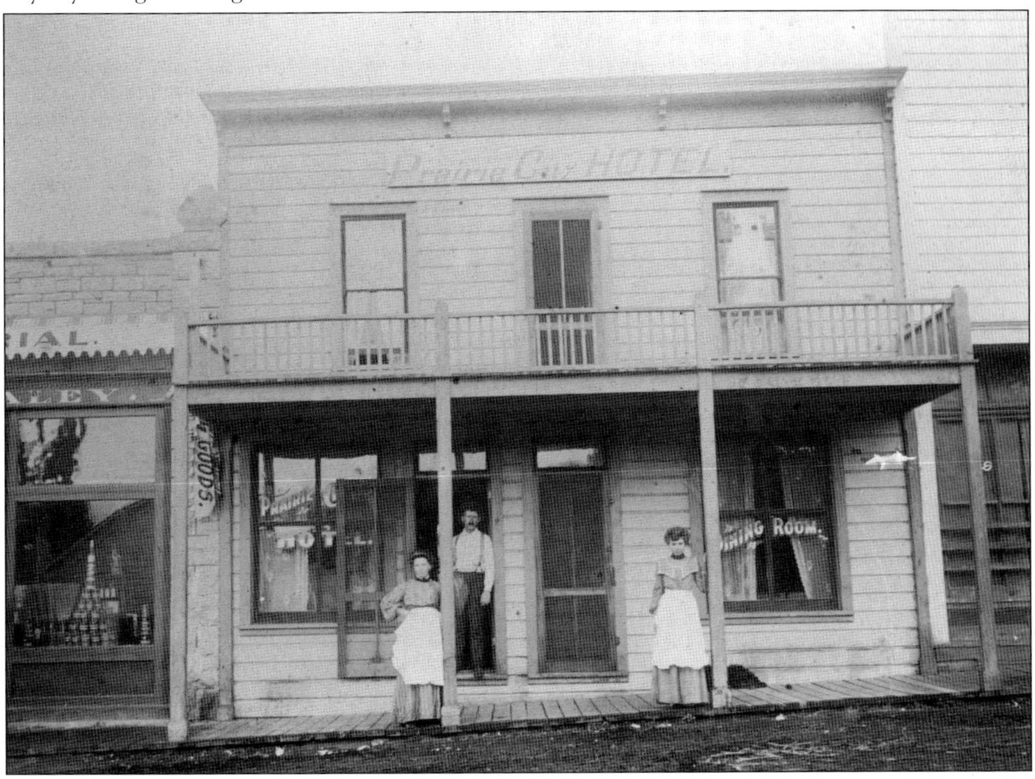

The Prairie City Hotel lies along Front Street or Highway 26. This c. 1890 photograph shows the front of the hotel. There was a dining room on the first floor with rooms on the second floor. Today the hotel offers modern facilities to travelers.

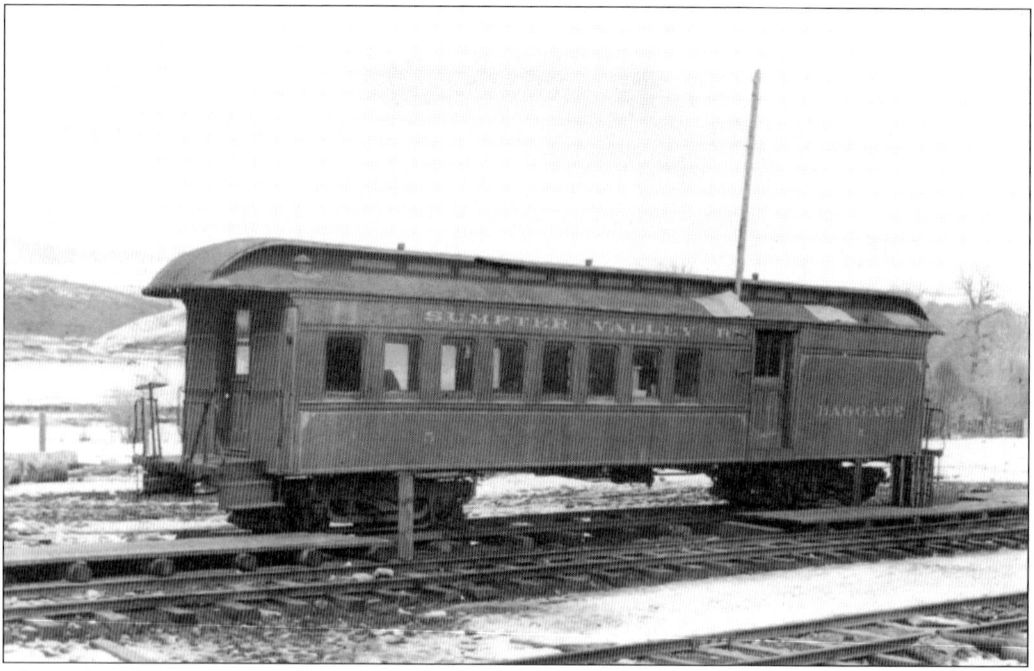

The railroad came to the John Day Valley in 1910. A man by the name of David Eccles began building the railroad to haul the vast sources of timber back to Baker City. It was called the Sumpter Valley Railroad. As the timber in an area was cut, the spur line was torn up and placed farther up the valley. It eventually reached the top of the divide and continued into lower elevations. John Day Valley residents noticed this and raised over $10,000 for Eccles to extend the rail line into Prairie City. As miners from Idaho began coming into the John Day Valley from the east, they rode the train. Being a smart entrepreneur, Eccles began charging them to ride his train and eventually raised enough money to buy a passenger car, shown above. A loaded log train is shown below. (Above, courtesy of Sumpter Valley Railway Depot/DeWitt Museum.)

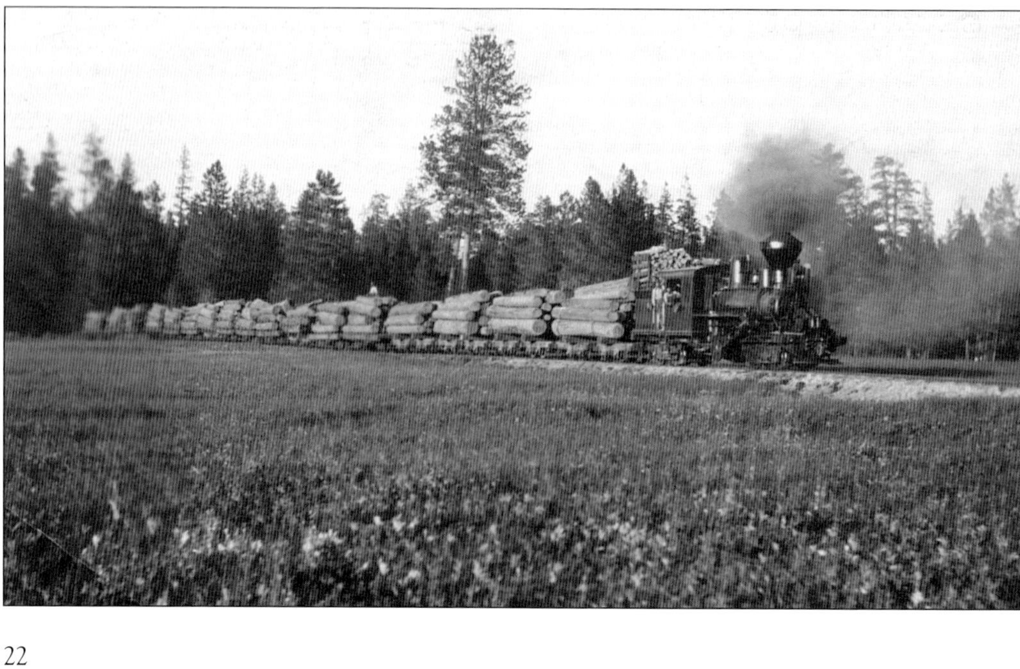

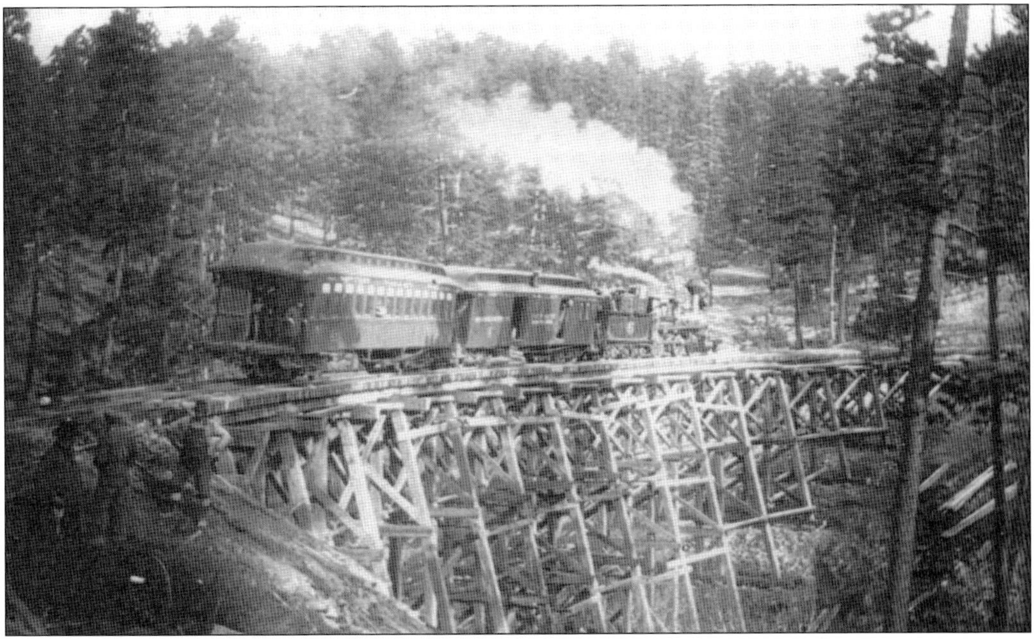

The Sumpter Valley Railroad had to cross many steep canyons as it climbed from Baker City up and through the Blue Mountains and then down into Prairie City. This required the building of several trestles, lengthy and tedious work. It was a long trip from Baker City, but this did not discourage many of the dignitaries from the town who were present for the dedication at Prairie City in June 1910. (Both, courtesy of Sumpter Valley Railway Depot/Dewitt Museum.)

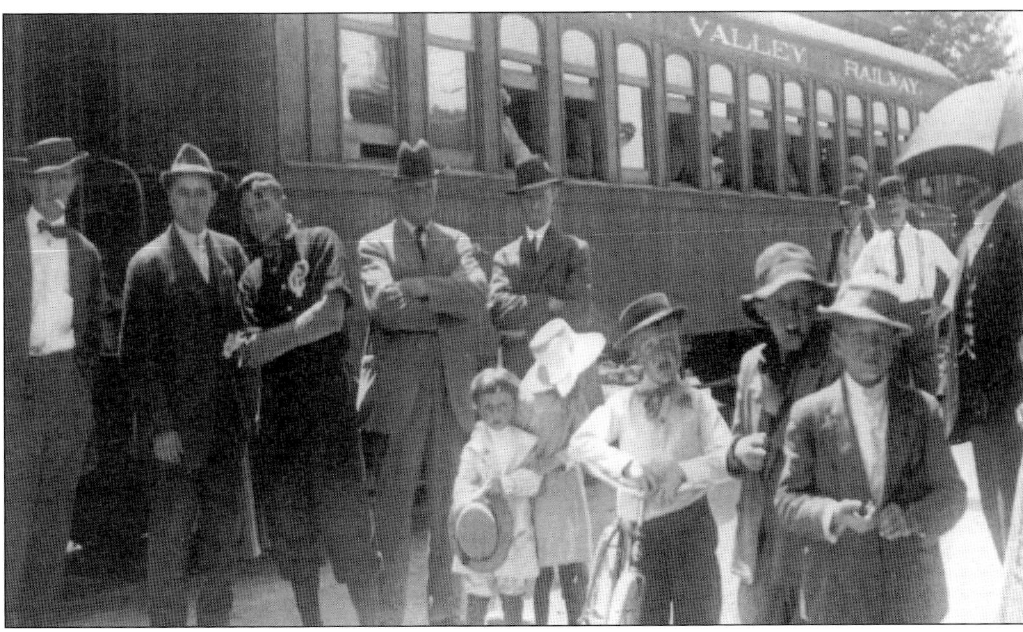

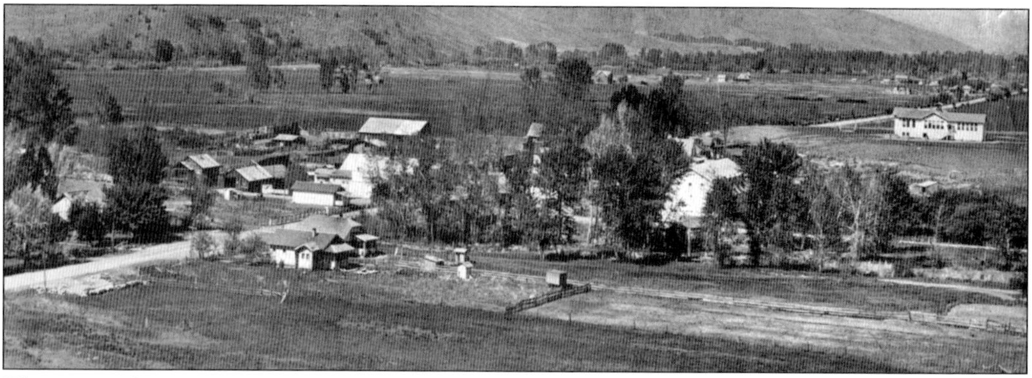

The town of Mount Vernon lies about 10 miles west of John Day along the John Day River. This c. 1935 image was taken looking northeast and shows Highway 26 a mile east of Mount Vernon, running from lower left to upper right. The schoolhouse is the building in the upper right. The stone structure resident David Jenkins built for his precious horse during the Bannock Indian War is still standing on the north side of Highway 26 as it passes through Mount Vernon.

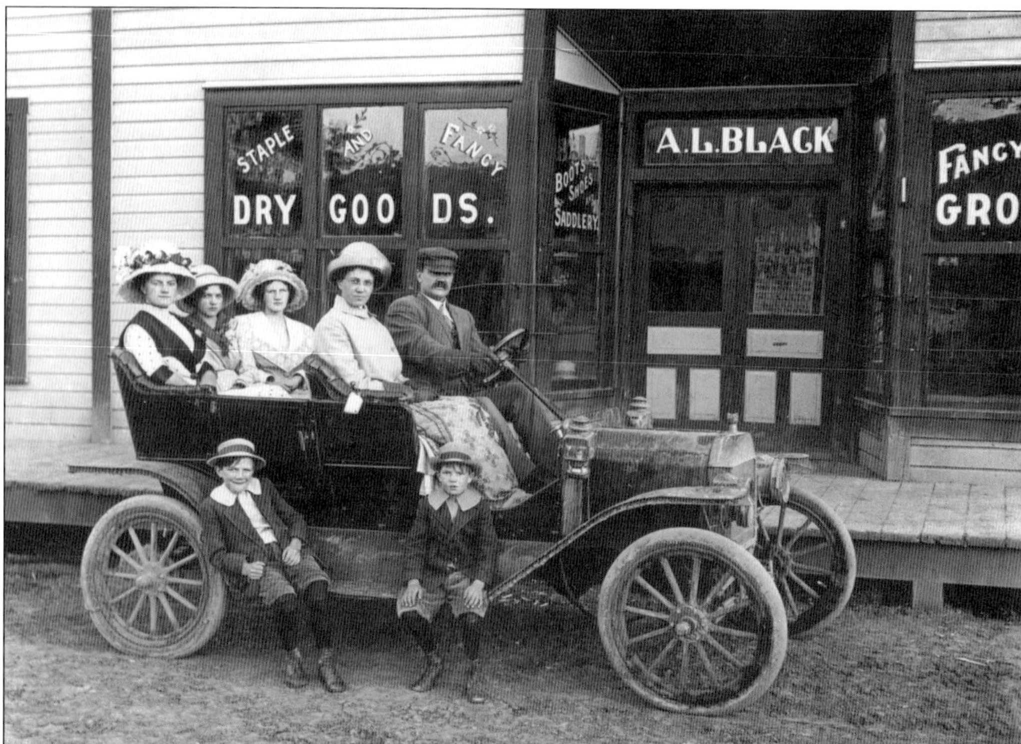

Automobiles had a difficult time coming to the John Day Valley. They had to be disassembled in Baker City, placed on the railroad, and reassembled in Prairie City. One of the first to own one in Mount Vernon was A.L. Black, who owned a successful business there, shown around 1912. In the front seat are A.L. and Mrs. Black. In the back seat from left to right are Etta, Grace, and Vinnie. On the fender and running board are Charles (left) and Howard. One daughter is absent from the photograph. The photograph was donated by Howard Black to the Grant County Historical Museum in 1953.

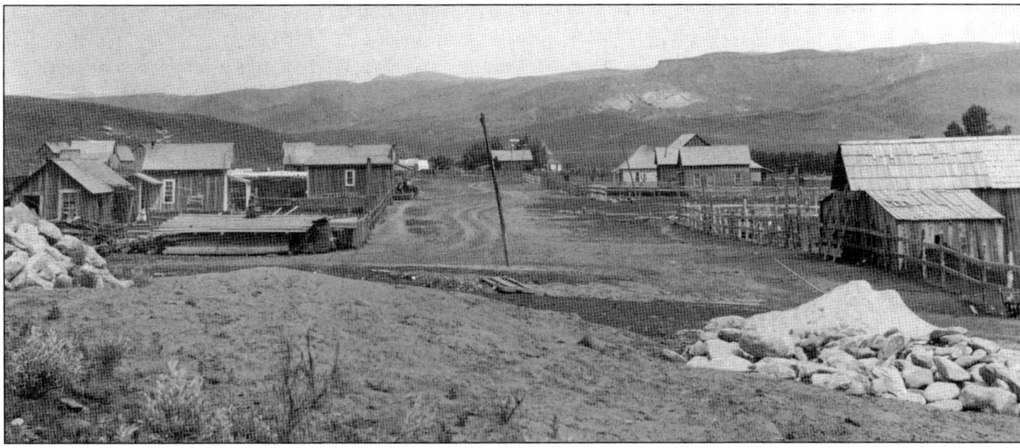

West of Mount Vernon along the John Day River is the town of Dayville. It was so named for its location near the river. It is in the far western portion of the John Day Valley. The Dayville Mercantile Company has been at the same location for nearly 100 years. It is not shown in the photograph.

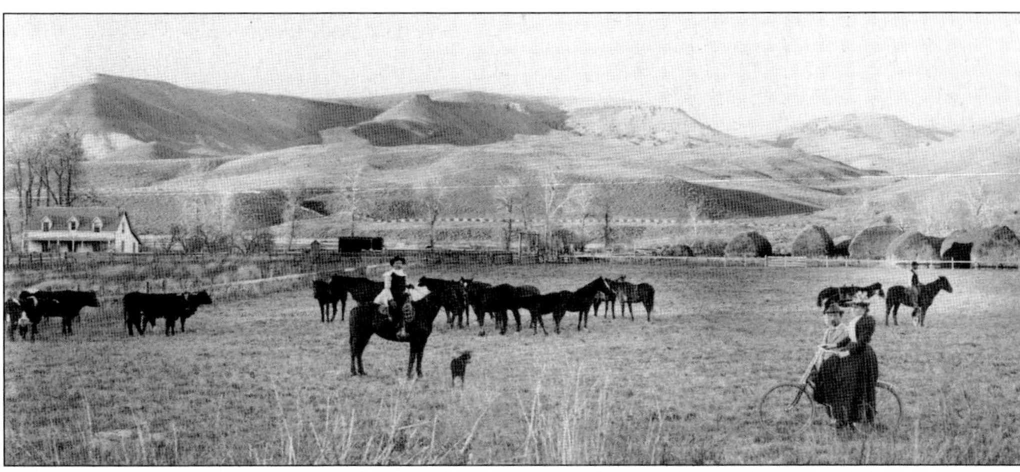

One of the more prominent ranches in the area around Dayville at the turn of the century was the Kenneth McCrae ranch. The ranch house is at far left. This c. 1897 image shows Mr. and Mrs. Farre near the bicycle. Farre was the ranch foreman. Note the large stacks of hay at far right. The photograph was taken in early spring.

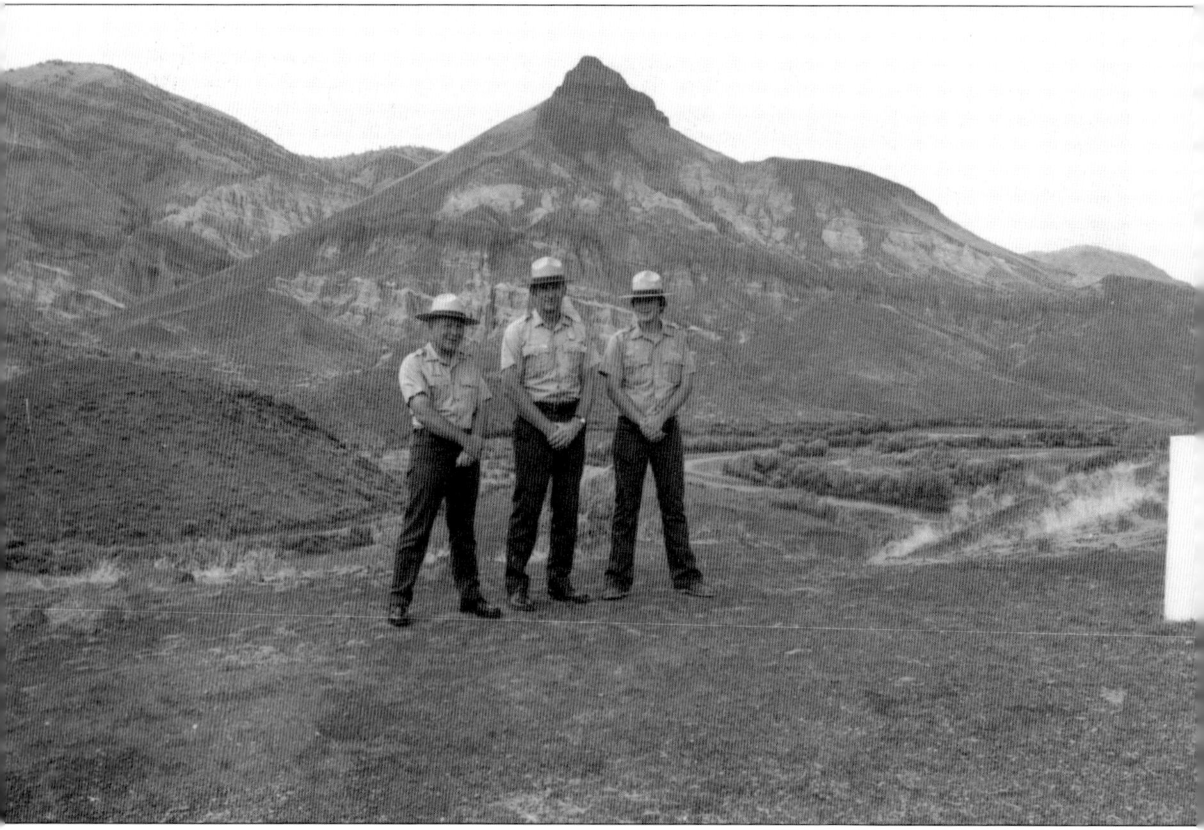

Part of the John Day Fossil Beds National Monument lies in the far western portion of Grant County. It is the Sheep Rock unit. Two other units are in Wheeler County to the west: the Clarno Unit and Painted Hills Unit. The three locations attract thousands of visitors to the area every year. Paleontologists are constantly discovering plants and animals that grew and roamed in the area millions of years ago. The monument was authorized by Congress in 1974 and established in 1975. This photograph, taken in 1976, shows three of the staff who first worked at the John Day Fossil Beds National Monument. From left to right are ranger Daron Dierks, superintendent Ben Ladd, and ranger Bob Johnson. Sheep Rock, a prominent feature in the area, is in the background. (Courtesy of the National Park Service.)

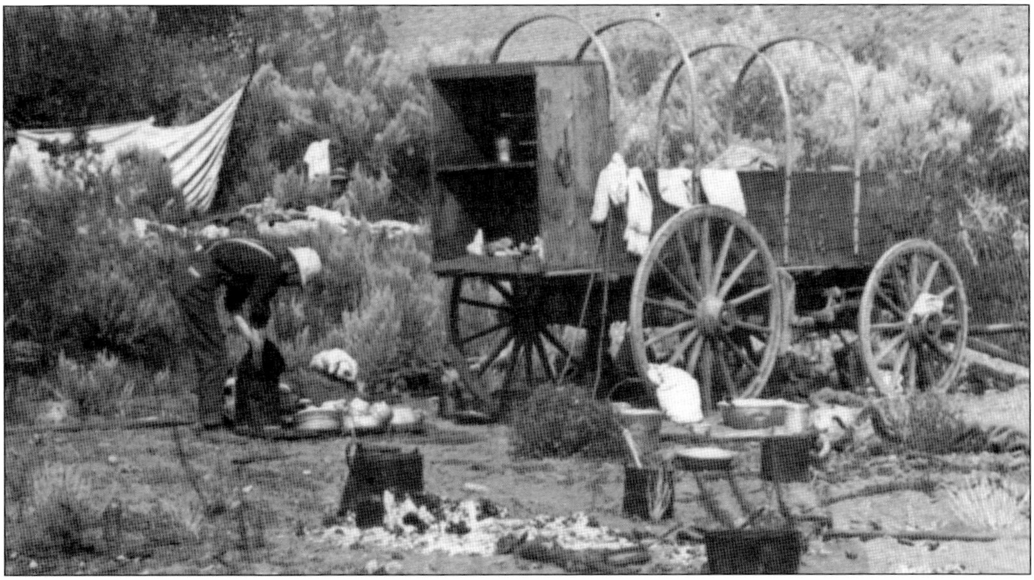

Although the national monument was not established until 1975, fossils were found in the area over 150 years earlier. In this image, taken during the 1889 Princeton Expedition, William Berryman Scott can be seen in the center, having made camp in the valley of the John Day River south of Kimberly, Oregon. (Courtesy of the National Park Service.)

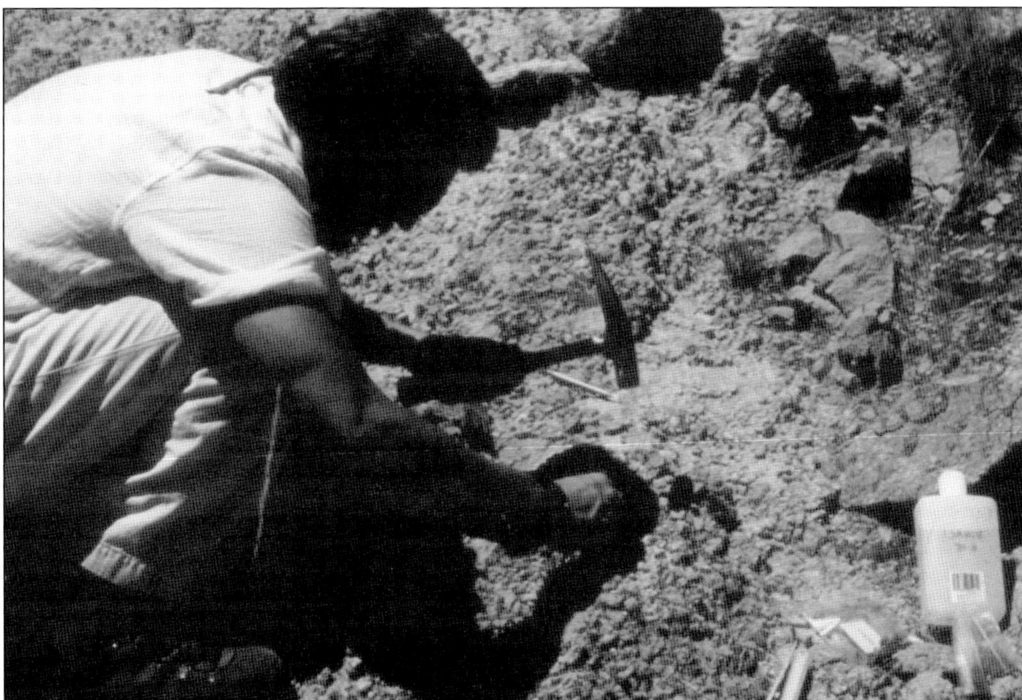

The work of a paleontologist is not all that glamorous. Quite often, long hours are spent in the field on hands and knees chipping away at the terrain in search of that one fossil or maybe even just a part of one. In the summer, temperatures can rise to over 100 degrees. The gentleman in the image is Ted Fremd, the monument's first staff paleontologist. (Courtesy of the National Park Service.)

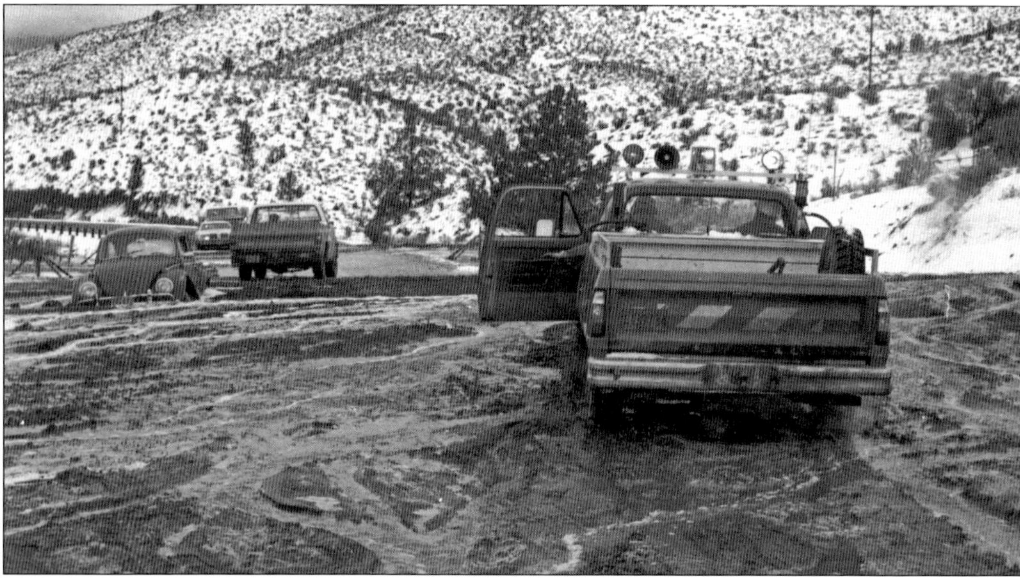

The terrain throughout the John Day Fossil Beds National Monument is generally sparse of vegetation. Heavy rain from summer thunderstorms or warm rain and rapid snowmelt in spring can cause flash flooding. Park rangers are shown rescuing a motorist caught in such a flood. Sometimes, as debris is washed away from the canyon walls, fossils are revealed that have been buried for millions of years. (Courtesy of the National Park Service.)

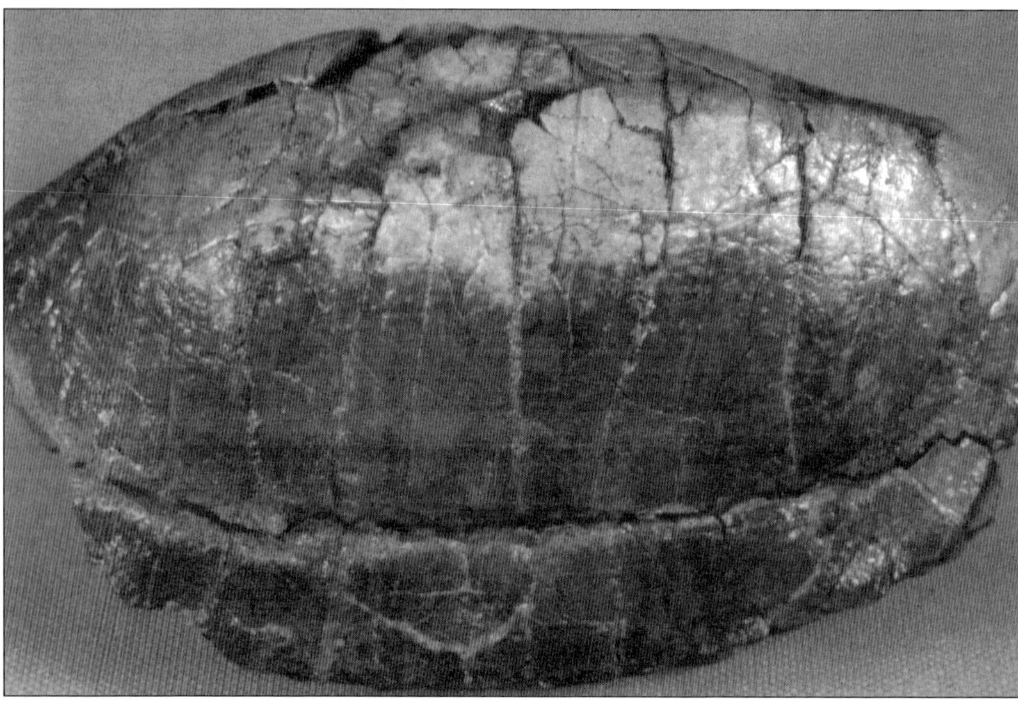

This tortoise is of the genus *Stylemys*. It was found in the Turtle Cove Member Rocks area of Grant County. *Stylemys* is the first fossil genus of dry land tortoise belonging to the order Testudines discovered in the United States. The genus lived in temperate to subtropical areas of North America, Europe, and Asia. (Courtesy of the National Park Service.)

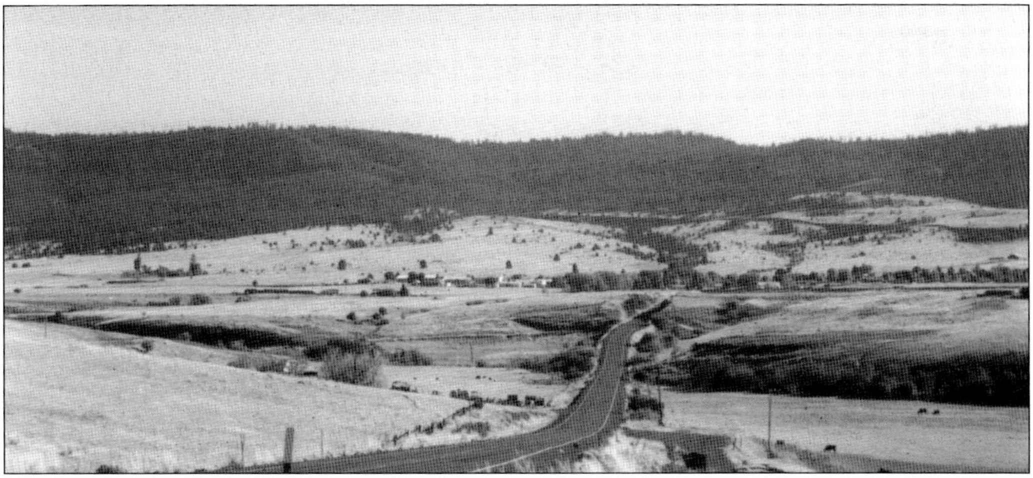

The image above shows the town of Long Creek in the Long Creek Valley. Below is a herd of Joe Oliver (pictured on horse) in a summer grazing area in one of the high-elevation valleys. This is typical of the many high mountain valleys in eastern Oregon. The valleys are surrounded by lush forests, as seen in both images. Note how quickly the vegetation changes from grassland to forest with only a slight increase in elevation. At night, due to the earth radiating heat, the slopes of the valleys cool. This cool, dry air then slowly drains down into the valley. During winter, these valleys are usually covered with snow, an excellent radiator. Light winds enhance the cooling, resulting in overnight low temperatures that can reach minus 50 degrees. Warm air lies above the cold air, resulting in higher temperatures in the forests above the valley. (Above, courtesy of the author.)

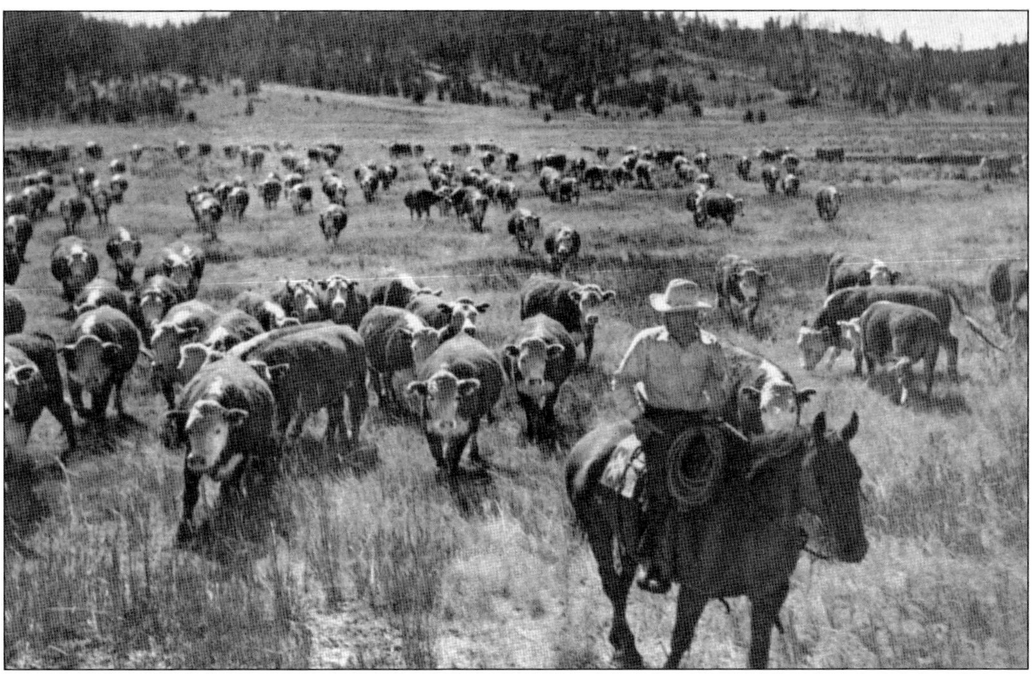

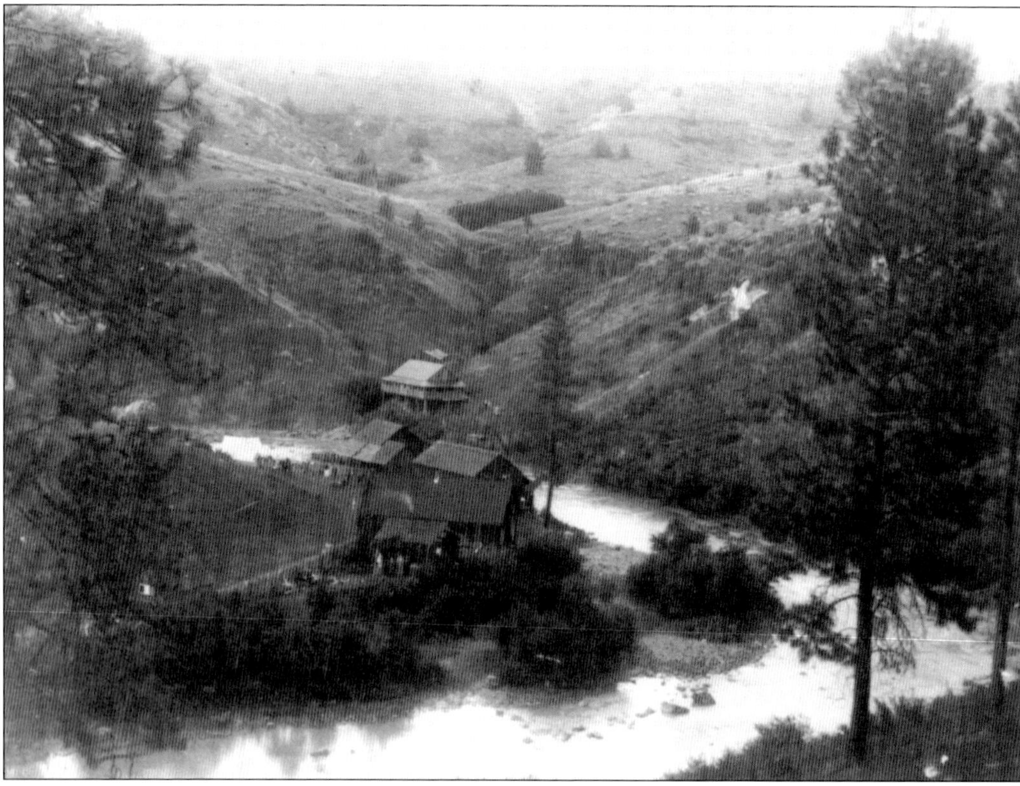

The above image shows the Ritter Hot Springs, near the town of Ritter in the northern portion of Grant County along the Middle Fork of the John Day River. Rev. Joseph Ritter was a pioneer Baptist minister in the area who named the town and established the first post office near his ranch.

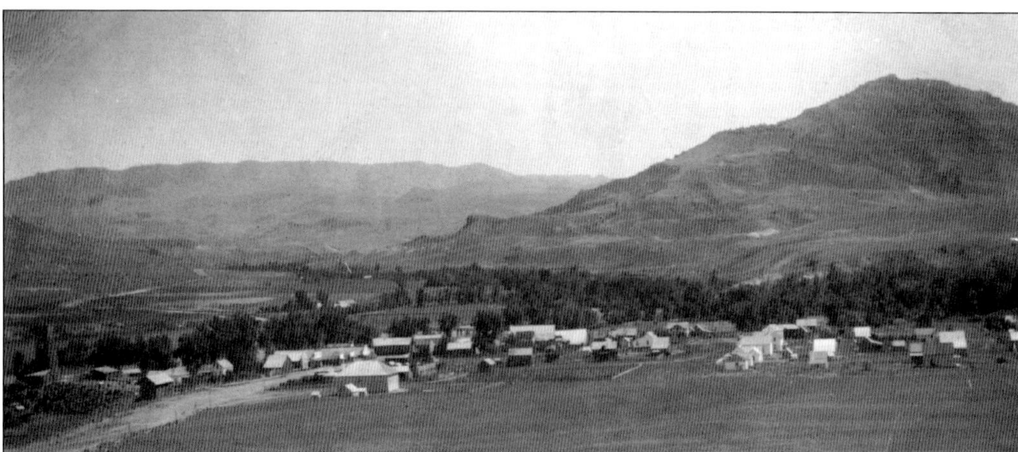

The small town of Monument is located near the confluence of the North and Middle Forks of the John Day River. Isaac Vilott, an early resident in the area, was said to have given the town its name in 1869 due to the mountain nearby that he thought resembled a pulpit. The mountain, shown in the upper right, is called Monument Mountain.

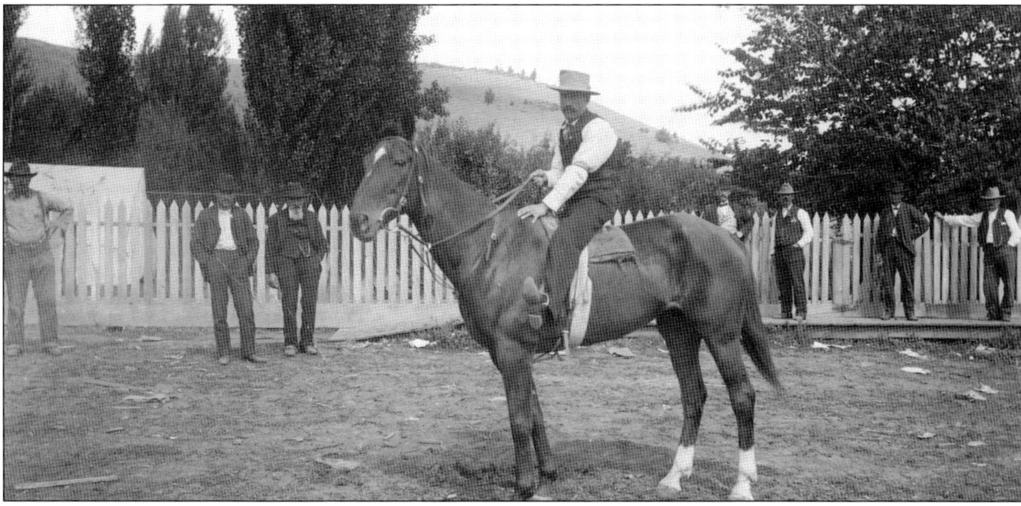

Although small, the town of Hamilton, a few miles west of Long Creek, boasted of a race track, general store, post office, and school around 1900. Pictured are Louis Morris, the rider, and, from left to right, Richard Blackwell, Leet Paine, J.H. Hamilton, Jim Barber, Douglas Hinton, George McHaley, and unidentified. The horse is Lazy Jane, owned by Leet Paine.

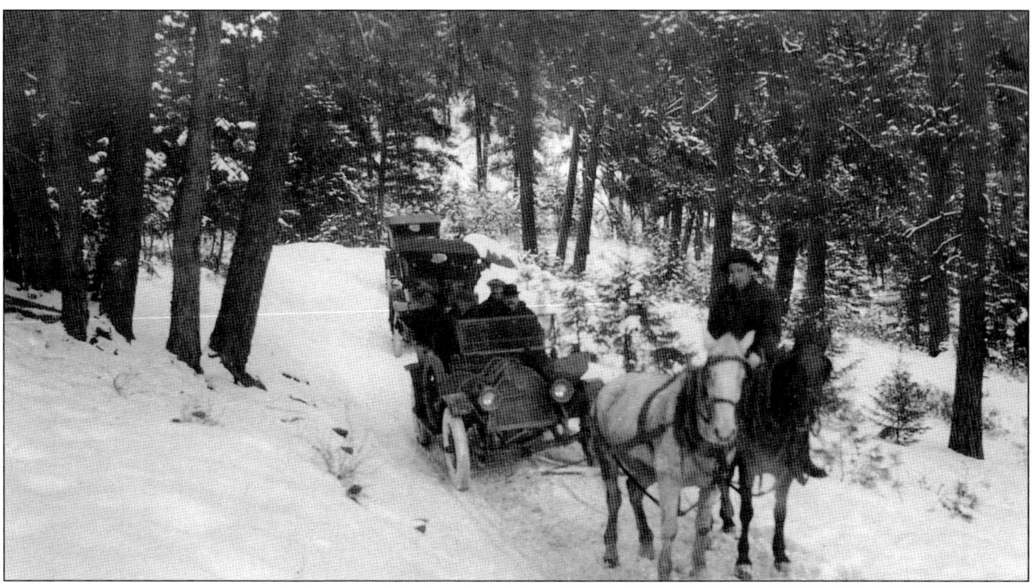

With snowplows nonexistent around 1910, not only were horses used to round up cattle, race, and pull wagons, there were also other duties. Early automobiles in Grant County were often stuck in deep mud or snow banks as they ventured into the mountains. A horse team would come to the rescue.

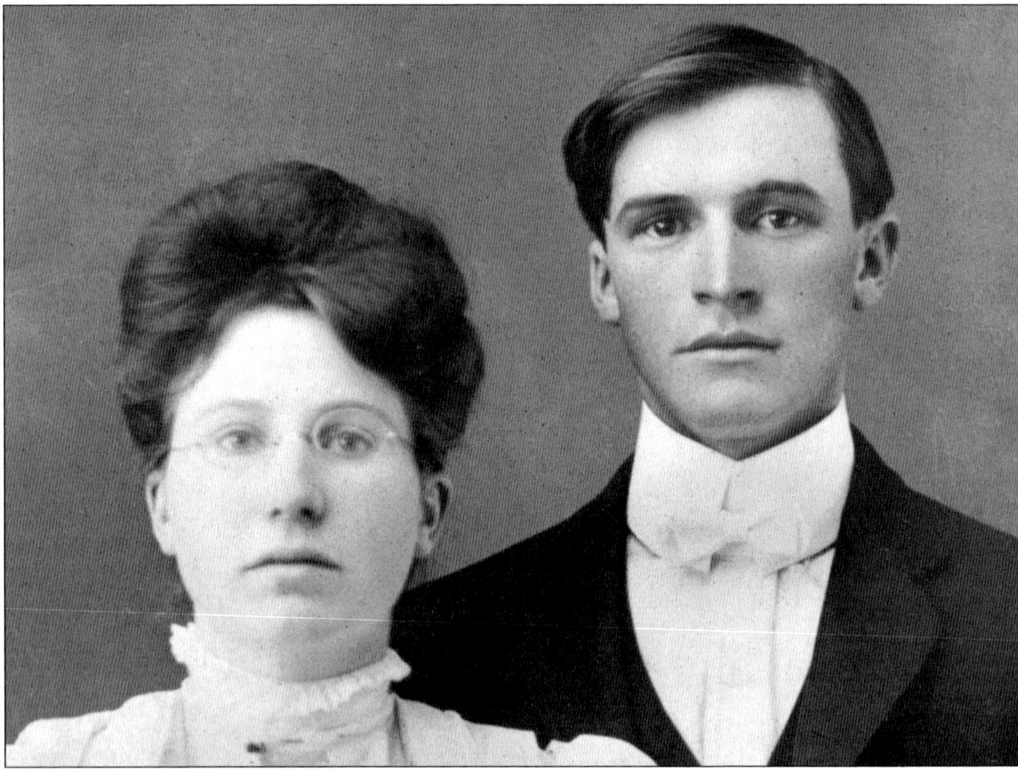

Herman and Elizabeth Oliver are shown here in an early photograph. Much has been said and written about Herman Oliver. Elizabeth kept most of the ranch records and loved children. She often took care of the children of relatives, friends, and ranch hands.

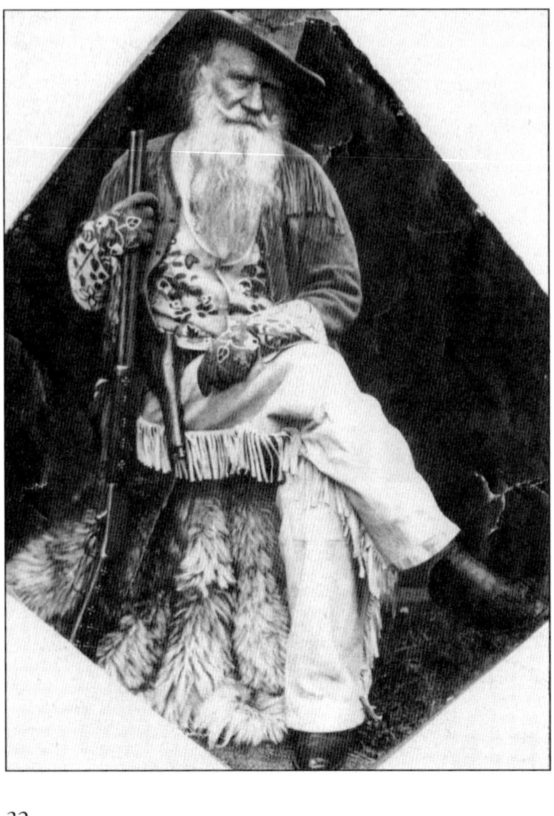

Joaquin Miller was probably one of the most colorful characters in Grant County. He was a poet, a newspaper editor, and a miner, among other trades. He once joined an Indian tribe and married one of the women. He lived in many locations, among them Canyon City. His cabin has been preserved next to the Grant County Historical Museum.

The gristmill at John Day was built in 1865 by A.R. McCallum and G.I. Hazeltine (pictured at right). Hazeltine came to the John Day area from California when gold was discovered in 1862. Other than a small mill at the Marcus Whitman mission in southeast Washington, it was the first flour mill east of the Cascades. Machinery for the mill was packed in by horses and mules from The Dalles. The mill could produce 20 barrels of flour per day and was water powered from its location on the John Day River near the mouth of Canyon Creek. McCallum and Hazeltine operated the mill until 1869. The mill was later purchased by William M. Basford. In the c. 1898 photograph below, the gentleman in the doorway is unidentified.

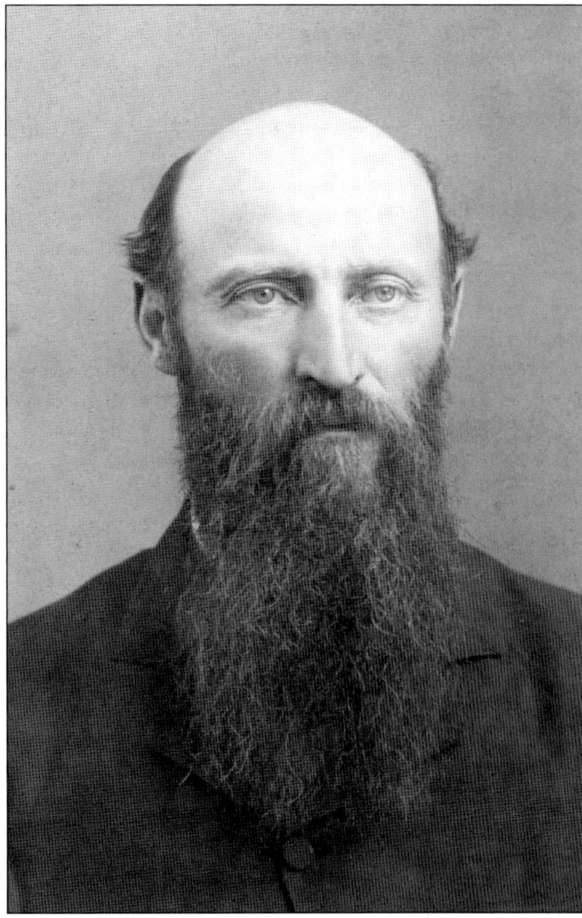

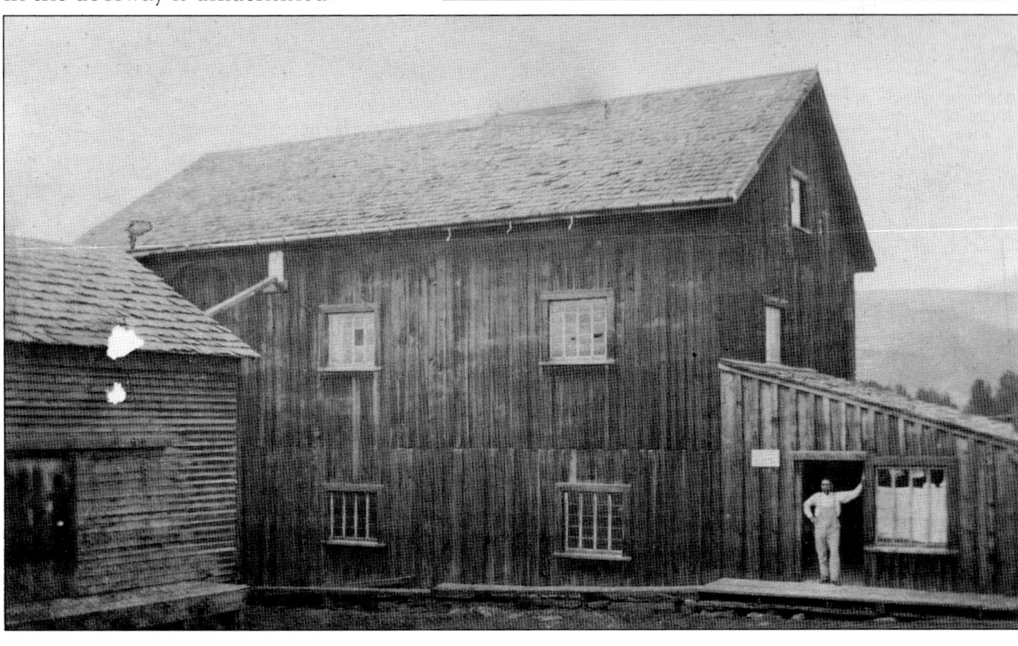

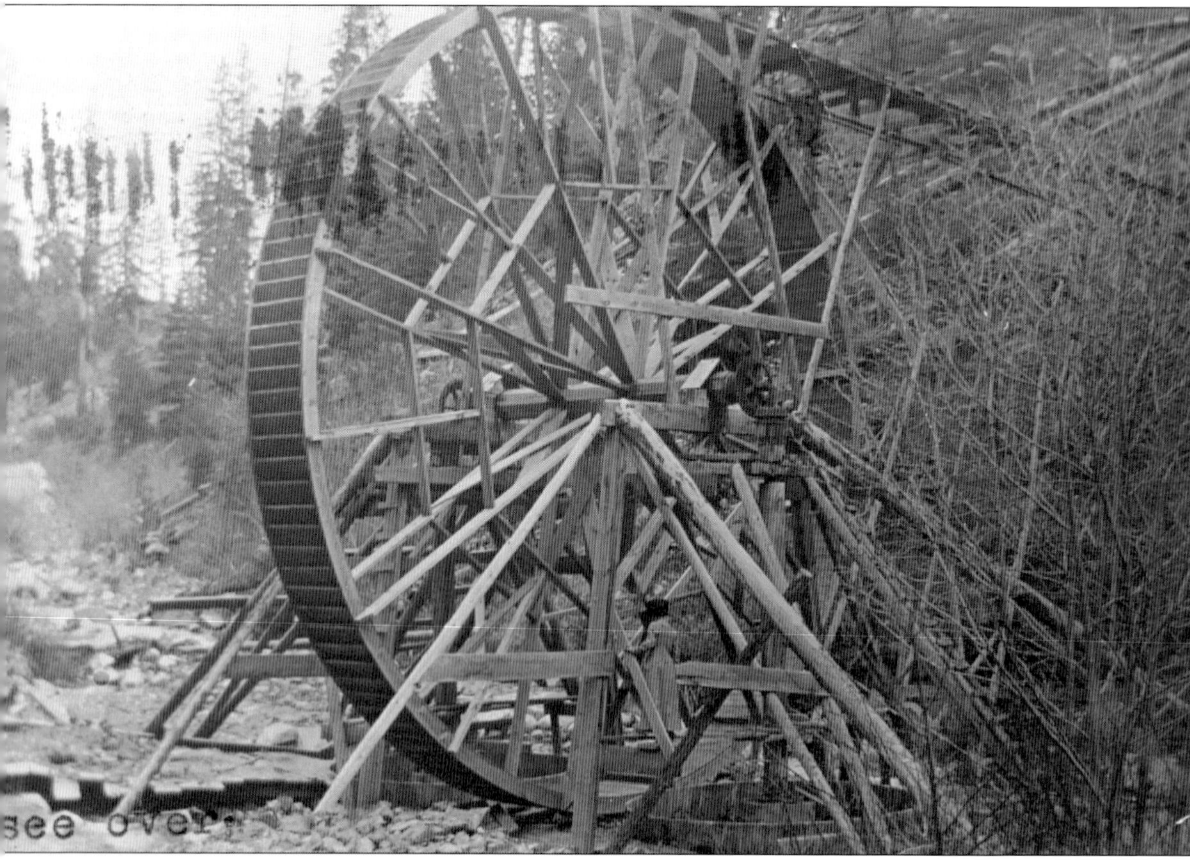

Grist or flour mills were powered by waterwheels similar to this wheel. This one was on Dixie Creek and was used to mine gold in the area. In milling, the wheel drove two sets of burrs (or burs). As the two burrs came together, the wheat was ground into flour. Smaller sets of burrs were used for corn, barley, and oats. Flour was a very important commodity for the miners.

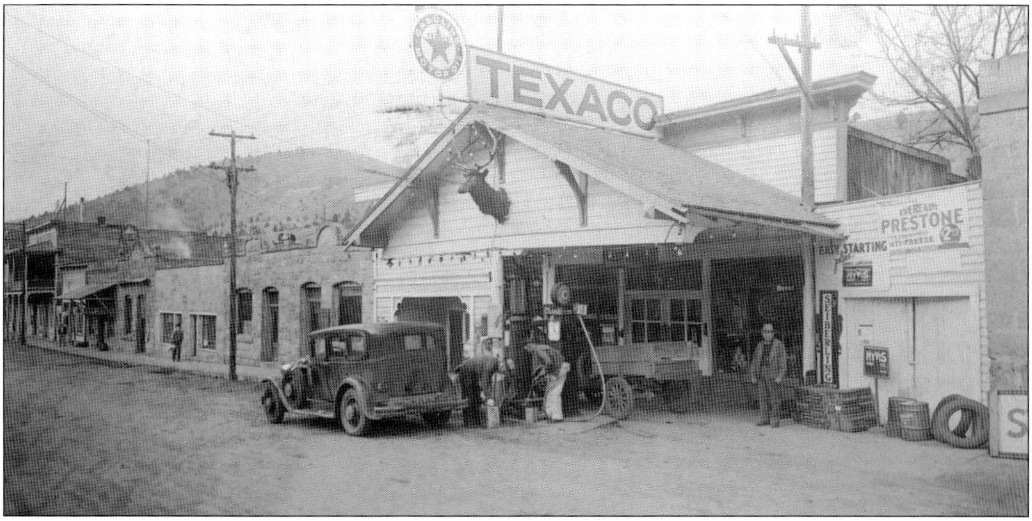

The Charles Brown Texaco station on Washington Street in Canyon City was a popular spot in the 1920s and 1930s. Gas stations in the early days sold tires, car parts, antifreeze, and other equipment. Many also had repair shops attached, unlike today's modern gas stations offering beverages, food, and a variety of grocery items.

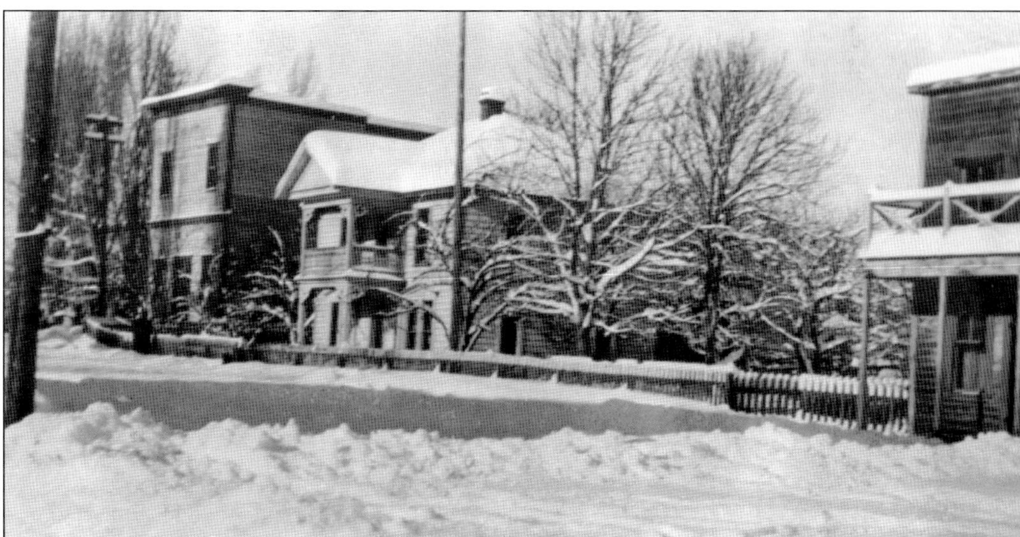

Snow usually falls in eastern Oregon from November through March. This image in John Day at the corner of Main Street and Church Street shows a substantial accumulation of snow. Grant County residents are well equipped when snow falls, unlike residents in western Oregon, where massive traffic jams occur when only two to three inches of snow falls.

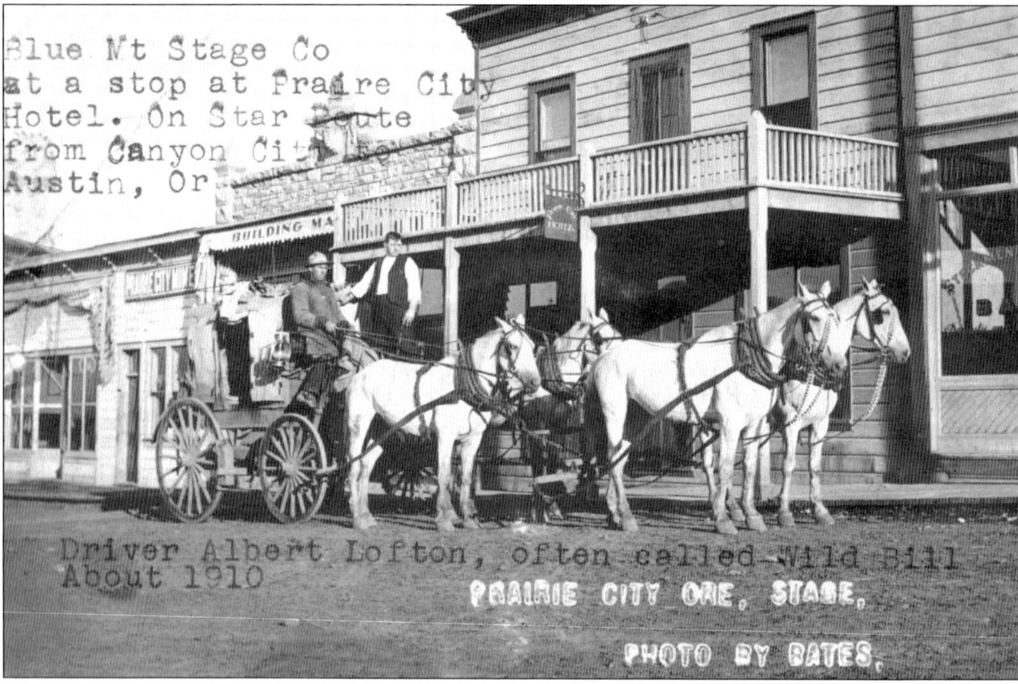

This image shows the Blue Mountain Stage Company stopped in front of the Prairie City Hotel in 1910. Stagecoaches ran from Prairie City to Burns to the south, Austin to the northeast, and The Dalles to the northwest. The driver is identified as Albert Lofton, often called "Wild Bill."

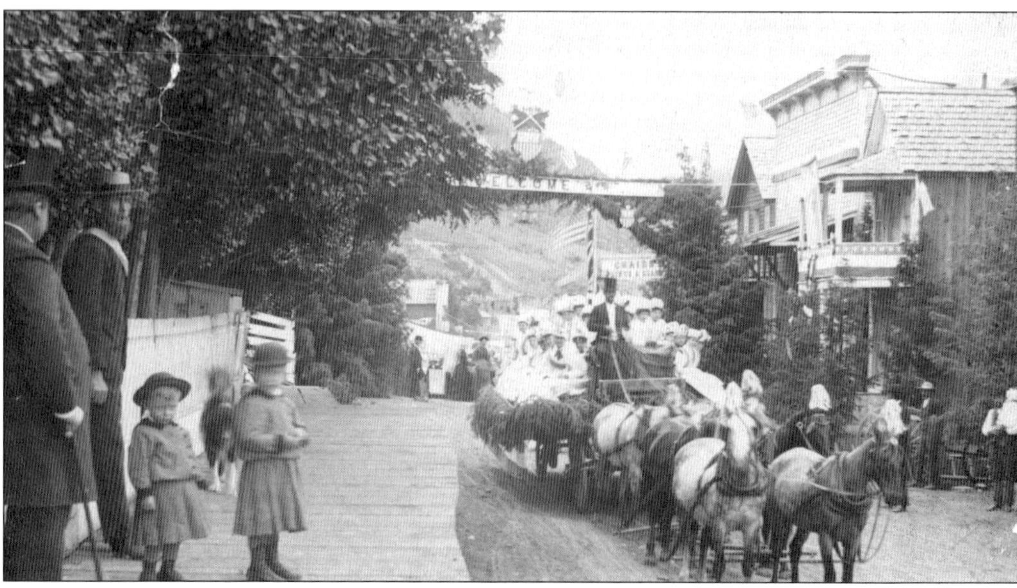

Fourth of July parades were popular throughout Grant County. This image shows the Canyon City Fourth of July parade. Because the Fourth occurred on a Sunday that year, the official parade was held on Monday. Such would not be the case today.

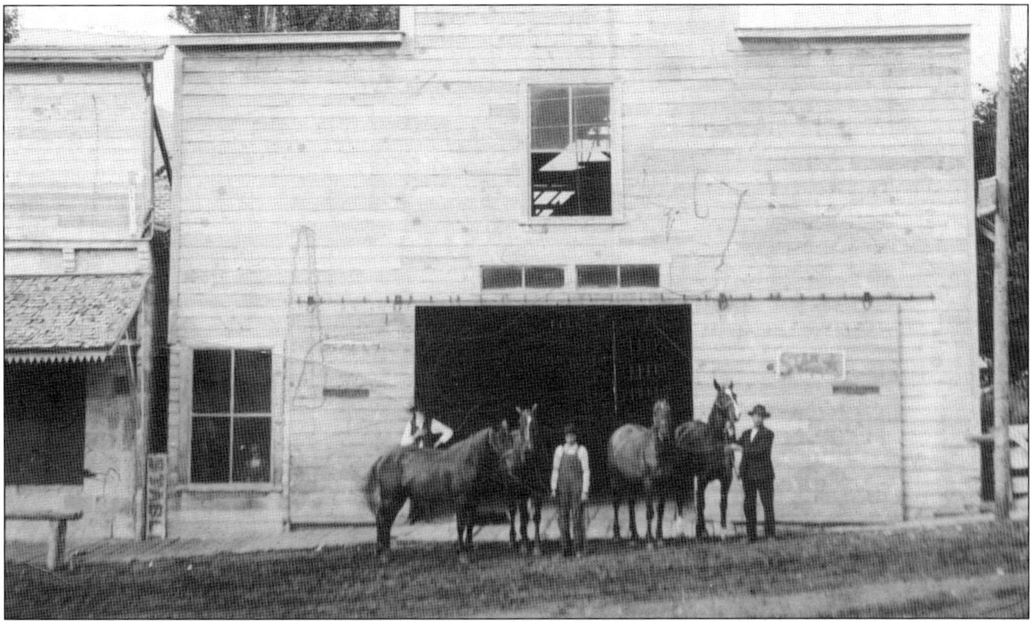

The above image shows the Blue Front Livery Stable in John Day around 1900. A livery stable or livery yard is where horses were kept. If the horse owner did not have sufficient acreage to comfortably house a horse, he could put it into a livery stable and pay the owner a weekly or monthly fee.

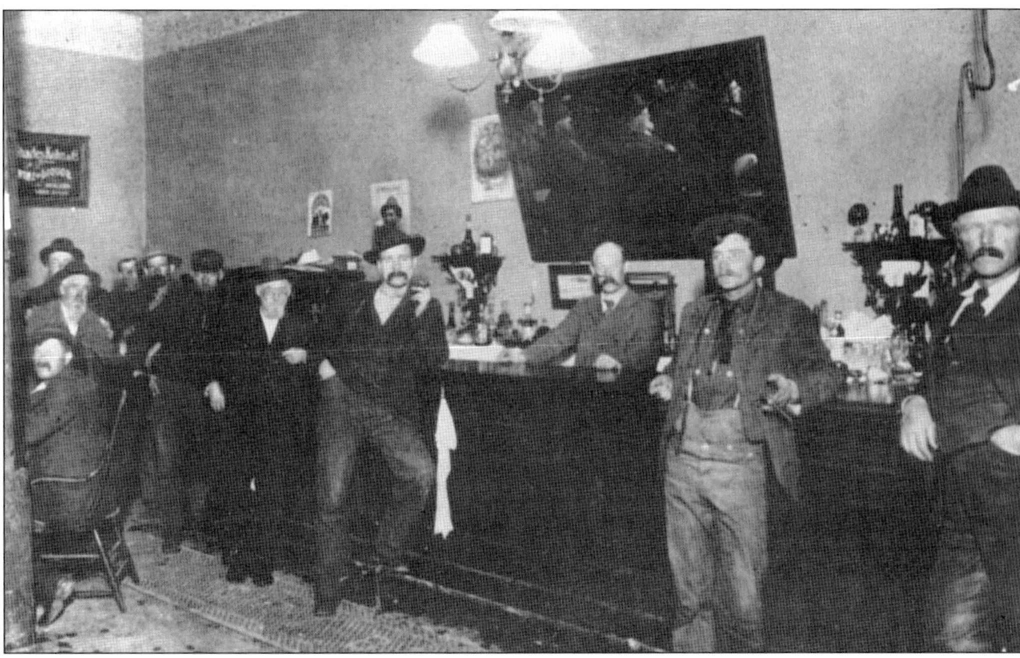

The City Brewery in Canyon City was a popular gathering place around the turn of the century. There appear to be no firearms belted to the hips of the individuals, so the bartender was enforcing his code of no pistols in the bar.

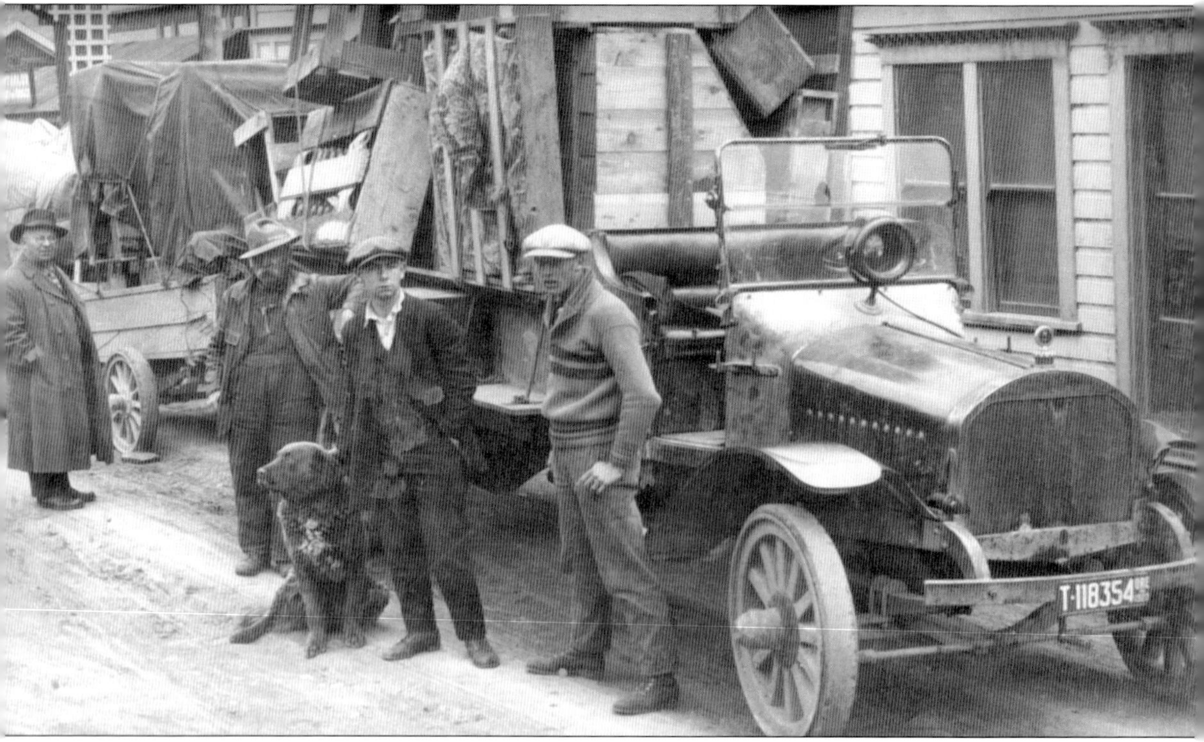

After the gold rush had subsided, people were still moving into Grant County. John Day began growing faster than its neighbor to the south. That did not stop the Pierpont family from moving to Canyon City from Washington state in 1923. They came by train to Prairie City. From there, the Wollenberg Freight Line brought all their belongings, including furniture, to Canyon City. Quite likely, their automobile was reassembled in Prairie City. The photograph was taken outside the Leucks' house on Main Street in Canyon City. From left to right are Louie Wollenberg, Russ Pierpont, Bill Pierpont, and Homer Morrison.

Two

Mining and the Chinese

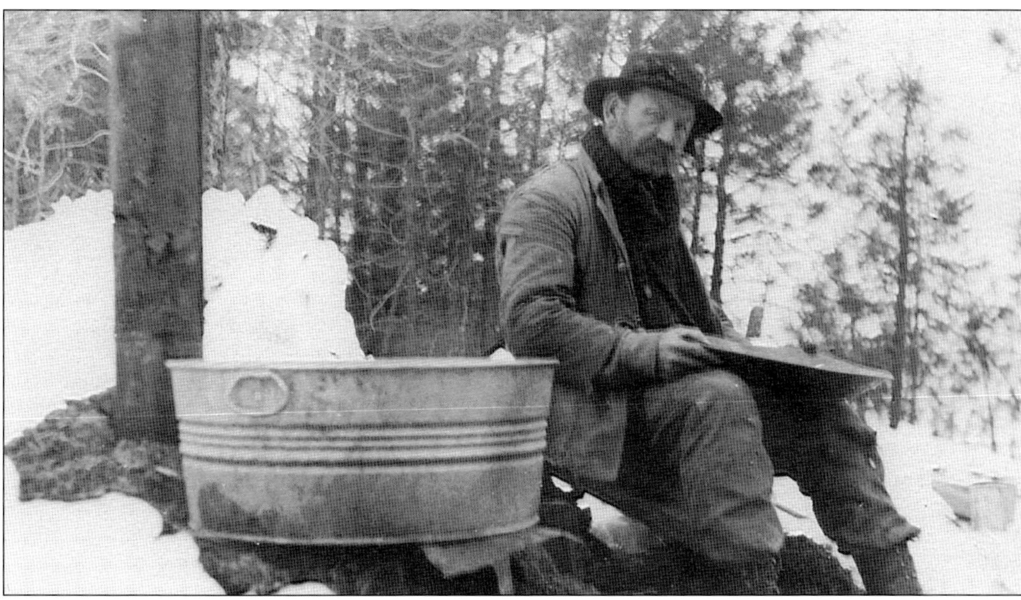

When the term "mining" is heard, one immediately thinks of a grizzly old man with a pan in his hands, kneeling by a creek, sloshing water around in the pan to separate out the gold flakes. That may be one method, but it was not the major method of extracting gold from the Canyon City goldfields. Isaac "Ike" Guker, pictured above with his gold pan, was one of the more famous and industrious miners in the area. He was born in 1860 in the Black Forest area of Germany. He was one of 10 children born to Johannes "John" and Anna Streib Gucker. Somewhere in his travels across Ohio, the Dakotas, and Montana, the *c* in his name was lost.

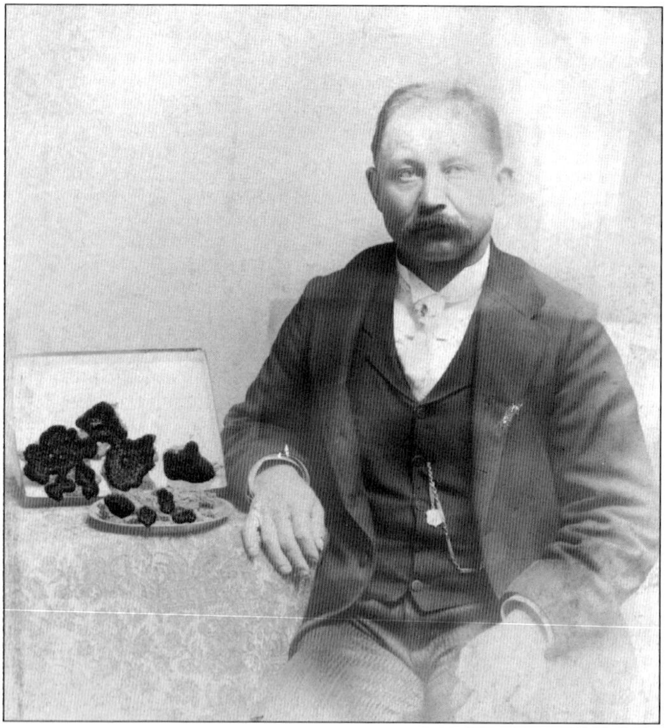

Initially, most of the gold removed from the creeks was probably done with gold pans, picks and shovels. Ike Guker, without his mining attire, is shown dressed in a smart suit and vest, displaying some of the gold nuggets removed from his mine. He reportedly took $50,000 worth of gold from a very small area and then sold his interests.

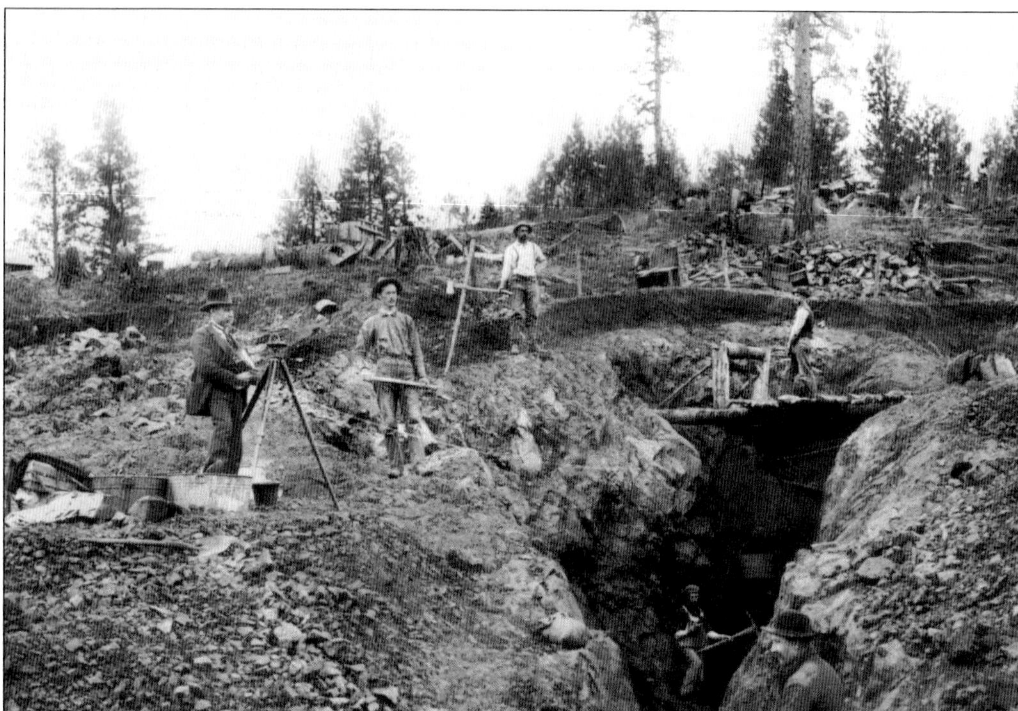

This mine shaft was one of Ike Guker's, called the Great Northern. The picture was taken around 1898, but the shaft was dug many years earlier. Guker is standing at left. Note the bucket inside the mine, hooked on a cable. This was likely one way to get the ore out of the mine.

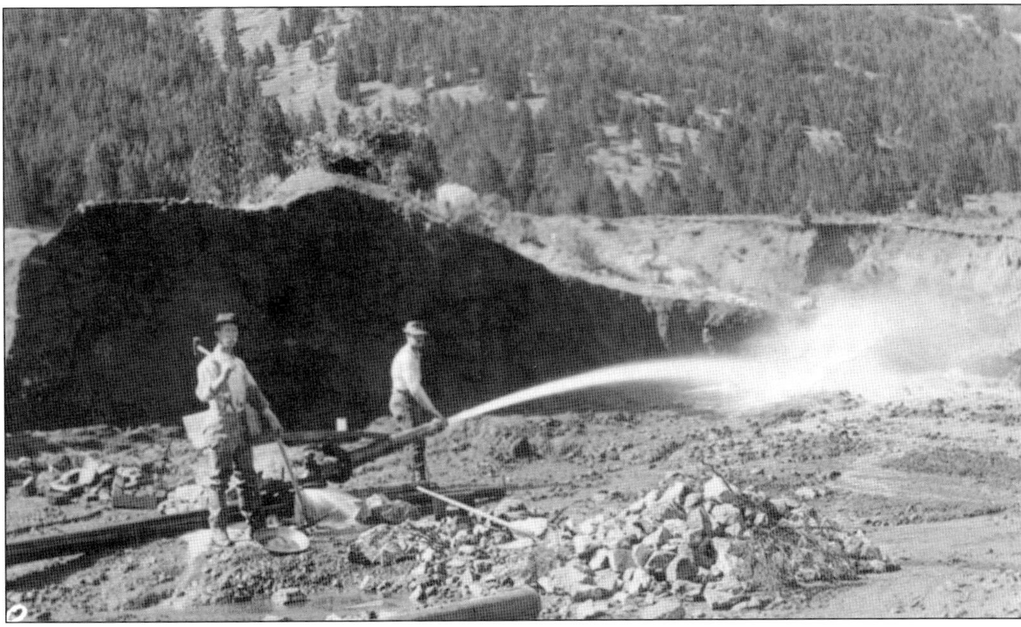

Placer mining involves the use of water that has been fed through a narrow opening just like a garden hose. The pressure then flushes out the rock and soil. In some cases, it is fed through a sluice box (below, at right) slowly so the gold flakes drop out. The two gentlemen above are Finlay Finlayson (left) and John Masson. Both photographs were taken around 1900.

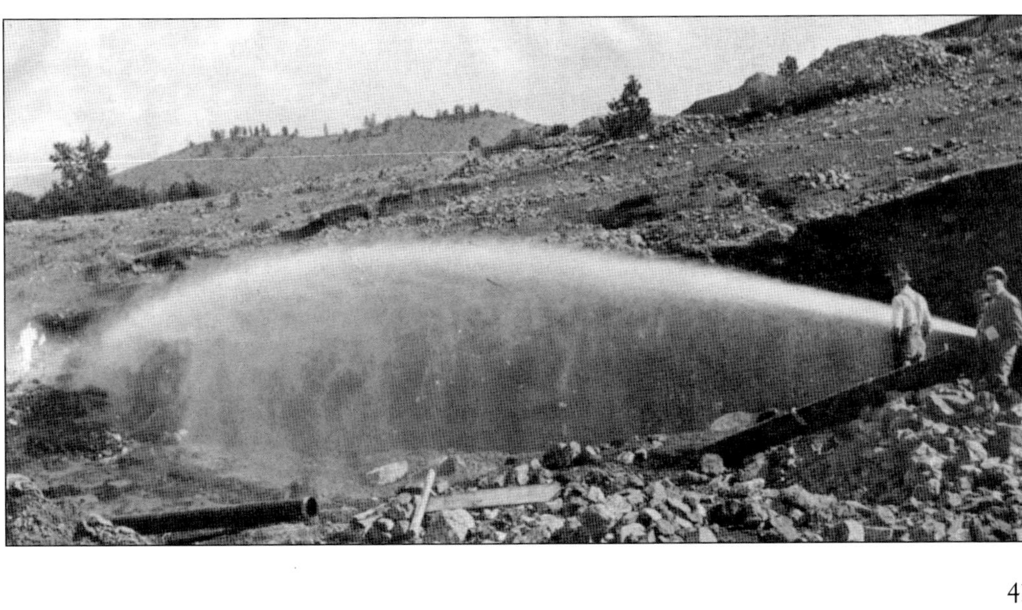

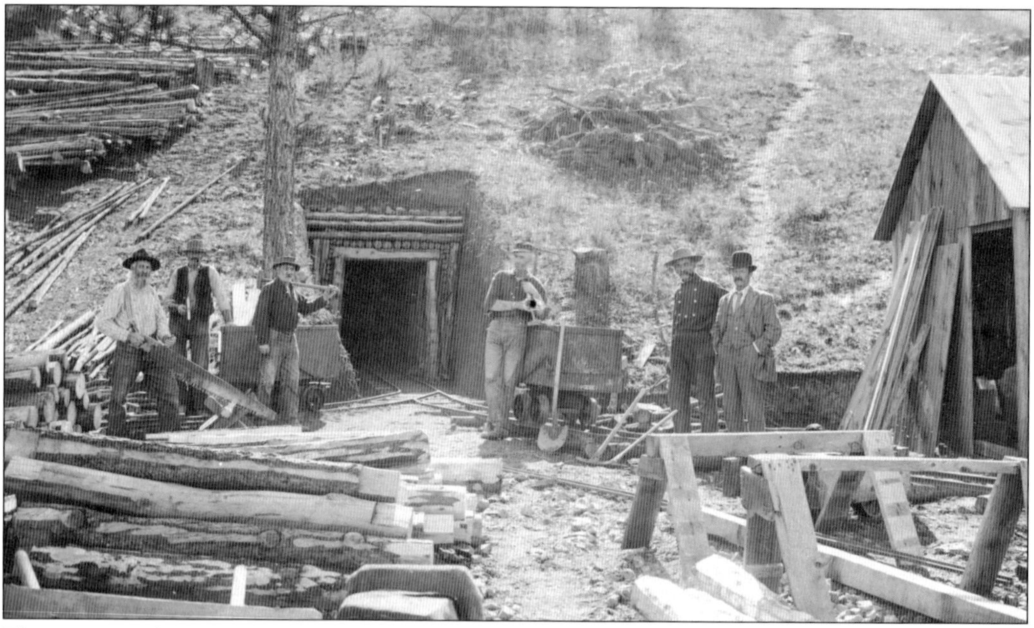

There were other prominent mine owners in the late 1880s. One of them was Jack Chambers. This image shows the Chambers mine around 1900. Note the timbers stacked in the lower left corner. They were used inside the mine to keep it from collapsing on the miners. Chambers is the man in the suit at right.

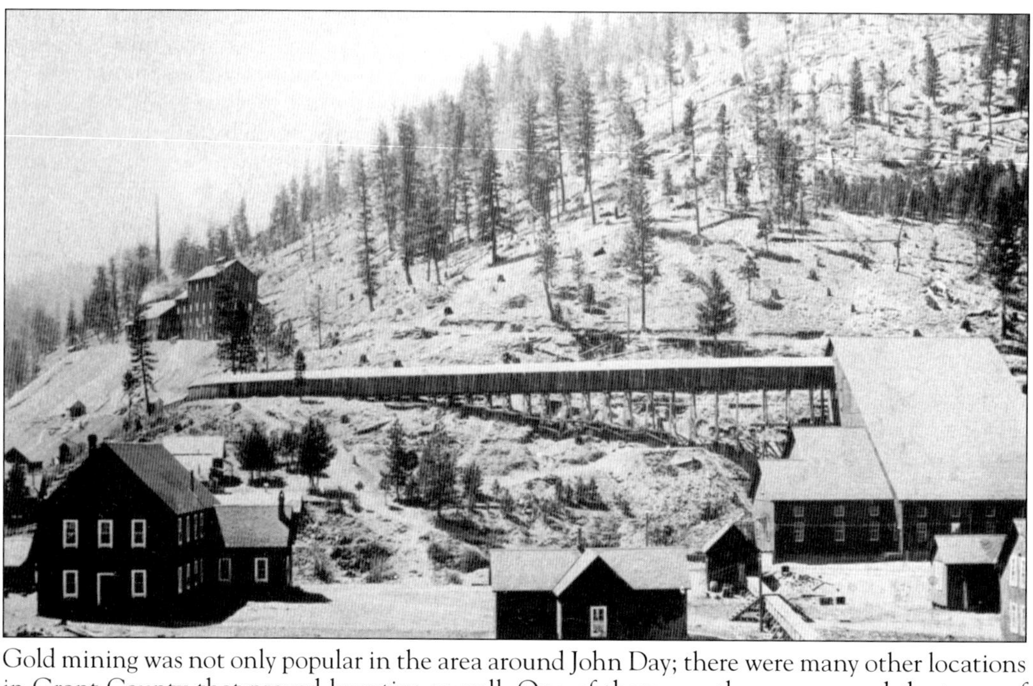

Gold mining was not only popular in the area around John Day; there were many other locations in Grant County that proved lucrative as well. One of them was the area around the town of Granite. Gold was discovered in this area around July 4, 1862. This image is of the Red Boy mine around 1898. The town's name comes from the large deposits of granite in the area.

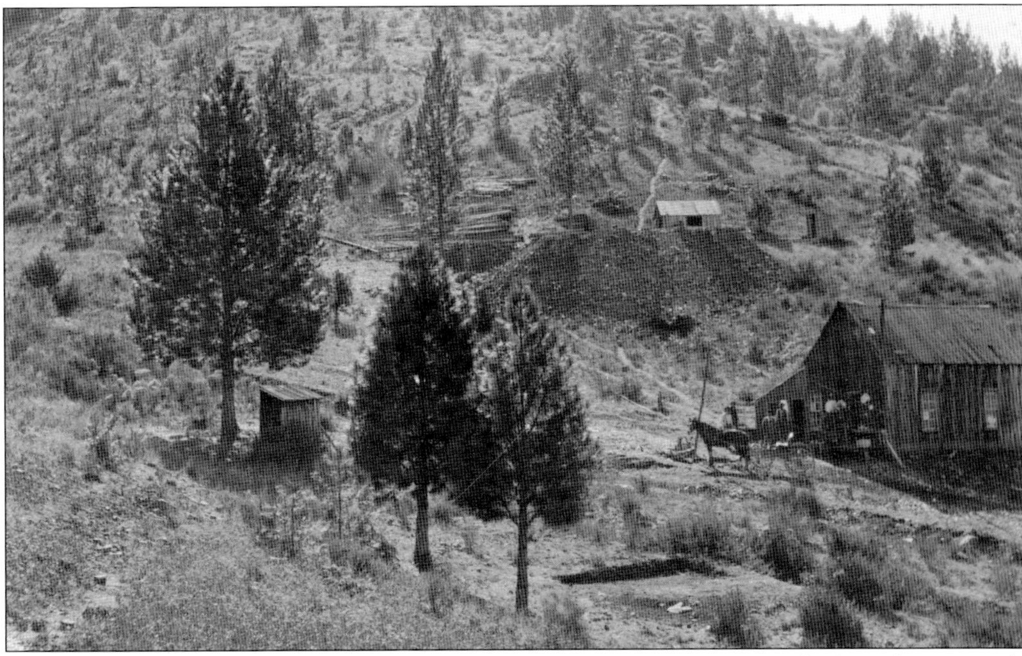

As the supply of gold diminished, some mine owners in Grant County switched to other minerals. One was chromium, and Jack Chambers was one of those who added this mineral to his holdings. This photograph shows his chromium mine shortly after 1900.

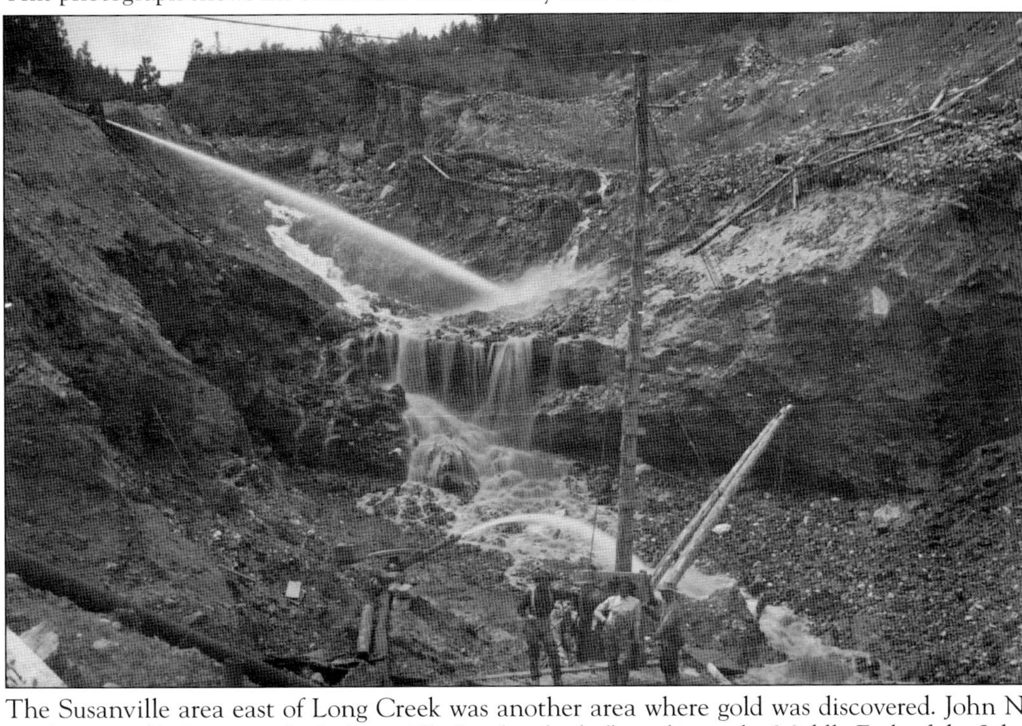

The Susanville area east of Long Creek was another area where gold was discovered. John N. Reid reportedly discovered a lode on Elk Creek, which flowed into the Middle Fork of the John Day River nearby. As with a lot of early gold-mining towns, a post office was established in 1888, changed to Galena several years later, and then dropped as the mining interests decreased.

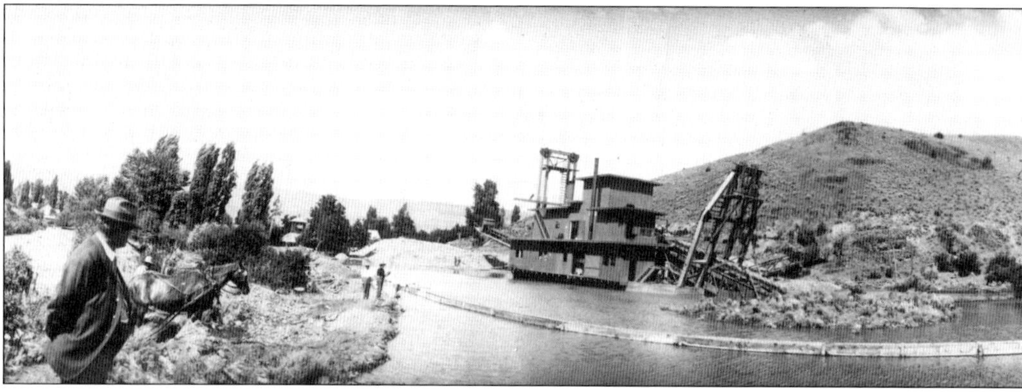

Mining for gold underwent a major change at the beginning of the 20th century. Although placer mining still existed in some areas, dredges became more common. Dredges worked on the rivers and large creeks. Tons of river gravel, sand, and dirt was scooped or drawn out with electrical or steam power. Once washed with water, the heavier gold would settle to the bottom. Some of the dredges were large and covered an entire streambed, as the image above shows. This was the gold dredge on Canyon Creek around 1910. The image below shows the John Day River much later. Dredge mining remains a controversial environmental issue due to its harmful effects on the streambed and surrounding area.

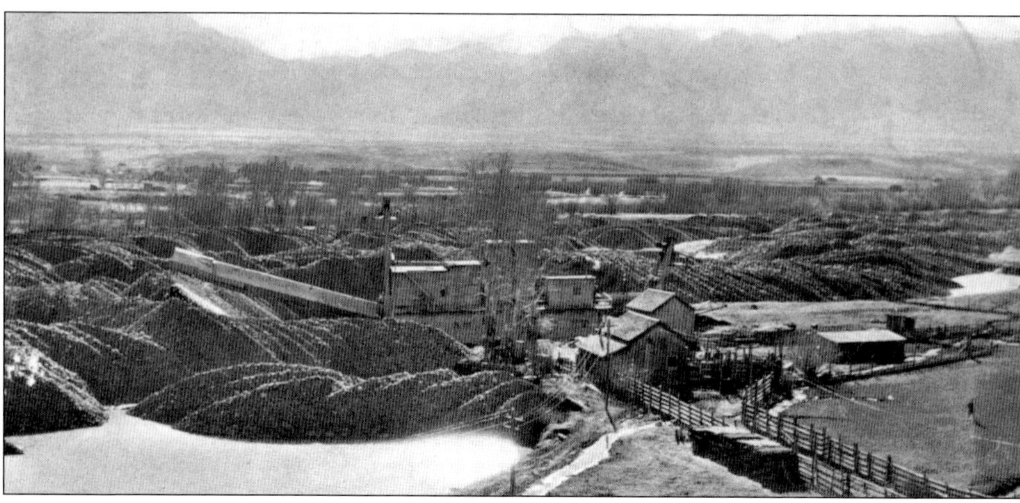

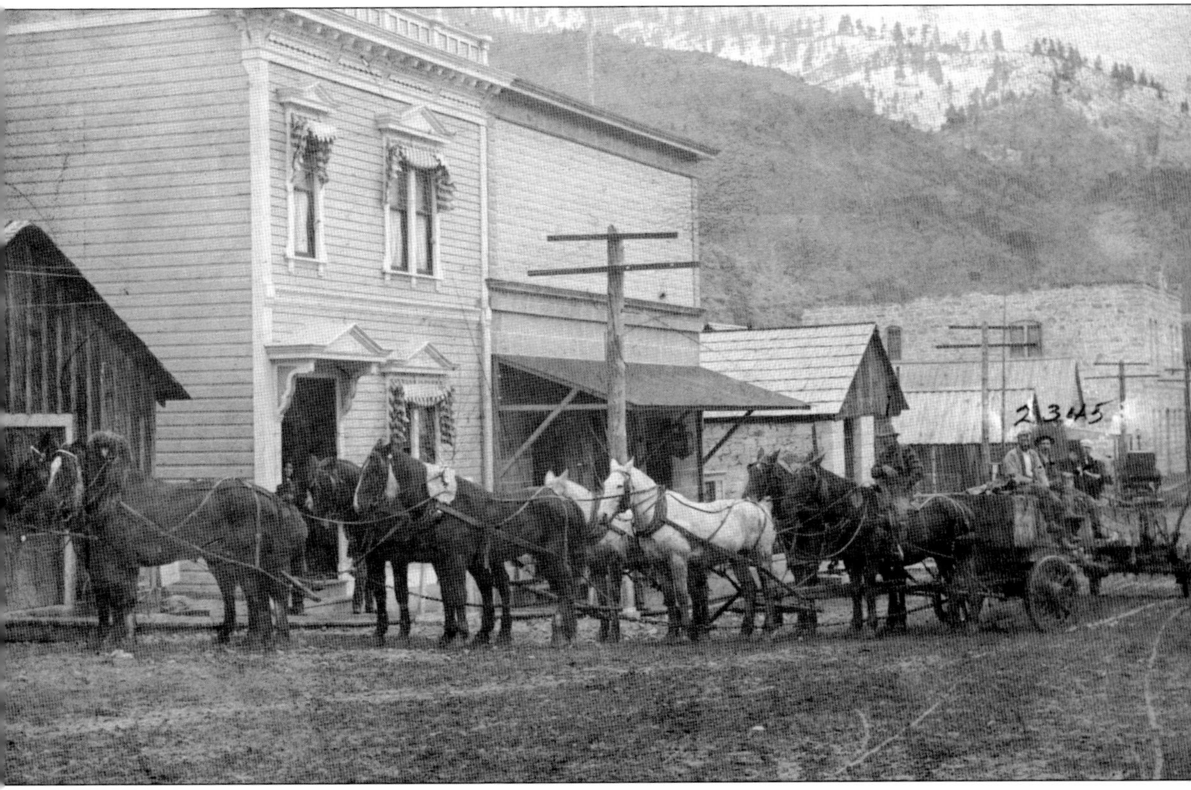

Around 1900, Jack McCullough's freight wagon is parked on South Washington Street in Canyon City in front of the Canyon City Market (extreme left). The Anna Sels House is the building with fancy gingerbread. The building next to it with the awning is the City Brewery. That building is still standing today. Farther south (at the right edge of the photograph) is the Masonic hall, a two-story stone building. Today, it is known as the Community Hall. The John Day Timber Dredge was reportedly built on the Porter Ranch in John Day but never left the ranch for lack of steam power. The freighting company brought timbers in from Bear Valley. From left to right are Jack McCullough (on horse), Al Sollinger, Oliver Peone, Horace Johnson, and Bill Loren.

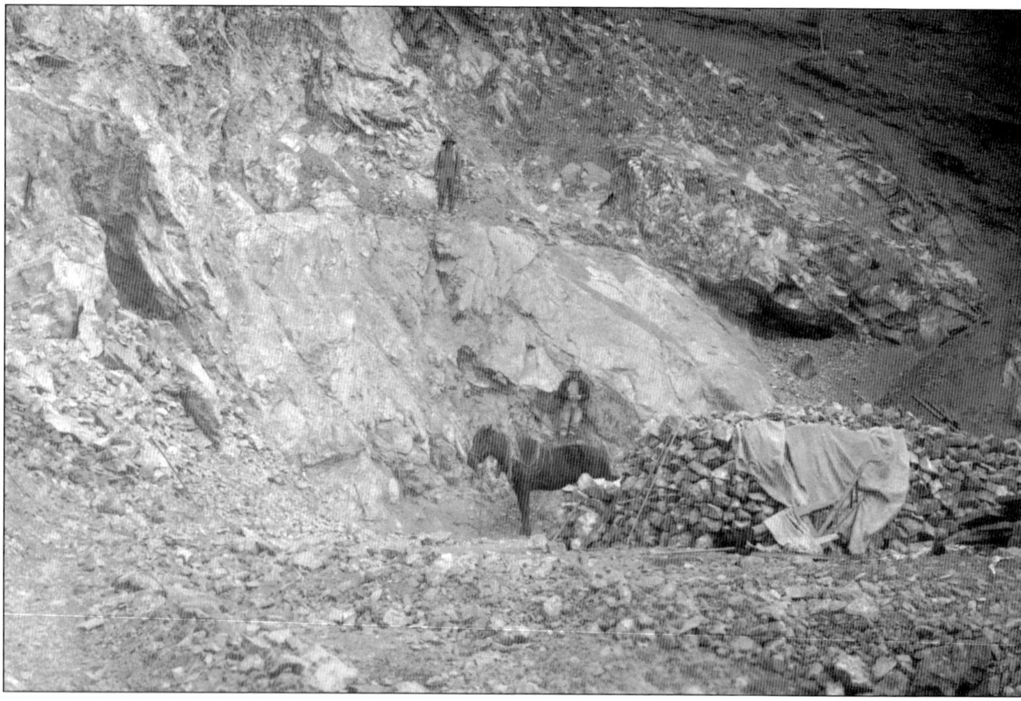

Hard rock mining consisted of three major steps. First, the rocks were sorted by size. The rocks, stacked in piles called "grizzlies," are generally all the relatively same size. The rocks were then sent via a conveyor belt or pulled on a sled down to a conveyor belt. Next, the rocks were crushed into a half-inch diameter or less. The larger fragments were then fed into a crusher machine. The final product could then be fed into a sluice box, where the heavier gold fragments were removed in the third step. Placer and hard rock mining were going on at the same time, as Canyon Mountain is riddled with tunnels from miners seeking gold. There is also evidence around Sumpter where the Chinese piled the rocks in long piles called "Chinese walls."

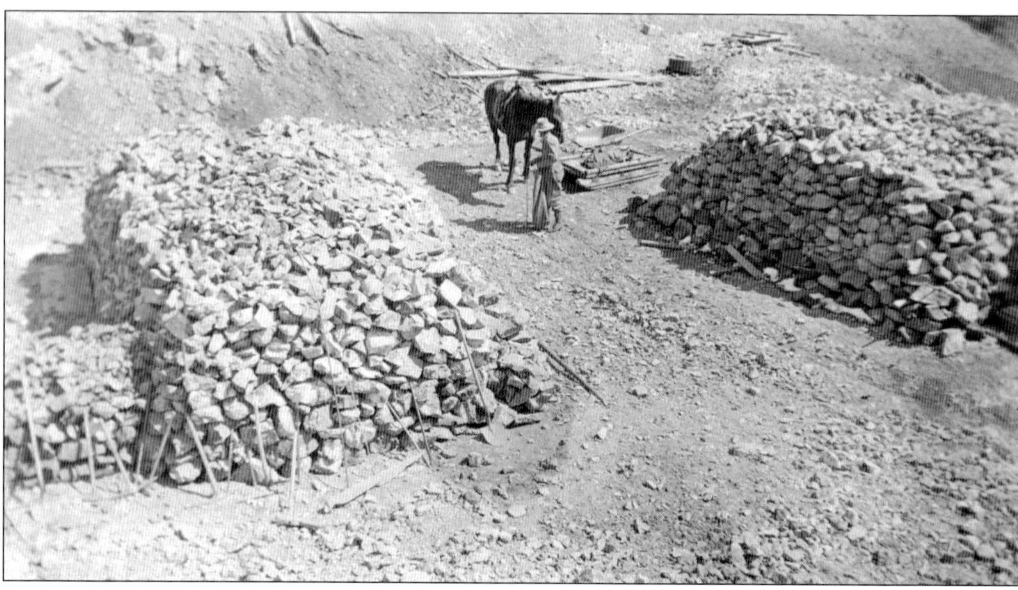

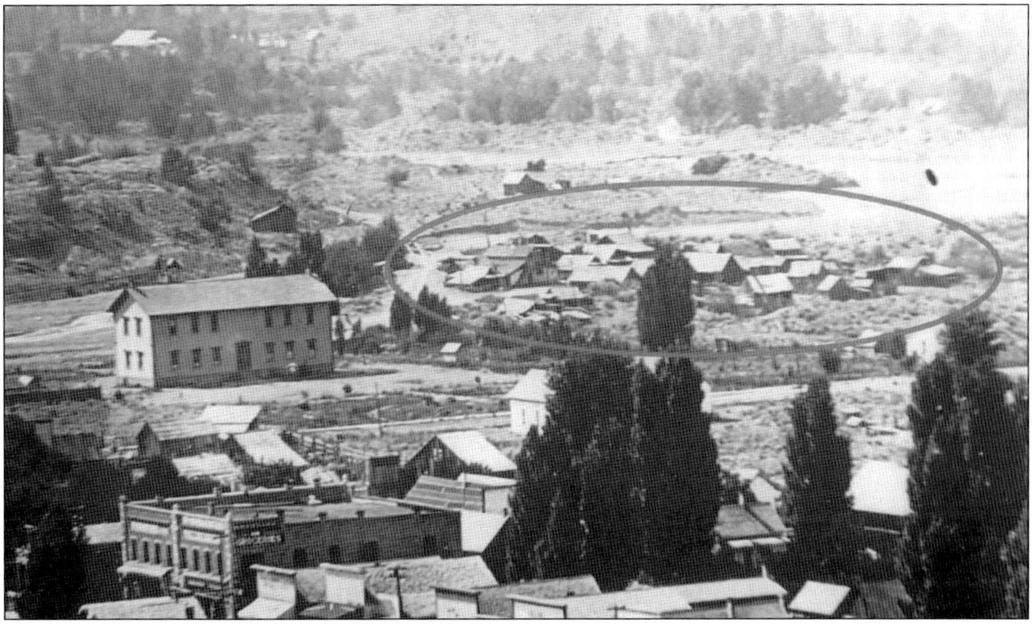

With the discovery of gold around John Day, miners arrived along with hundreds of Chinese. The Chinese were primarily used as laborers in the mines, but several began their own business, such as laundries, vegetable gardens, or even mining. The Chinatown erected in Canyon City burned to the ground in 1885 under suspicious circumstances. At that time, the Chinese population was estimated at 1,000, but no one really knows the exact number. Their attempt to rebuild at that site was refused by local authorities, so many of them moved a few miles north and rebuilt in what is now John Day. Above is John Day around 1920 with Chinatown circled. Below is what is now Clark Street in Canyon City. (Above, courtesy of Oregon State Parks, Kam Wah Chung State Heritage Site.)

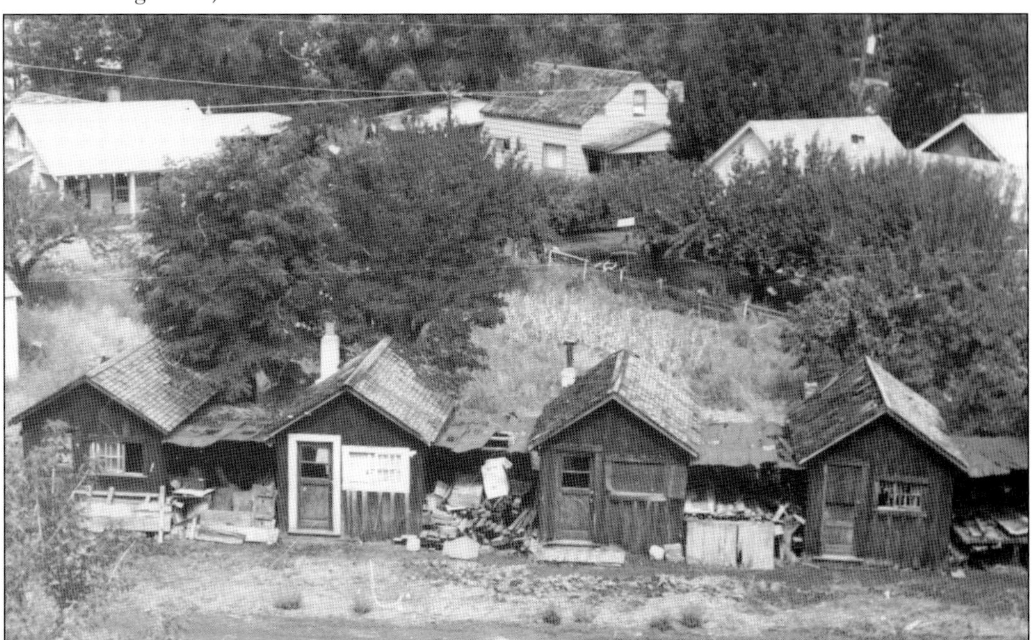

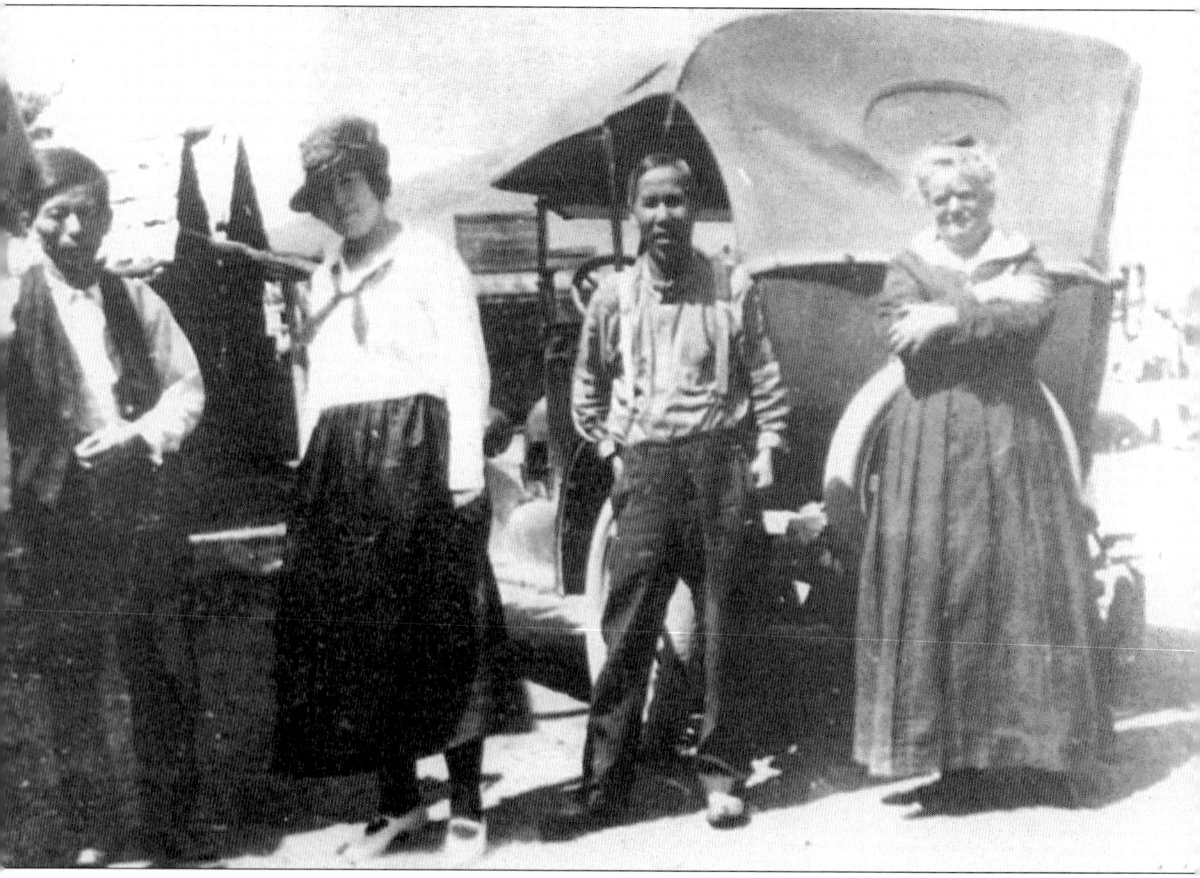

As the production of the mines decreased, some white miners sold their claims to the Chinese. The Chinese managed to survive by panning in the debris left behind by the hydraulic mining. It was tedious, but the Chinese were hard workers, and for some, the work paid off. There was a certain amount of animosity between the white residents and the Chinese. The Chinese had very little legal authority, and there were incidents of claim jumping. However, in 1887, a man by the name of Ing Hay, also called "Doc Hay," arrived in the area. At that time, the Chinese community was thriving. He was soon joined by another Chinese, Lung On. Both were from the same area in China. One was a doctor and the other a businessman. Together, they built the Kam Wah Chung building. From left to right are Lung On, Mable McGirr, Doc Hay, and Mrs. McGirr, the mother of Mable. (Courtesy of Oregon State Parks, Kam Wah Chung State Heritage Site.)

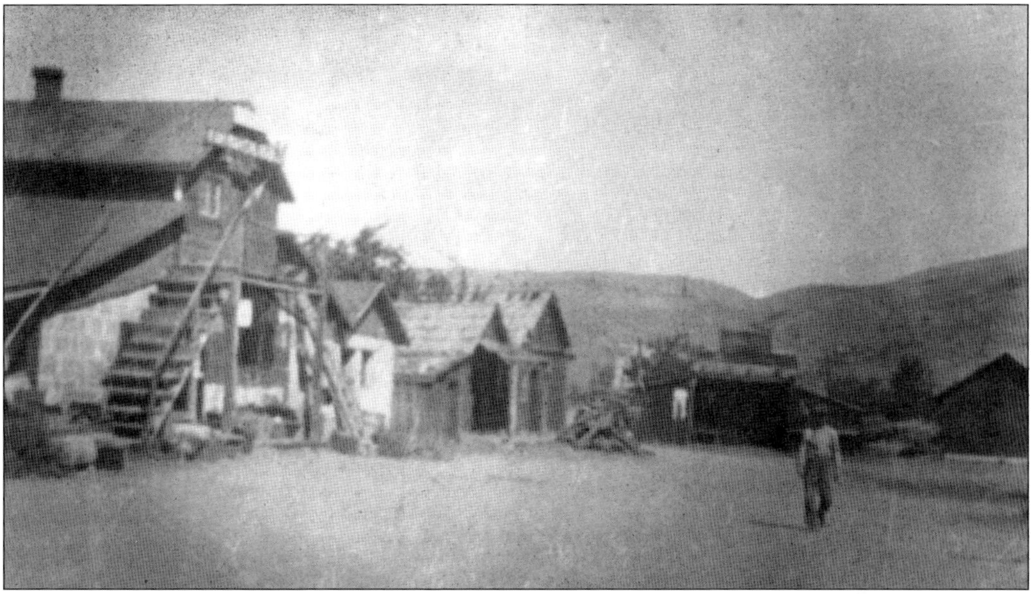

The Kam Wah Chung building was constructed in the late 1880s by Lung On and Ing Hay. It served as a gathering place for the local Chinese. It was a pharmacy, general store, doctor's office, and home for the two men. Doc Hay was famous throughout the area. Using many of the herbal medicines and diagnoses he had learned in China, his treatment of many illnesses and diseases brought thousands of patients to his practice throughout his life. He often just held the hands of patients and felt their pulse. He traveled miles, taking his medicines on the road. Lung On was the businessman. He adopted many Western standards. He invested money, learned how to drive, bought land, and sold automobiles, among many other activities. (Both, courtesy of Oregon State Parks, Kam Wah Chung State Heritage Site.)

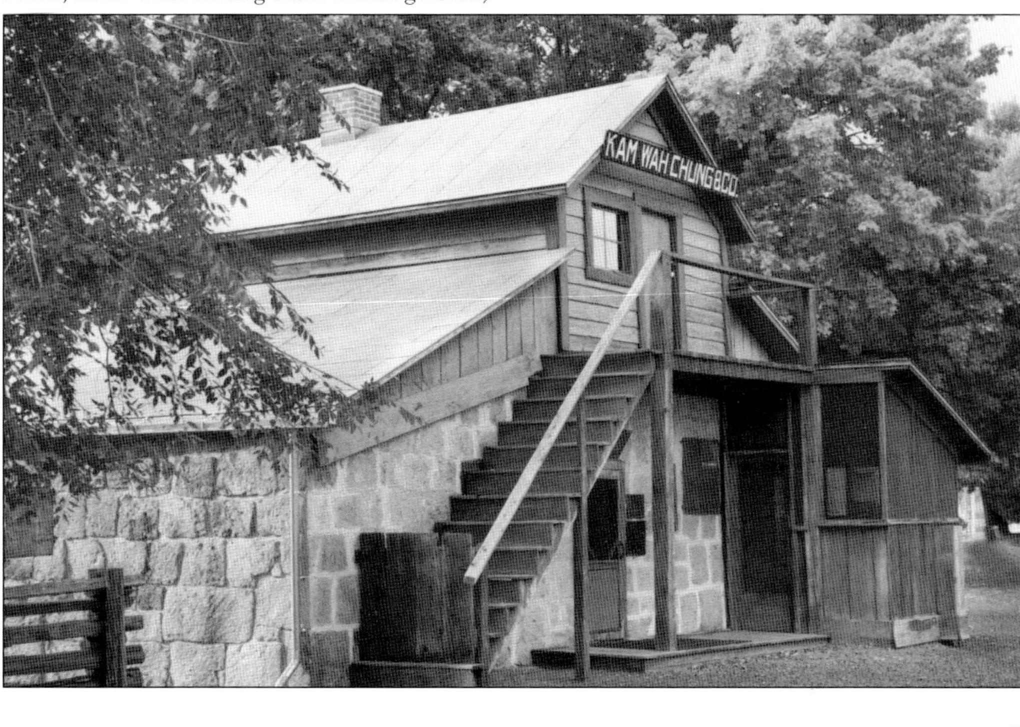

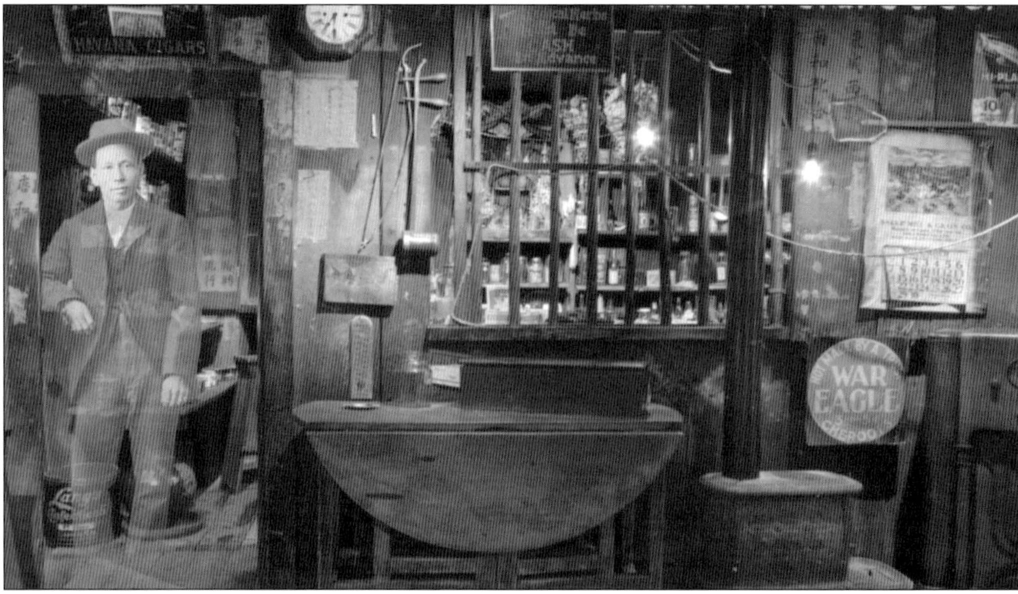

Long On is superimposed above, while Ing Hay is superimposed below. Guided tours of the heritage site are available daily when open and should be arranged prior to visiting. The interior of the building remains much like it was 100 years ago. For years, the building remained unattended, and some vandalism occurred, but it remains remarkably the same as when Lung On and Ing Hay lived and worked there. The desk in front is the same, as is the small stove. Beyond the window, one can see shelves stacked with items used by the two individuals. Old catalogs and other items are arranged on the walls. (Both, courtesy of Jody Brown Photography Art and Design and Oregon State Parks, Kam Wah Chung State Heritage Site.)

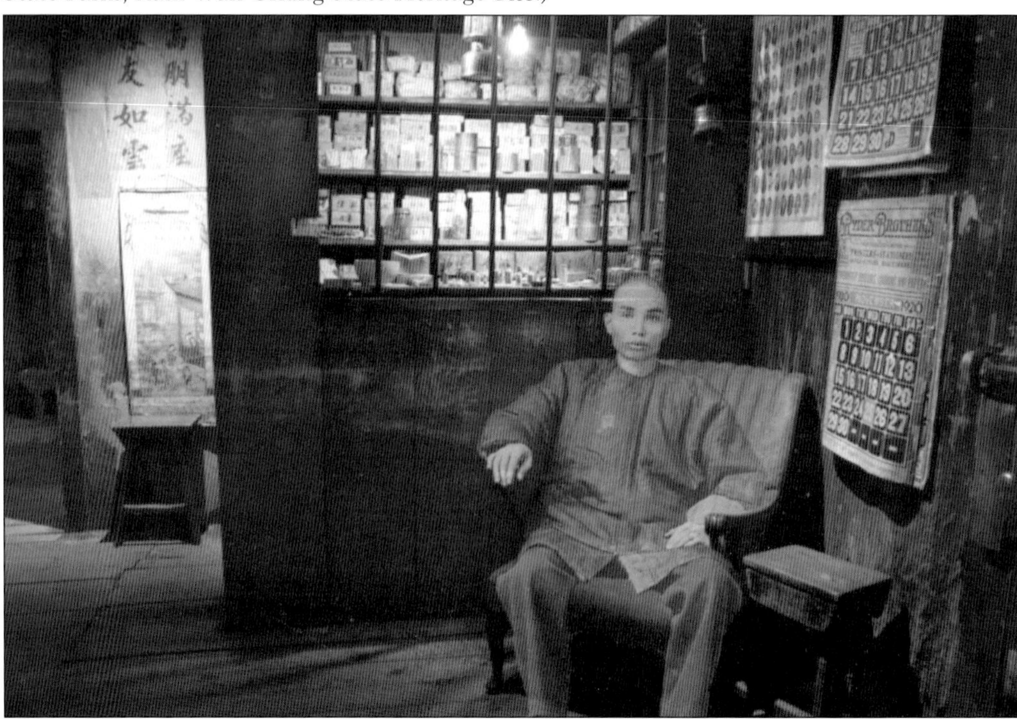

Three

Cattle, Sheep, Farming, and Timber

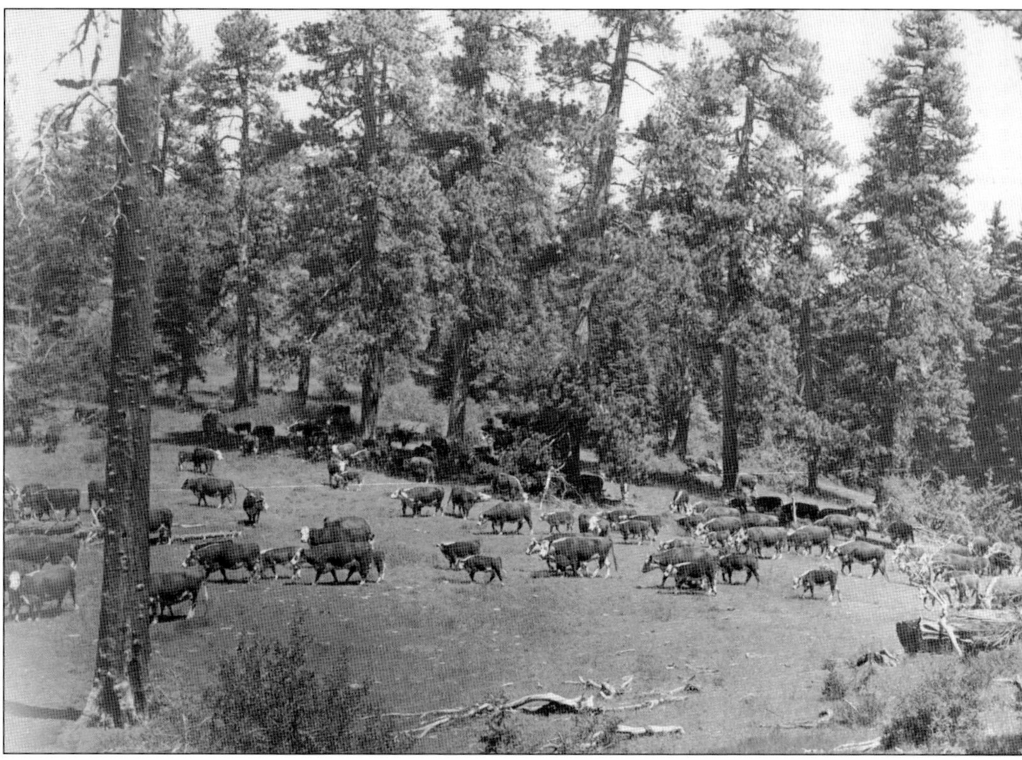

After most of the miners had left to search for gold elsewhere, remaining and new residents took notice of other ways to be productive. Large stands of ponderosa pine grew in the forested mountains, cattle and sheep were raised in the valleys, and rich soil was available for farming. The image shows where cattle grazed during the summer.

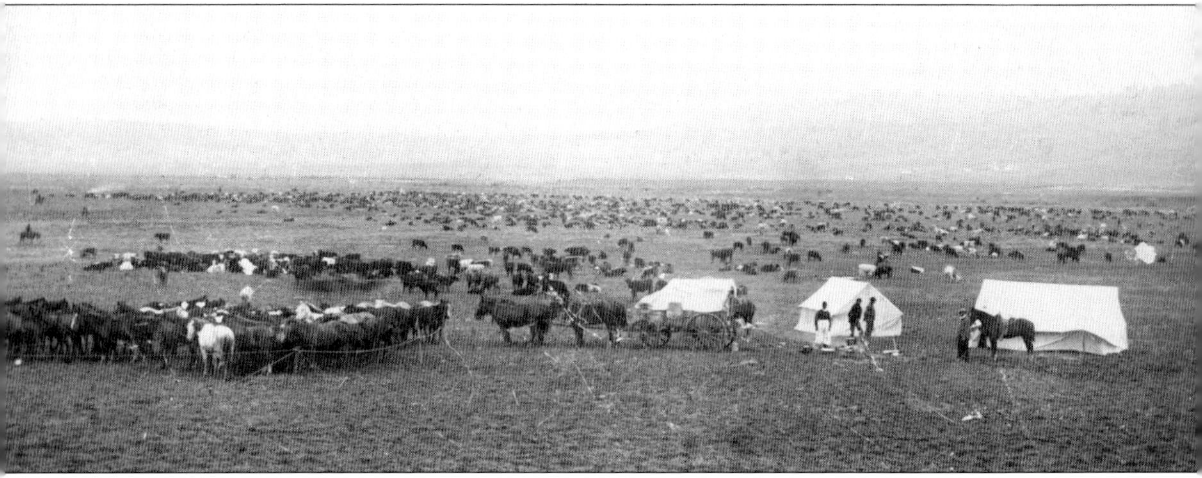

It sometimes seemed like cattle stretched for miles in the valleys where they were grazing. The two images show the McGirr herd in Fox Valley around 1901. Above is a temporary encampment and a wagon that brought supplies to the location. Horses are corralled at left. Seventeen cowboys worked the herd, which numbered around 2,500. The cowboys and other helping hands are shown below during round-up. (Both, courtesy of the Mrs. E.R. Mumford Collection at the Grant County Historical Museum.)

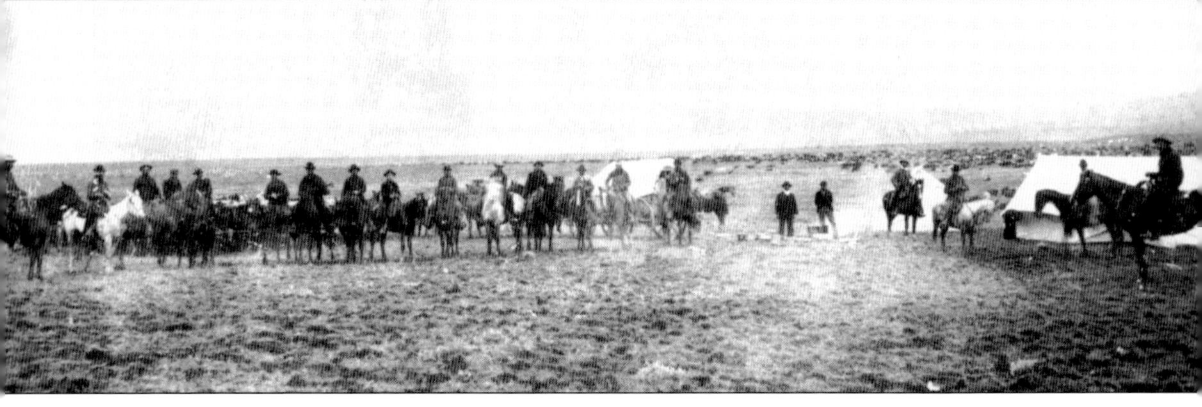

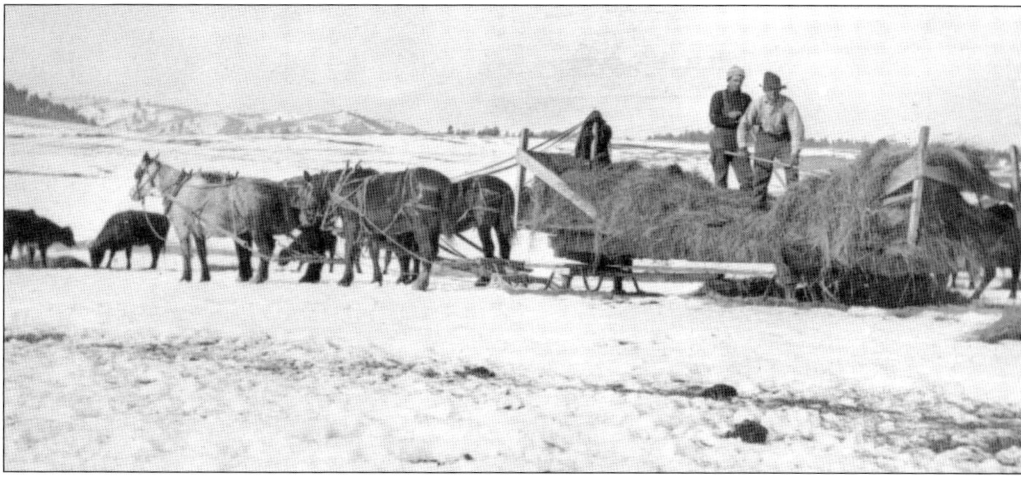

During the harsh winters in eastern Oregon, thousands of head of livestock often perish due to very cold temperatures, deep snow, and lack of food. Such was the case in Grant County in the mid-1880s.

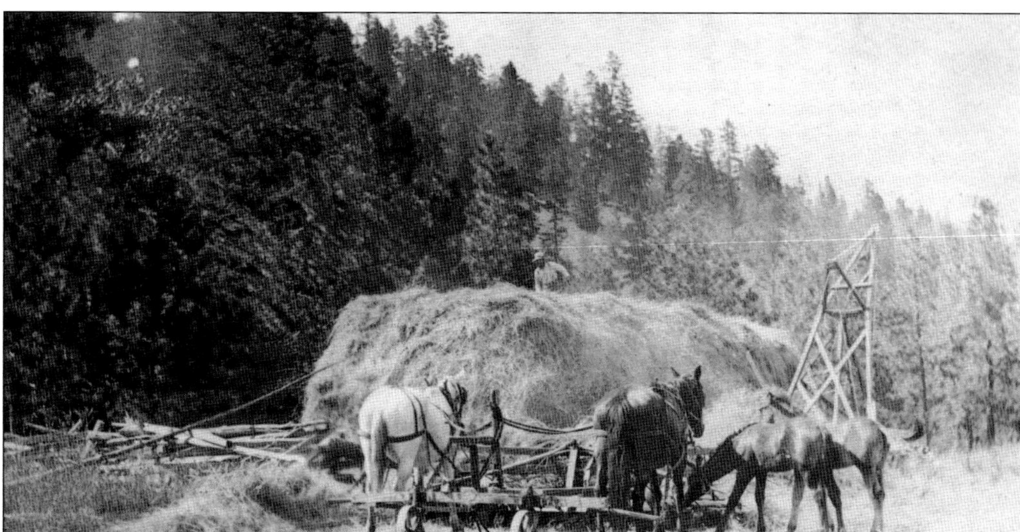

At first, cattle were left to survive without food for grazing during the winter. Ranchers could not suffer such losses. Hay farming provided an additional food source during the winter. The rich soil in the valleys led to an abundance of hay that would be stacked in piles for winter use.

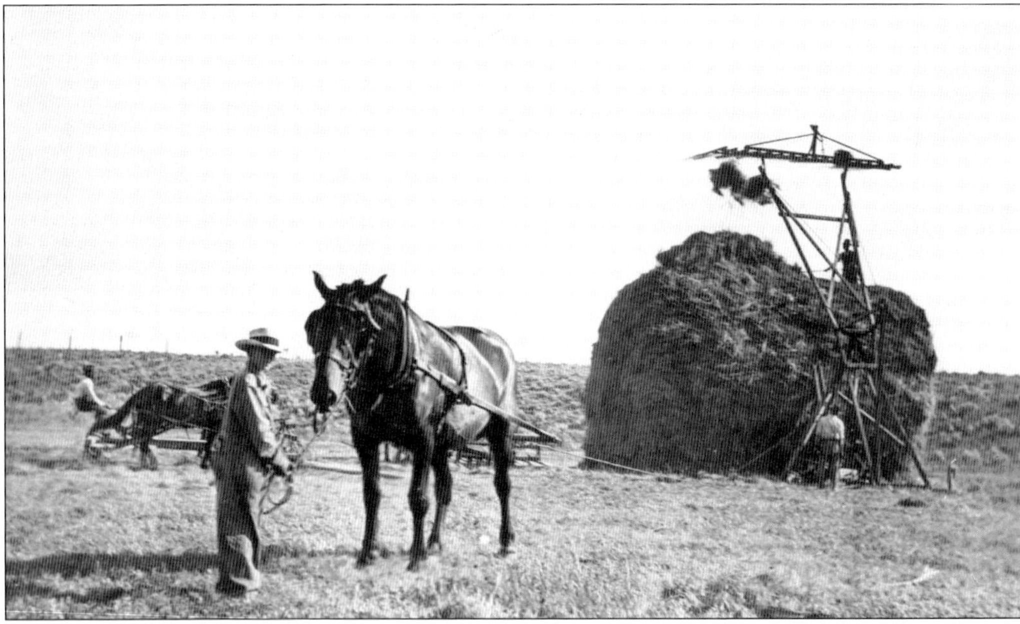

Haystacks could get quite high, and different means were used to stack the hay. Horses and a pulley system allowed the hay to be stacked in these large piles. To get the hay into tight bundles, a haystack needle with a rope tied on the end was pulled through the base of the pile of hay. Haystack needles were long, slender, metal poles with an opening at the end. The rope would then be untied and pulled through the pile. It would be thrown over the pile, tied to the haystack needle, and pushed through the stack again. Doing this several times allowed the hay to be compacted into tight bundles. Other means to stack hay involved the Jenkins stacker (above) and Mormon pole (below).

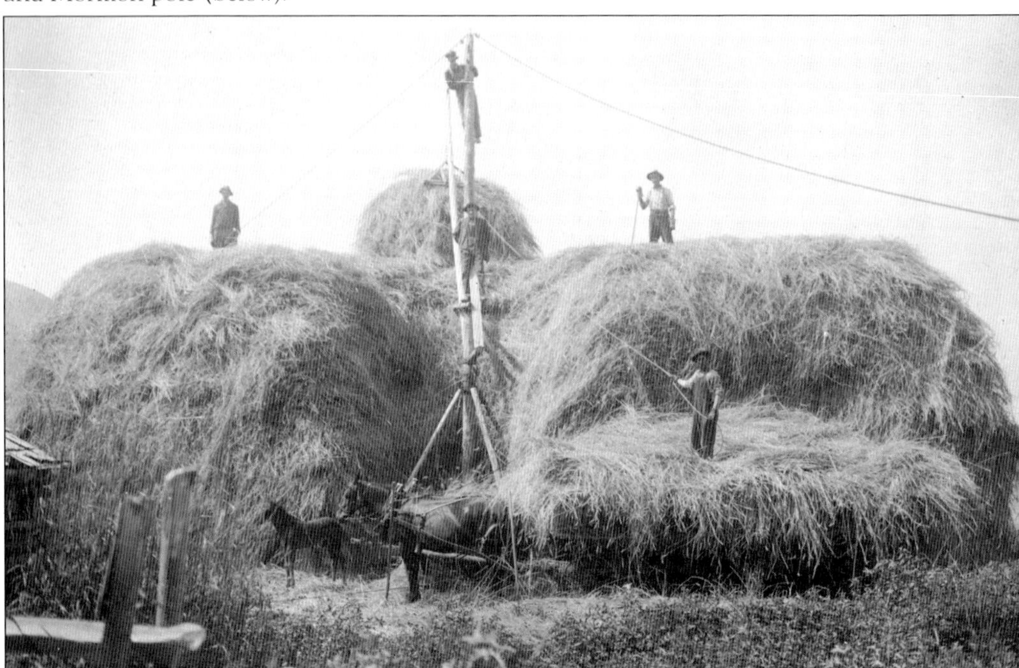

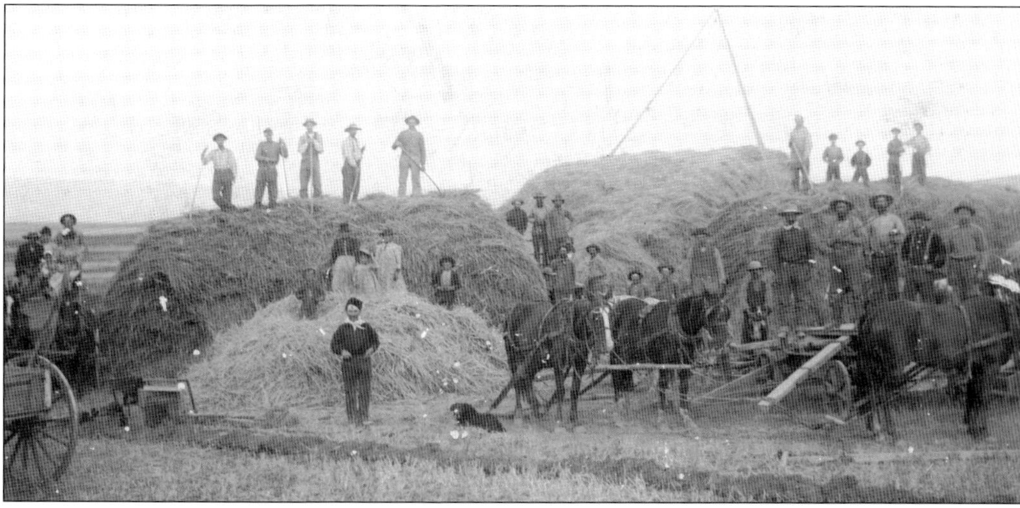

Various forms of stacking hay and storing it for the long winter months appear in these images. A Mormon pole is used in both images. Two gentlemen are identified in the lower photograph: Herman Oliver (on the wagon) and Frank Oliver (below the Mormon pole). The women are unidentified. Also in back of the team of horses driven by Herman Oliver is a dairy wagon.

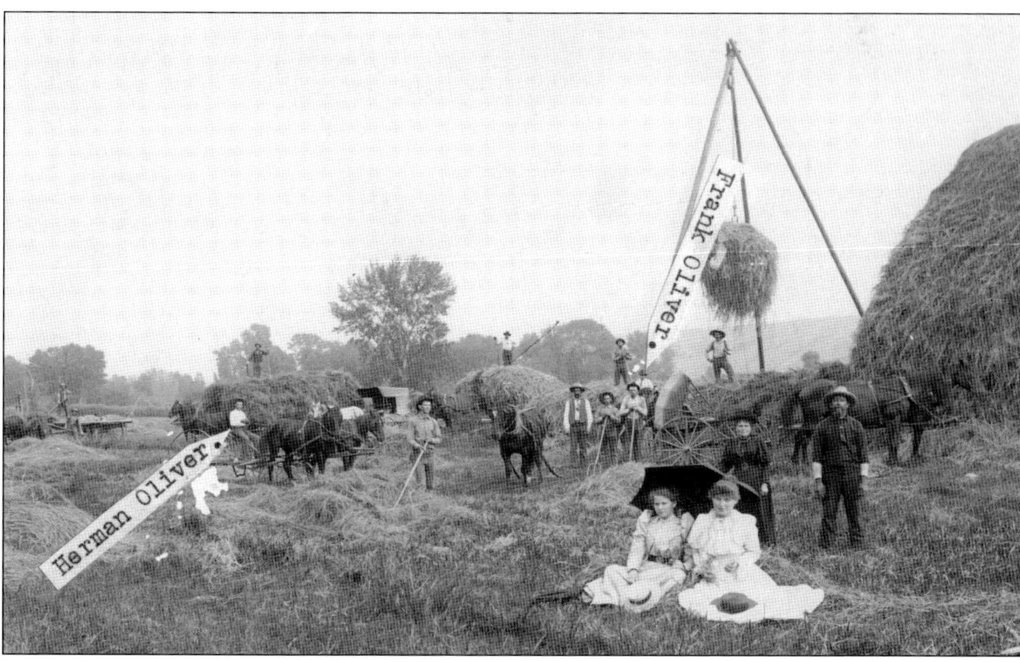

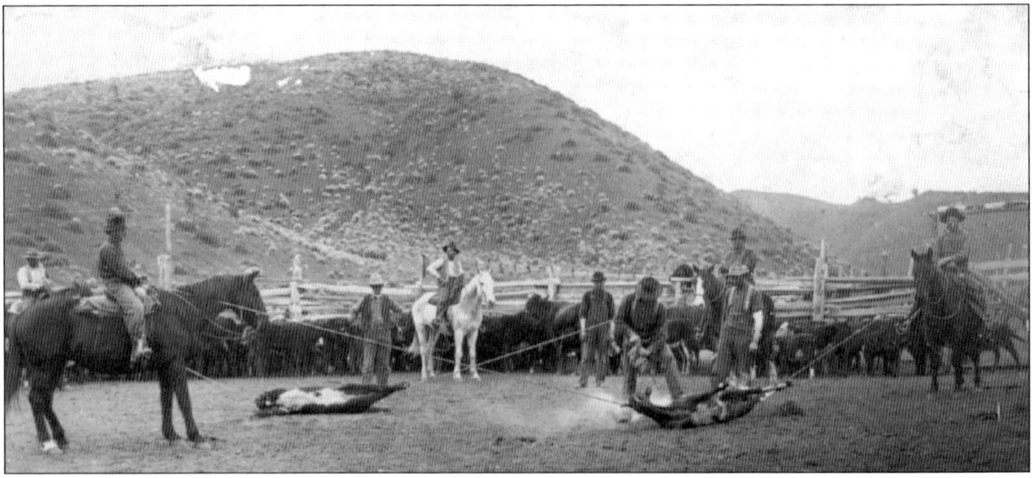

With cattle numbering in the thousands, it is obvious that some would stray from the main herd, especially at their grazing lands in the wooded areas at higher elevations. If a cowboy happened upon such cattle, how was he to know whose herd it belonged to? Branding was the answer. Each ranch had its own special brand. Throughout Grant County, there were well over 100 different brands. Joe Oliver's brand was simply JO. Others were a combination of symbols, bars, and whatever the rancher had in his mind. Cattle that had strayed could be returned to the main herd. If the cowboy was at a different ranch, it would be foolish to mix the different brands with his, since he could be accused of rustling. Above is the Henry Trowbridge Ranch in Izee. (Below, courtesy of Grant County Ranch and Rodeo Museum.)

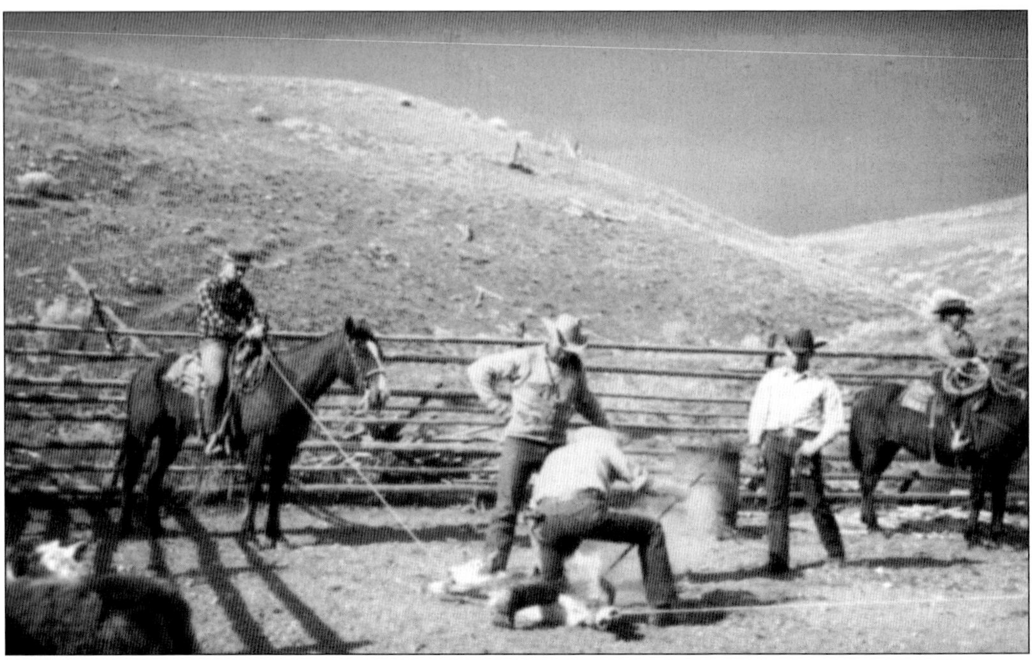

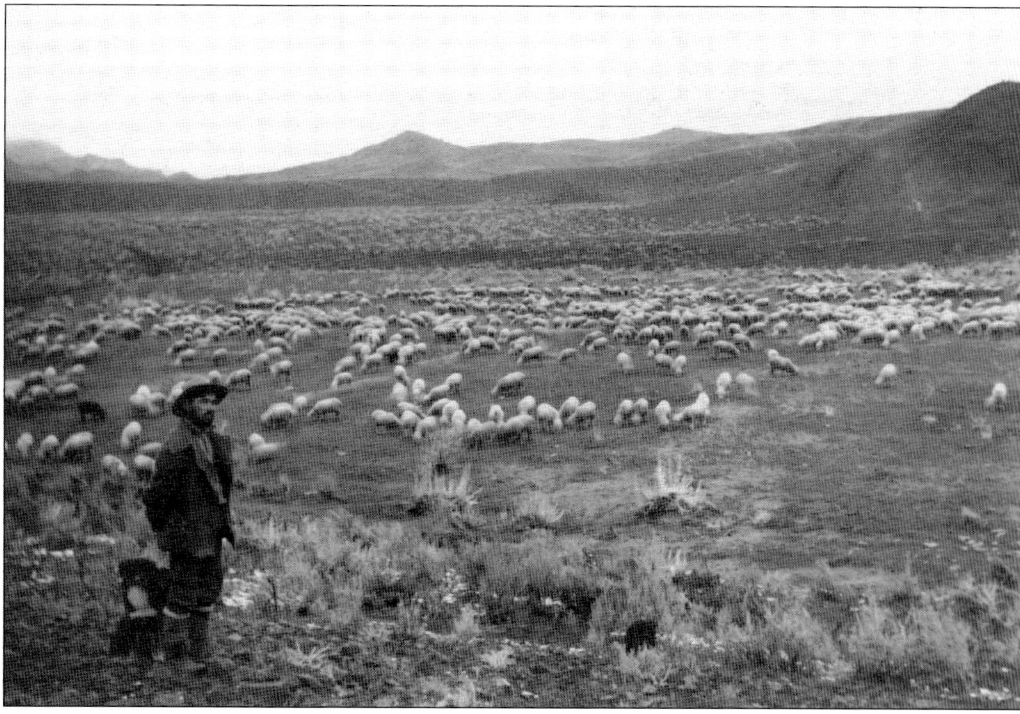

Cattle were not the only form of livestock raised in Grant County over the years. Sheep also became a lucrative business, and a band could number well over 1,000 sheep. There were often conflicts between cattle ranchers and sheep ranchers. Some believed that sheep were more destructive to the grasses, but certainly cattle did their share. Later, as ranchers turned to more environmentally conscientious practices, these fears were subdued. Above is the Tom Kennedy band around 1910. Below is the James Small Ranch. A sheepherder often spent long, lonely days as the only guardian of the band along with his dog or two.

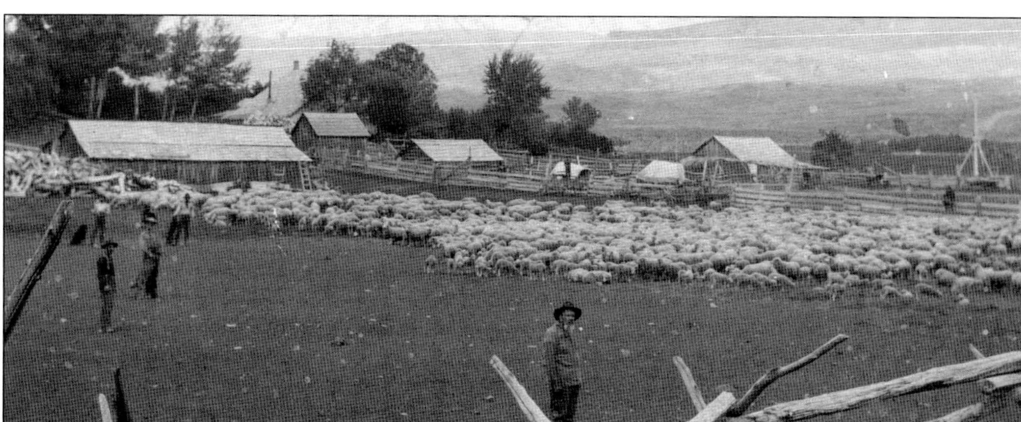

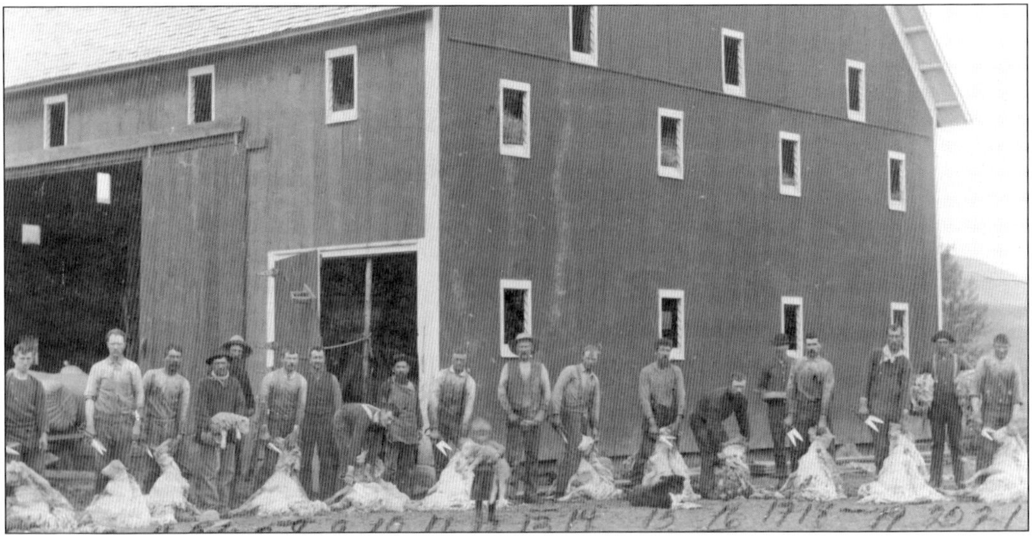

Unlike cattle, sheep had to be sheared of their fleece. This could involve many individuals. Above is the Billie Stewart Ranch in Dayville around 1882. From left to right, including the child in front, are R.L. Oliver, Sam Martin, Link Luce, Mr. Hill, Charley Ladre, Donald MacKay, Al Officer, E.E. Roope, Ward Swift, unidentified, Hi Munjar, Bob Fulkerson, Jim Angel, Jim Harrison, unidentified, Fred Goyon, Sam Winters, and Chas Kimball.

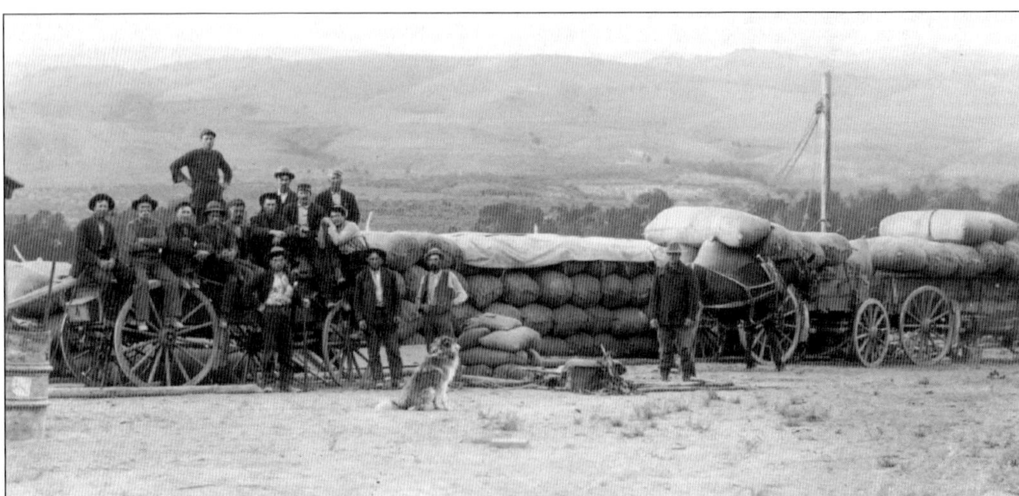

Once the sheep were sheared in spring, the wool was tightly packed into sacks and sent by way of wagon teams to The Dalles. A sheepherder was an individual a rancher put a large amount of faith in. After all, he could be gone for several months tending a band. Once the sheep were sheared, the wool would bring many thousands of dollars at market.

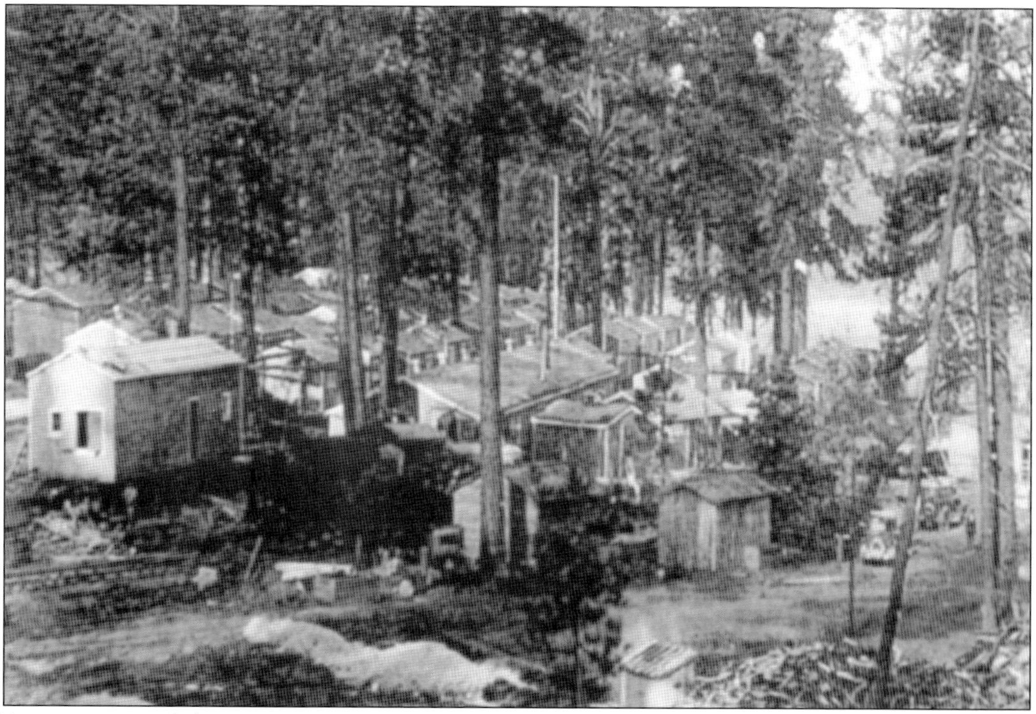

Logging entered the scene in Grant County in the late 1800s. The vast stands of straight timber led to many sawmills being built throughout the county. They seemed to come into existence in remote locations. But how was one to get a heavy log to market? It was Mr. Eccles who brought rail lines into the county for the logs to be sent to market. Note the rail line at left above at Camp One near Seneca. The image below shows something quite different. Note the skid trail leading out of the timber, with several logs on it leading to the pile at lower right. This sawmill was located near Canyon Creek around 1900.

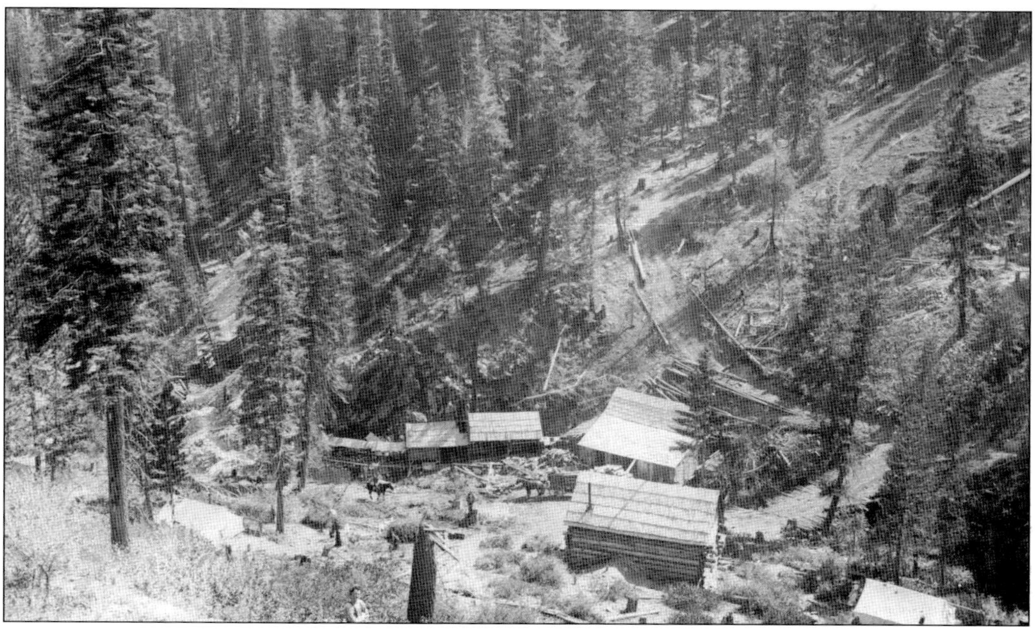

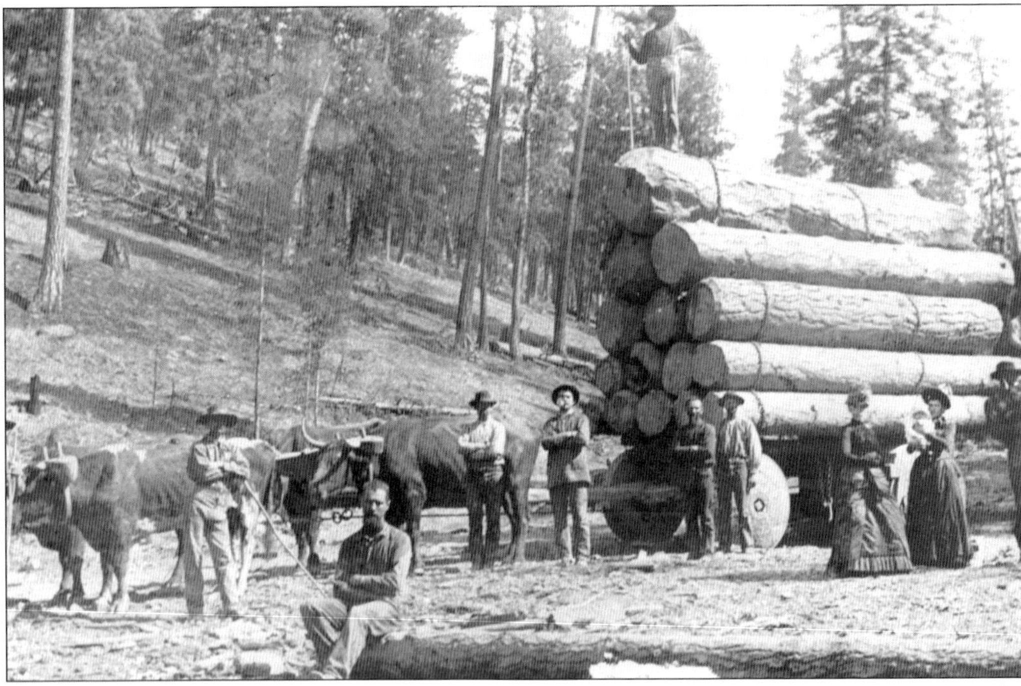

Before railroads arrived, logs were brought to sawmills by horse, mule, and oxen teams. If pulled by a team, the logs were dragged across small logs placed perpendicular to the route. This was called log skidding and is shown below. Generally, only one log could be skidded at a time. Above, a team of oxen pulls a large load of logs around 1900. Livestock would soon be replaced by motorized log trucks.

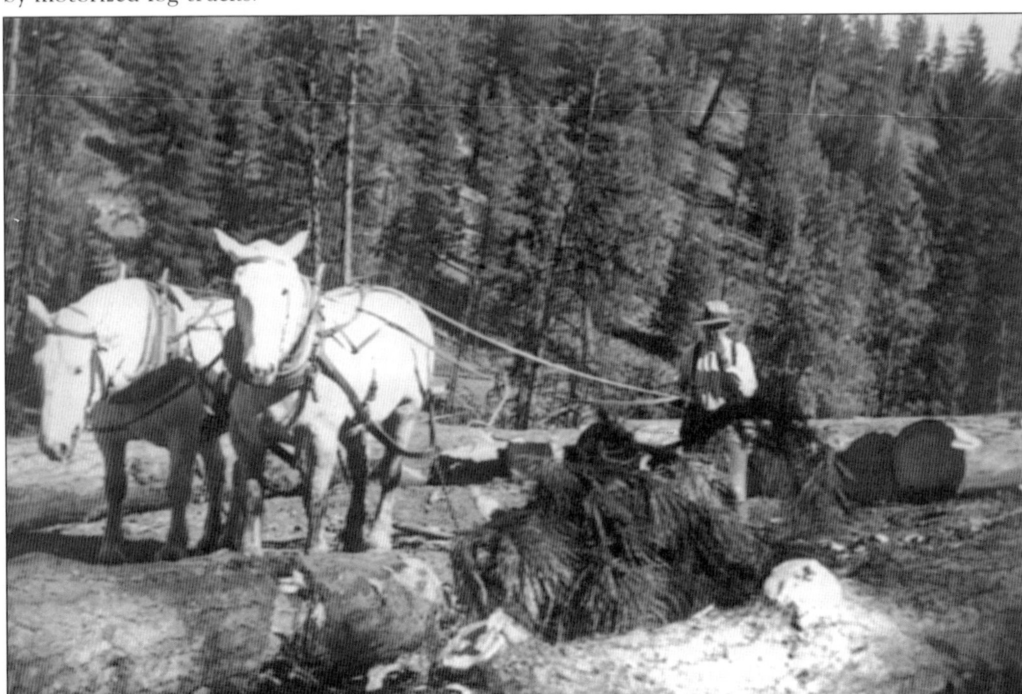

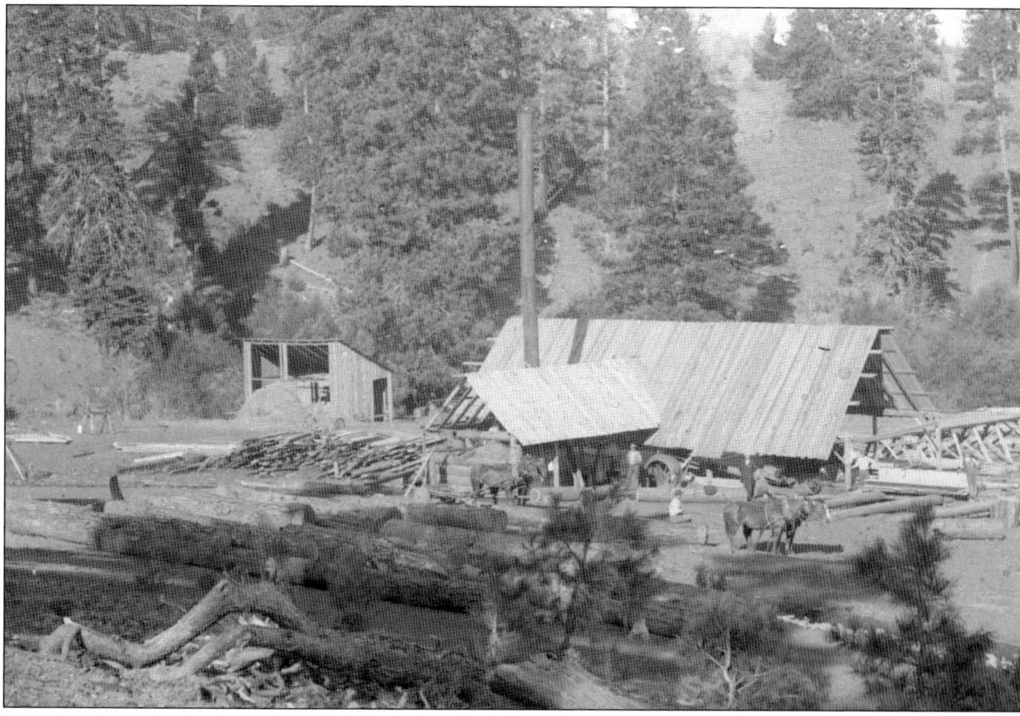

Fred Carlin was one of the prominent sawmill owners around the turn of the century. Below, a team of horses hauls a large log into the mill to be cut to appropriate lengths. The image was taken around 1910, and the men sitting on the log are unidentified. Above is the mill around 1900. Those identified inside the mill and around it, in no particular order, are Margaret Carlin Leuck, Deldon Carlin, Frank Baiers, George Carlin, Wilbur Carlin, Bill Bates, Catharine Carlin Mattson, and Wilbur Cresap.

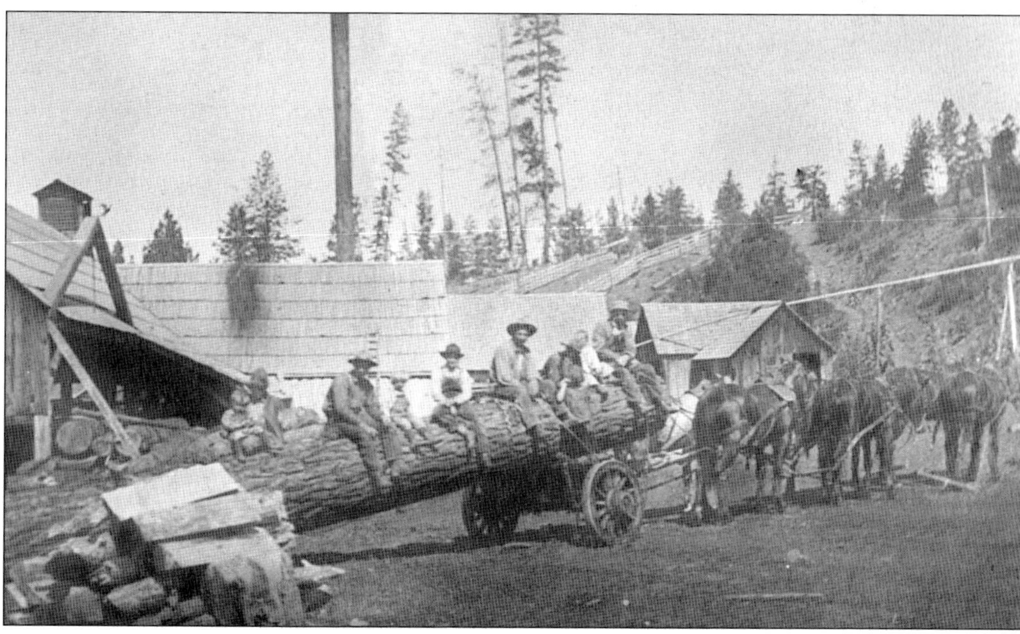

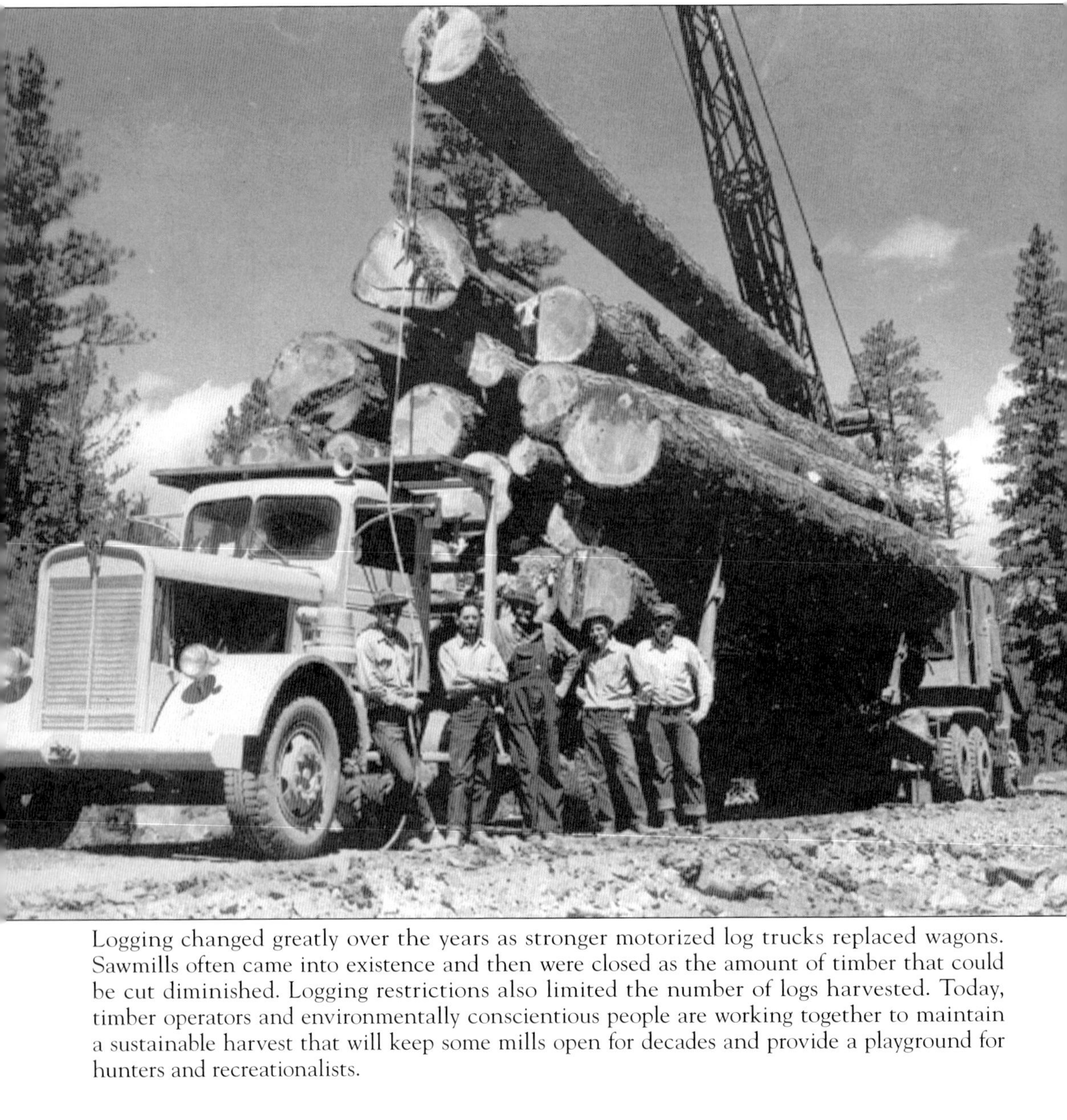

Logging changed greatly over the years as stronger motorized log trucks replaced wagons. Sawmills often came into existence and then were closed as the amount of timber that could be cut diminished. Logging restrictions also limited the number of logs harvested. Today, timber operators and environmentally conscientious people are working together to maintain a sustainable harvest that will keep some mills open for decades and provide a playground for hunters and recreationalists.

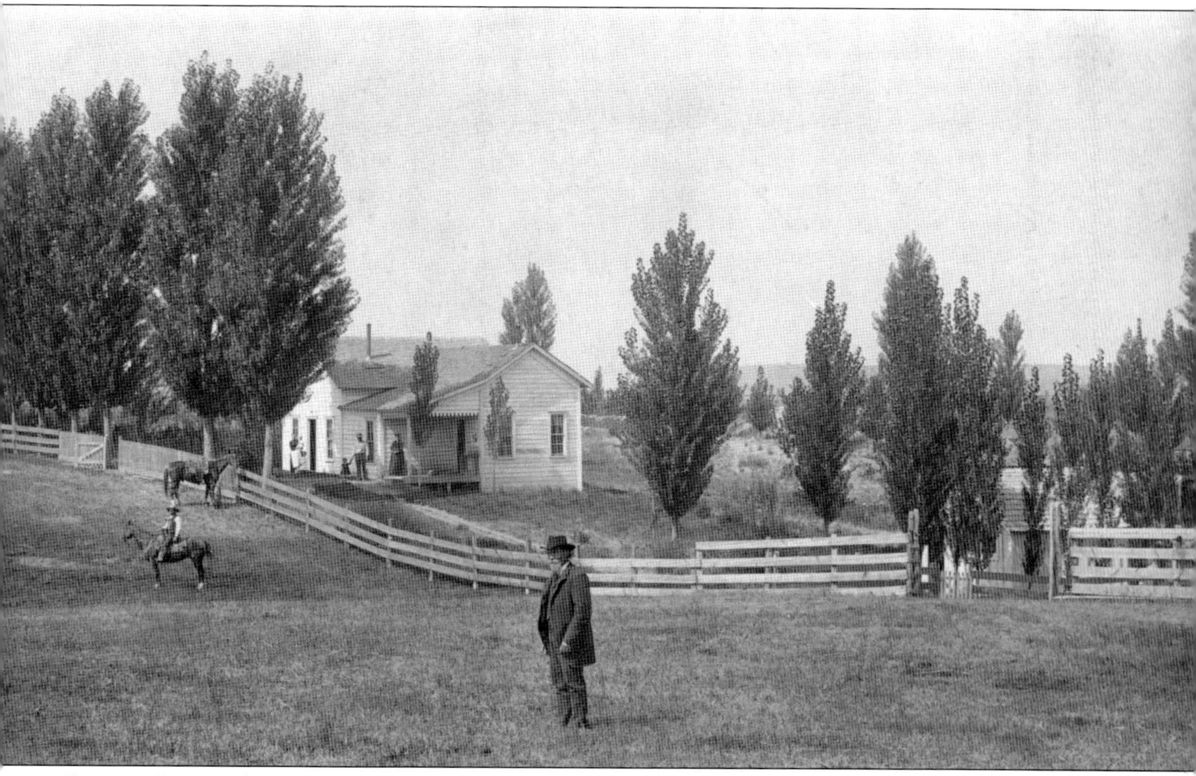

Eastern Oregon does not receive a notable supply of rain during the year. Water, both for irrigation and home use, often comes from springs. In this particular innovative case, the house was built over a spring to ensure running water at all times. Shown in the image are D.B. Rinehart, standing in field; Dan Fisk, mounted on horseback at left; on porch far left, Eudora Wilson holding baby Florence with Nora Wilson (small child close by her side); on center porch, Frank Fisk holding daughter Stella by hand; Rosalia Fisk, wife of Frank, to his left in the doorway.

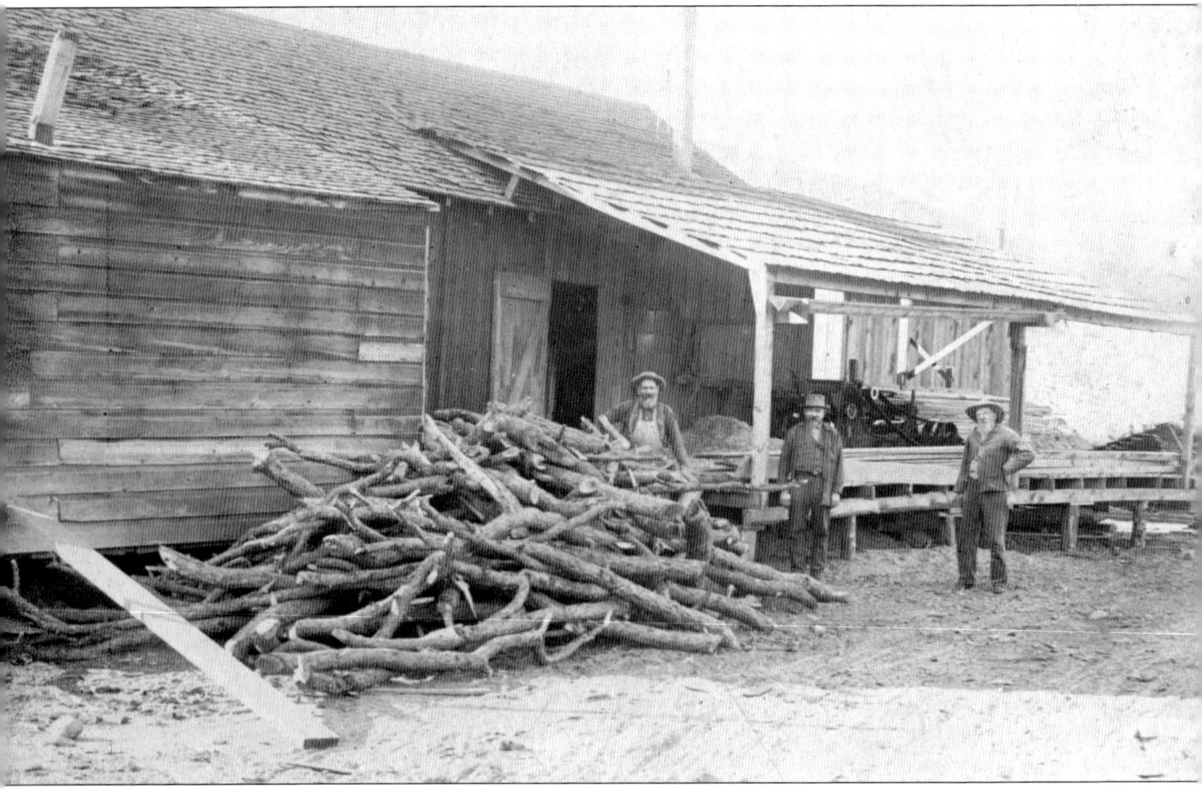

In the late 1800s, William S. Southworth (center) owned a sawmill on Fall Mountain and devoted his time to the mill. He sold a half interest in the mill to a man named Guernsey and then purchased the planer mill and door and sash factory in Canyon City, seen above. This business was on the old creek bank near the present Hicks Bottling Works site and escaped the Canyon City fire of 1898. Southworth provided the sash and doors to the county courthouse, which later burned down in 1951. He was elected county clerk in 1878 and served one term. In addition, he served as deputy sheriff under O.P. Cresap from 1890 to 1892. (Courtesy of Jo and Jack Southworth.)

Four

SCHOOLS, CHURCHES, AND SOCIAL ORGANIZATIONS

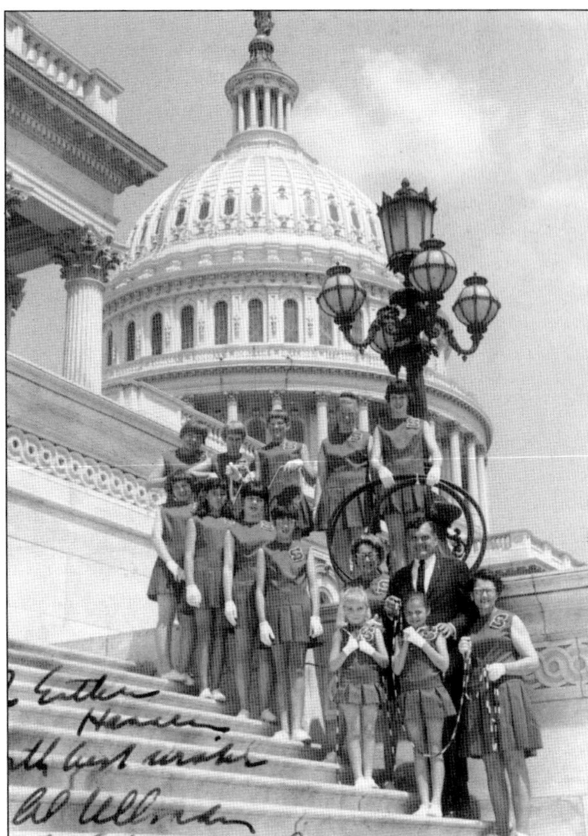

The Seneca Rope Jumpers made a historic trip to Washington, DC, in 1967 to perform at the invitation of US Representative Al Ulman. The 11-member group traveled by the Union Pacific Railway, stopping at various locations to perform. The jumping group was formed in 1946. They always wore bright red uniforms.

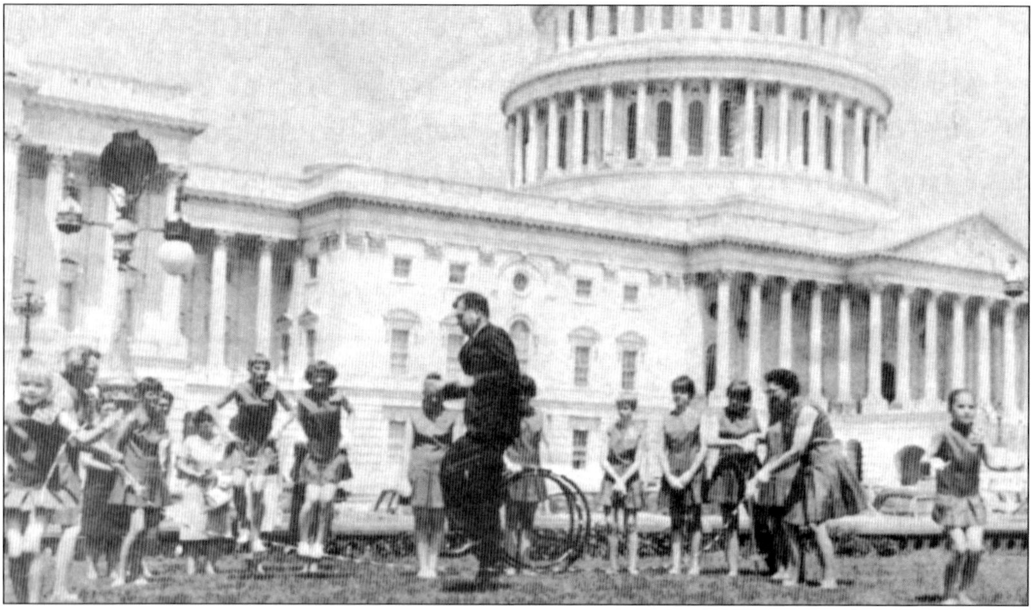

On their trip to Washington, DC, in 1967, the Seneca Rope Jumpers performed on the US Capitol grounds and entertained the Oregon delegation, which at that time included Mark Hatfield, Wayne Morse, and Wendell Wyatt, in the Caucus Room of the Canon Office Building. They toured the nation's capital and other locations in the area. Various organizations and businesses helped sponsor the group, including Edward Hines Lumber Company. The group, all from the Seneca Elementary School, included Nan Sproul, Lori Smith, Glenna Thissell, Darlene Lissman, Linda Smith, Georgene Hansen, Sherry Walker, Patty Tout, Pam Roswell, Karen Griffith, and Sharon Thissell. Esma Reynolds was director and group founder, and assistants were Dorothy Klabo, Jean Sproul, Phyliss Lissman, Zora Thissell, and Nadine Lissman. (Courtesy of Georgene Hansen.)

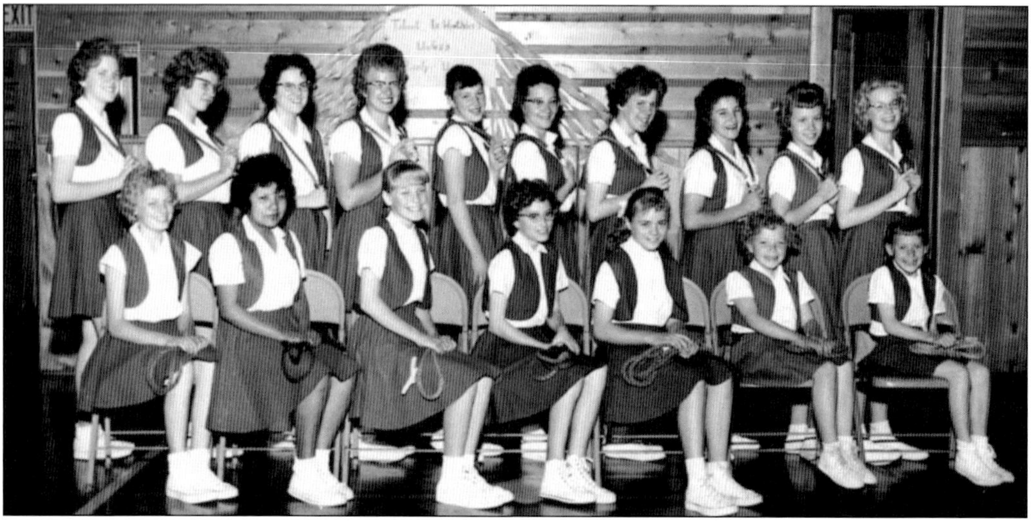

This 1961 photograph of the Seneca Rope Jumpers shows, from left to right, (first row) Kathy Griffith, Betty Hawley, Bonnie Lenz, Irene Poovey, Kristy Lindley, Sherry Walker, and Susie Davis, (second row) Sharron Southworth, Linda Shields, unidentified, Helen Seebart, Betty Johnson, Janet Beverage, Nancy Baxter, Margaret Tout, Linda Weeks, and Linda Wright. (Courtesy of Seneca Elementary School.)

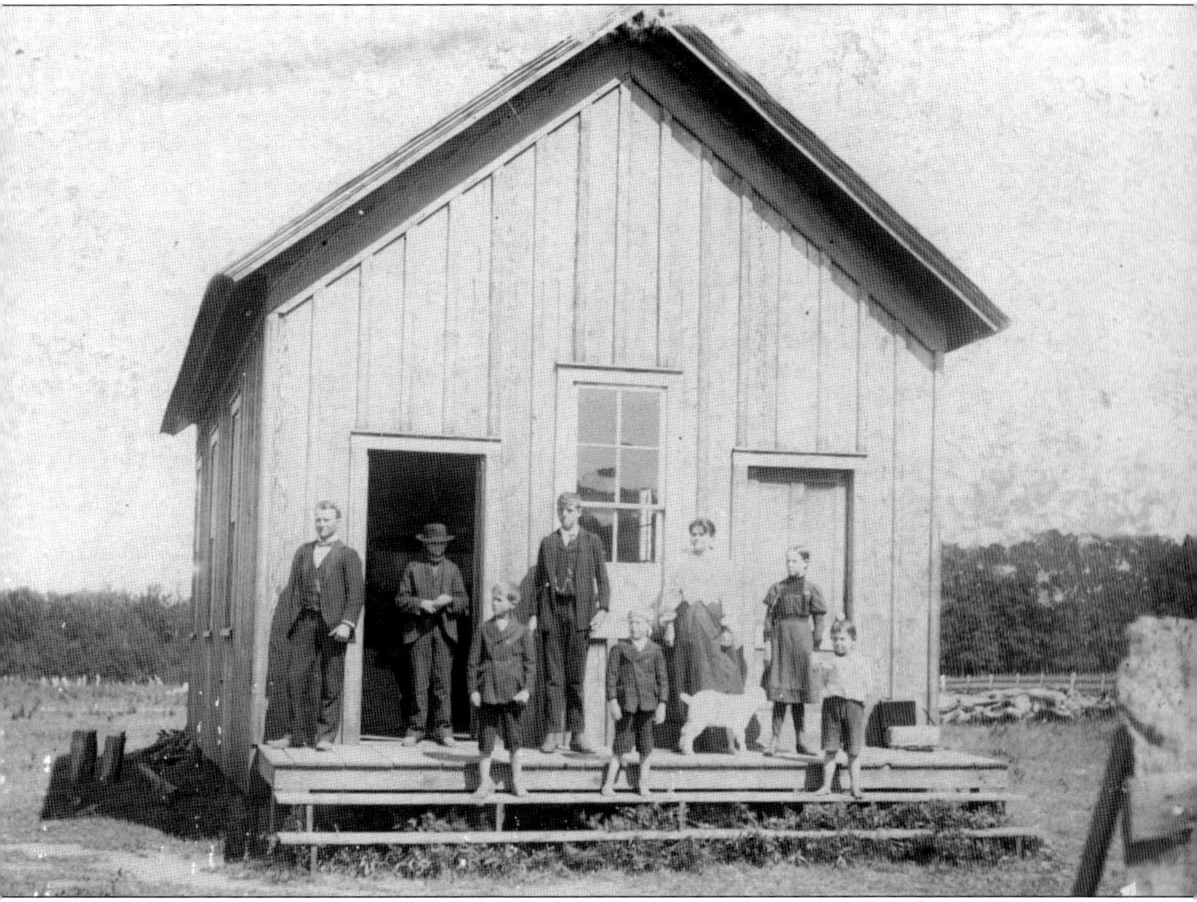

Shortly after gold was discovered in the county, the need for schools became apparent, as families followed the miners. The Strawberry School was located above Prairie City. It is reported to have been one of the first schools in Grant County. It was on the left side of the road and river going toward the Blue Mountain Hot Springs. Ala O. Mosies, the teacher, is likely the individual pictured in the doorway. He later served as Grant County treasurer for a number of years. The students are unidentified, but note the large difference in ages. Some students in these remote locations rode to school on horseback, and there was usually a hitching post out back where the horse would have to wait all day for the student to finish classes.

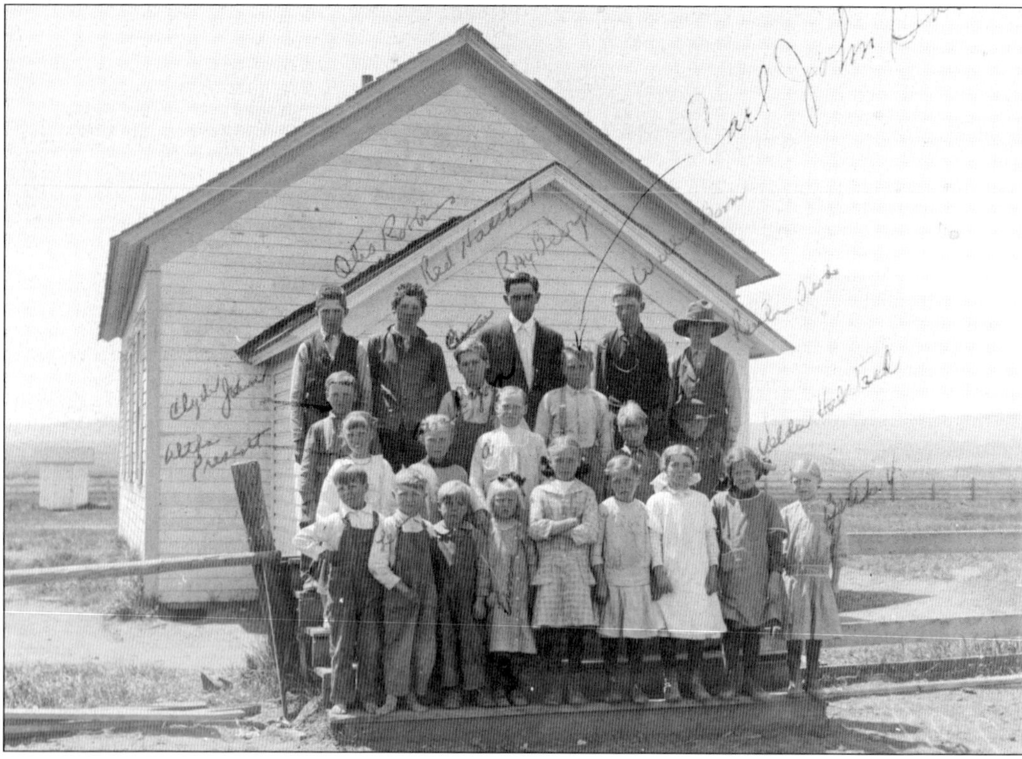

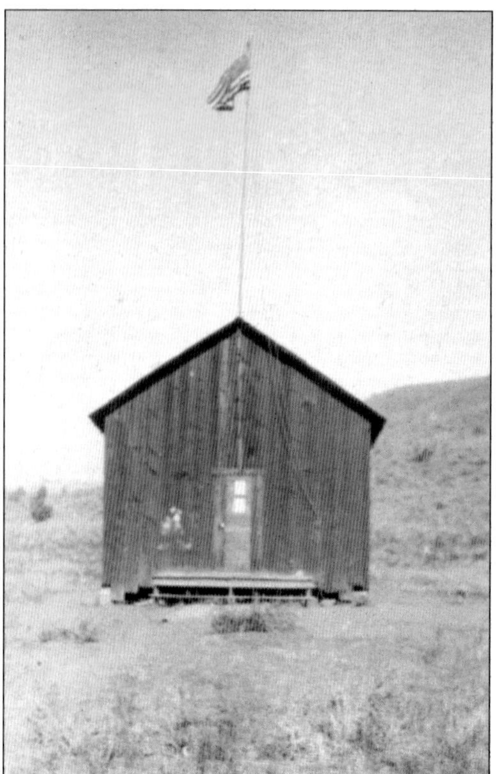

This photograph shows the Fox Valley School in 1914. From left to right are (first row) Ray Prescott, Leet Vaughan, Melvin Snyder, Erma Robbins, Velma Snode, Lenora Snyder, Lavern Johns, Velma Halstead, and Bertha Vaughan; (second row) Altha Prescott, Aura Robbins, Zella McBride, Francis Crossett, and Clarence Snode; (third row) Clyde Johns, Byrm Berry, and Carl Born; (fourth row) Otis Robbins, Homer "Red" Halstead, teacher Ray Berry, Willie Born, and Reuben Snode.

This image shows the Cupper Creek School around 1915. Cupper Creek is in the northwest corner of Grant County and flows into the North Fork of the John Day River just west of Monument. Henry Cupper, his wife, Cordelia, and their three children left England in 1877. Their excursion took them through southern Oregon to Prineville, Heppner, and finally along with a freight load of provisions to the local Bill Welch Ranch, where they settled and raised cattle.

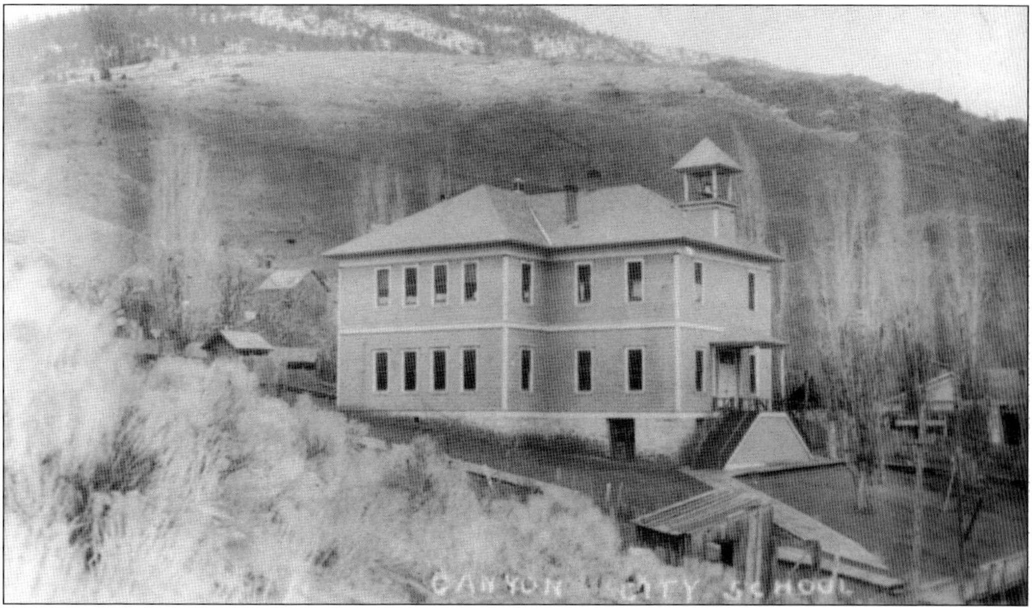

Schools built in larger towns were much larger than those built in outlying locations to serve the greater number of students and the differences in ages. This image shows the Canyon City School in 1904. It was built on the east side of Canyon City.

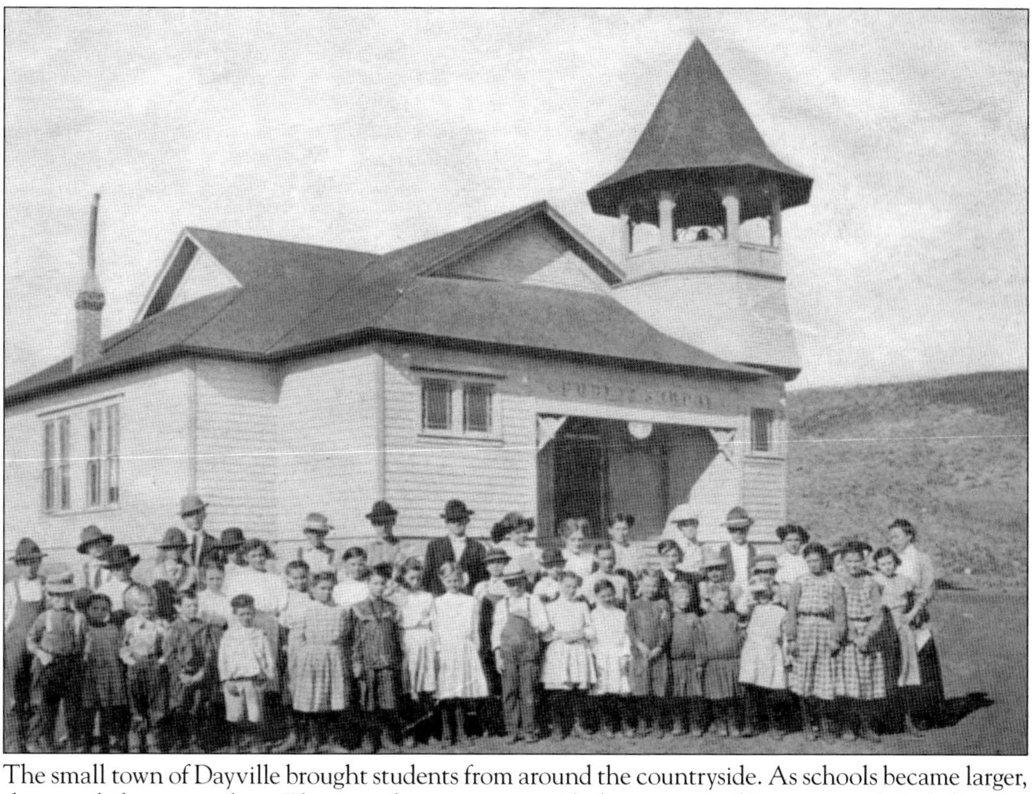
The small town of Dayville brought students from around the countryside. As schools became larger, they needed more teachers. These teachers were not paid a large sum, and it was more their dedication to instructing young people that kept them from leaving or starting different occupations.

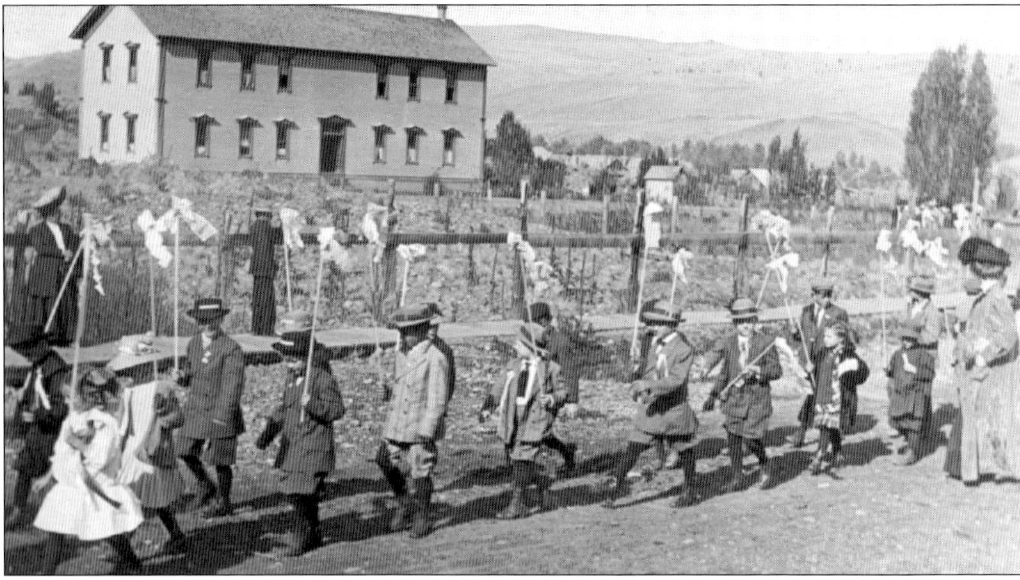

This image shows the John Day School around 1910 participating in the May Day parade. Note the garden growing between the fence and the school building. Could the students have been instructed in the art of gardening and cultivation, or was this information learned through their parents?

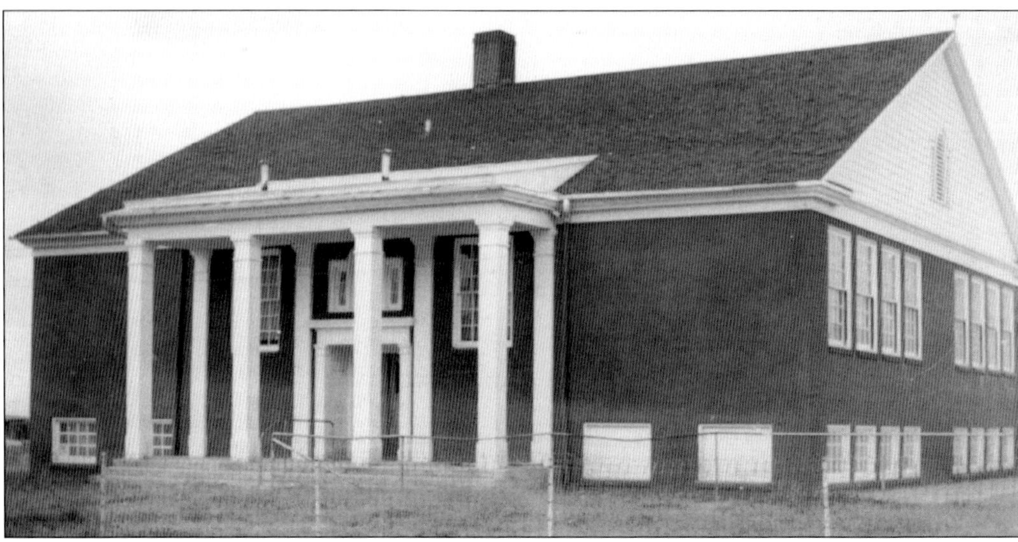

The Seneca School today is much larger than the earlier schools in small towns. It no longer has hitching posts for horses, and the school includes modern facilities.

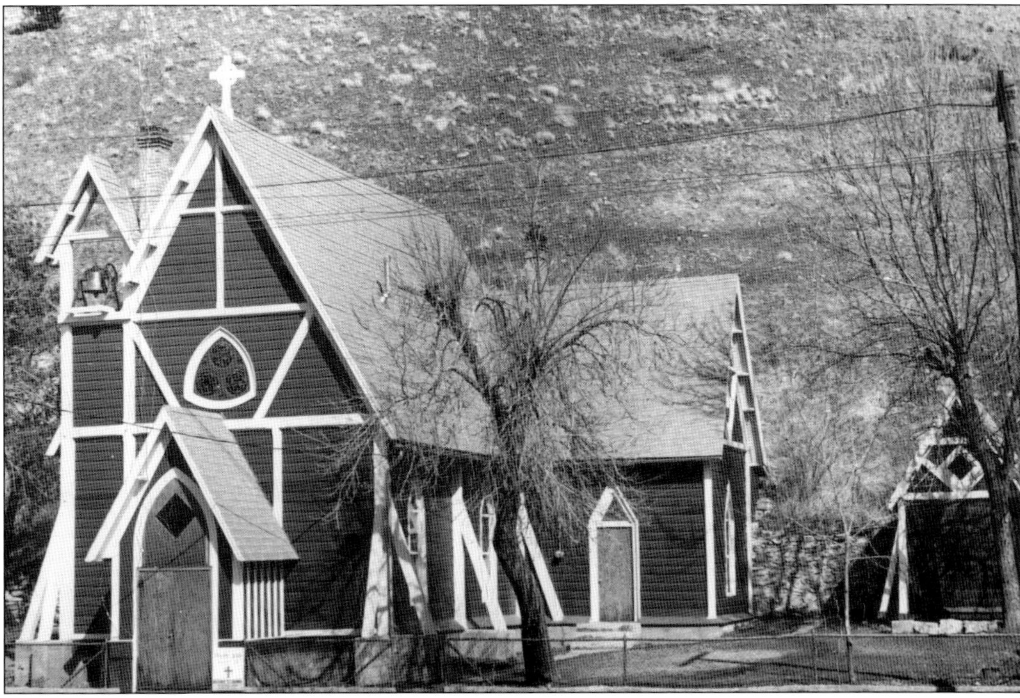

This image shows the St. Thomas Episcopal Church in John Day, first built in 1876. The church was built in the ashes of the 1870 fire. As with other congregations, traveling priests and bishops served, as there was no full-time pastor. The church had a group called the St. Thomas Guild that provided housing and food to the traveling clergy. It was organized by Minnie Southworth in 1889.

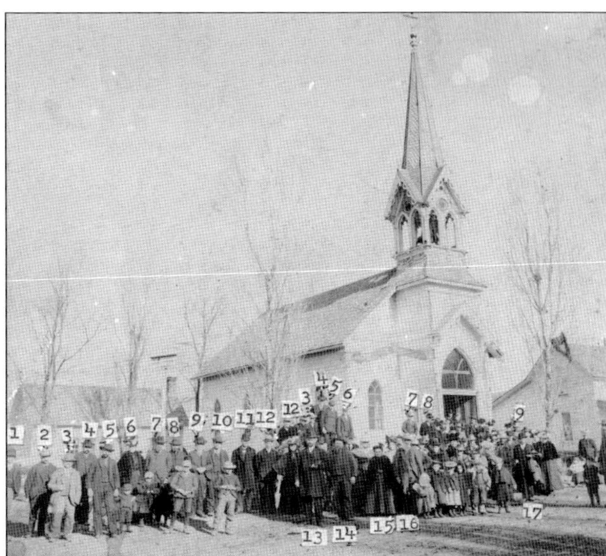

The Advent Christian Church is shown at its dedication in 1900. Members first began meeting in the home of Charles Belshaw and his wife, who came to the area in 1862. Property at what is currently the corner of Main Street and Bridge Street was purchased for $250. The church was designed by Samuel Hope, and he was the lead carpenter. At first, a traveling minister by the name of James Orchard served the congregation. Later, Mary Grove served as minister for a number of years. Pictured from left to right are (first row) unidentified, Al Gearing, Billie Jones, Chas. Timms, ? Shanks, Mrs. J.A. Laycock, Judge Laycock, unidentified, ? Penfield, two unidentified, Frank Hacheney and wife, John Luce, Mrs. Porter, Mr. Porter, Hotly Bunn, and Bill Bunn; (second row, starting after no. 12), Will Foreman, Jude Pope, four unidentified, Arch Timms, Horace K. Johnson, and unidentified.

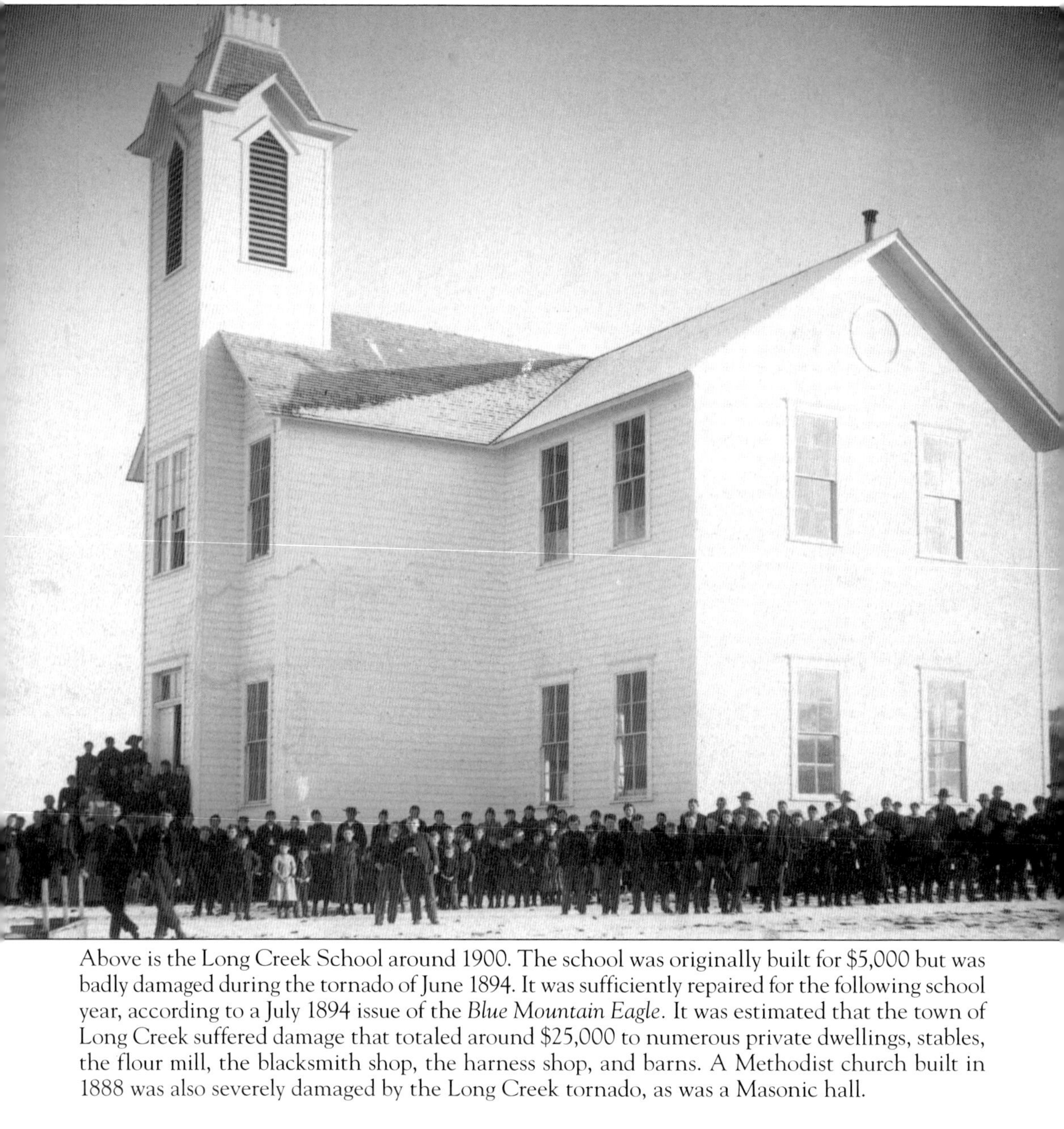

Above is the Long Creek School around 1900. The school was originally built for $5,000 but was badly damaged during the tornado of June 1894. It was sufficiently repaired for the following school year, according to a July 1894 issue of the *Blue Mountain Eagle*. It was estimated that the town of Long Creek suffered damage that totaled around $25,000 to numerous private dwellings, stables, the flour mill, the blacksmith shop, the harness shop, and barns. A Methodist church built in 1888 was also severely damaged by the Long Creek tornado, as was a Masonic hall.

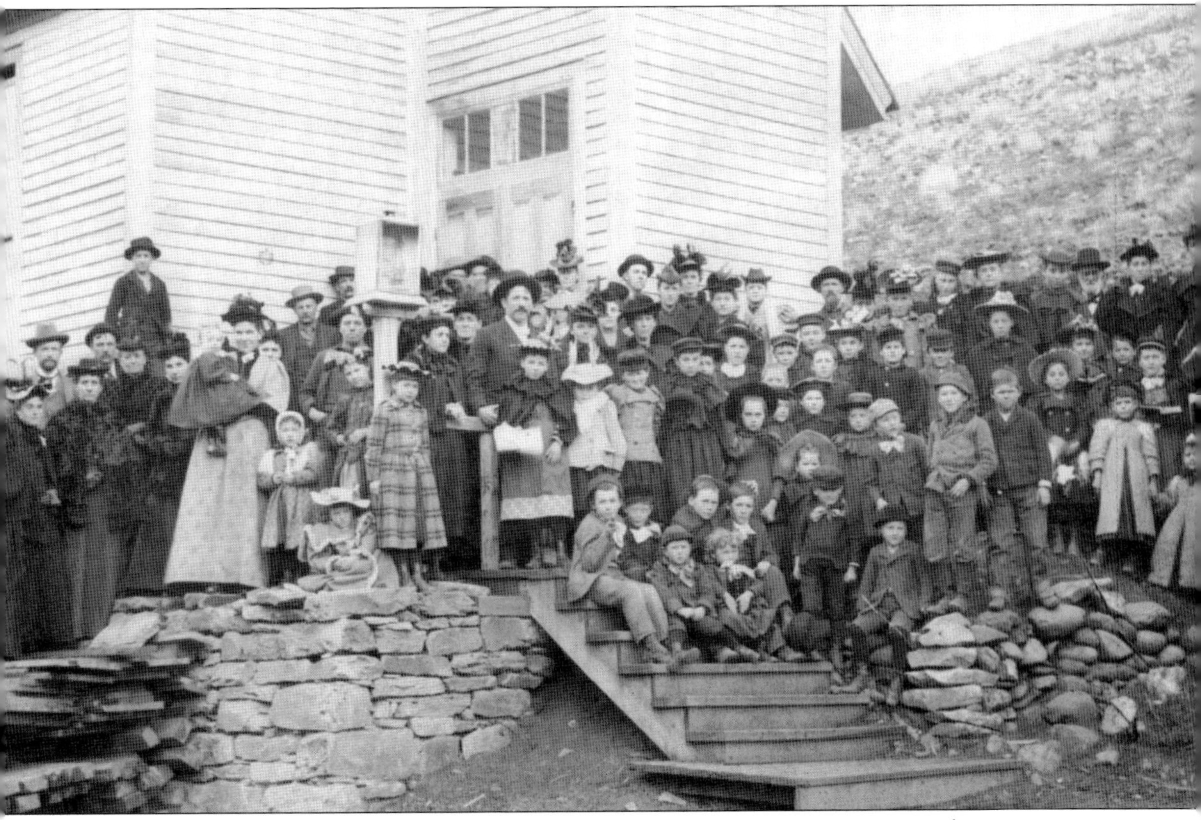

Just a few years after the discovery of gold, when Canyon City was a young, rambunctious town with several saloons, a traveling Methodist minister named W.H. Goddard held a church service in the town. There was no record of where the service was held, but it was likely in the home of one of the parishioners. For the next several years, the church was served by traveling ministers from The Dalles, one of whom was Noble Trowbridge. Under the leadership of Rev. G.W. Grannis, a church was started in Canyon City in 1875 and completed in 1876. The above image was taken at the dedication. As John Day to the north began to increase in size, a second congregation was formed in 1881. Ezra Hays served periodically as the same pastor to both churches. Mark White was one of the most memorable pastors. He served John Day, Canyon City, and Prairie City and initiated services in Seneca every other Sunday.

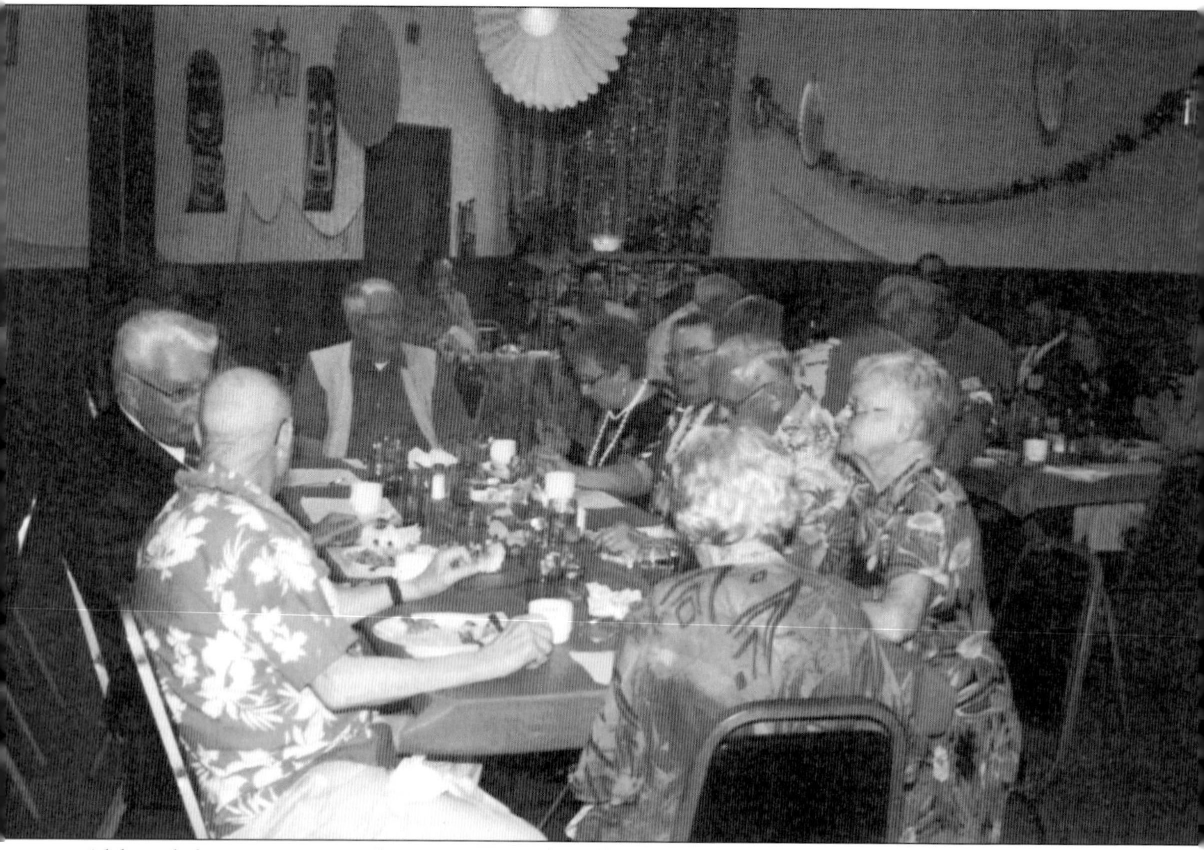

Although known as a social organization, the Elks have always been a strong supporter of area youth. The John Day Elks Lodge No. 1824 is an extraordinary example of that. It has sponsored youth activities from basketball to baseball. Christmas, Halloween, and Easter activities featuring the youth of the area are yearly events, and attention is given to handicapped youth. But it is not just the youth who have received attention. The Elks are involved in blood drives, the local hospital, local parades, and even the Seneca Rope Jumpers. Pictured at a fundraising luau event clockwise from the bottom are Pete Baucum, Don Hanson, Len Nelson, Marge Conlee, Bob Larkin, and Barbara Pollock. The John Day Elks began as an affiliate of the Baker Lodge No. 338. George Kern was elected president during the interim. Their official charter was received on September 9, 1950.

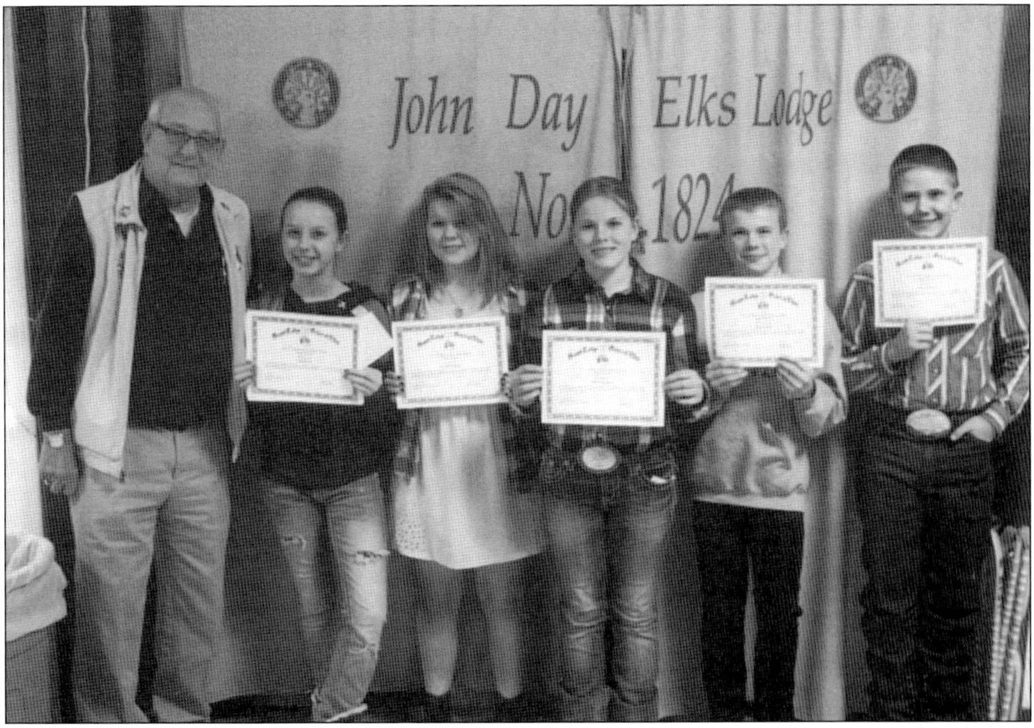

An outstanding event by the local Elks club gets area youth interested in writing and teaches them about the Constitution and history of the United States. The American Essay Contest winners in 2016 were, from left to right, Harli Grove, Krystle Douglas, Riley Robertson, Justin Hodge, and Cinch Anderson. Carl Lino, the gentleman standing at left, organized and supervised the contest.

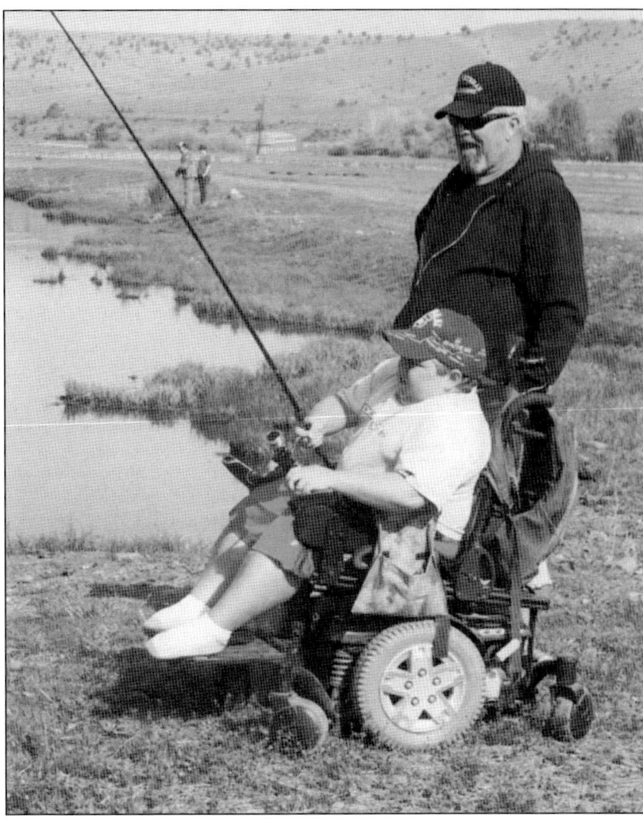

Through the dedication and supervision of the John Day Elks, handicapped youth in the area are given the opportunity to go fishing. A local rancher provides a pond that is stocked with catchable fish.

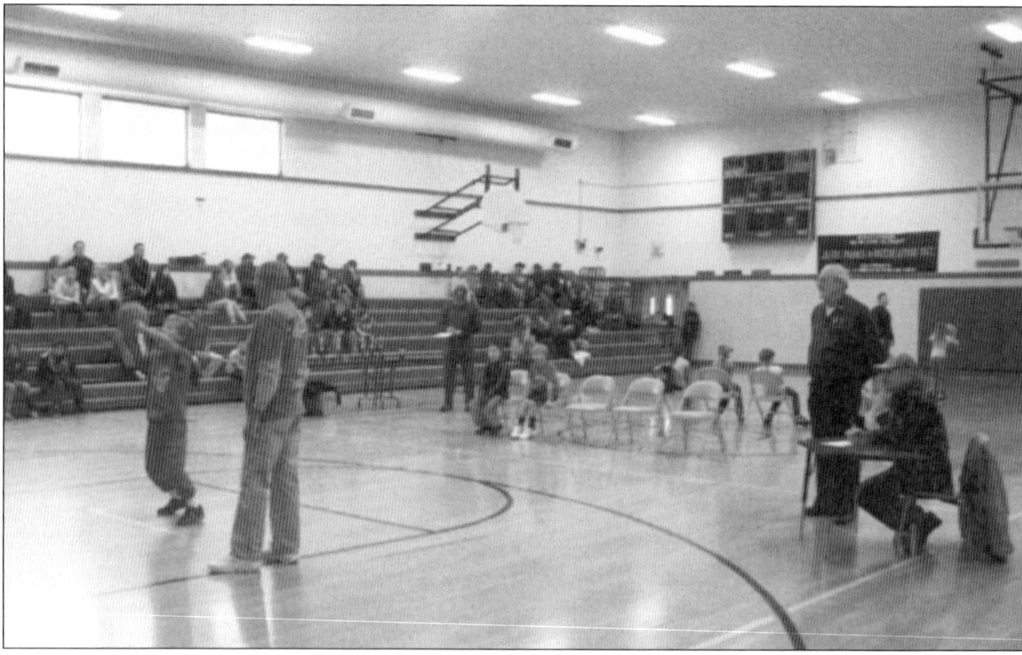

One of the more popular youth events held by the John Day Elks is the annual hoop shoot. The event is very popular because youth from all ages can compete. They are divided into different age groups, both girls and boys. The winners, those scoring the most baskets, can move up and compete with youth from other areas. The gentleman above standing near the foul line on the semicircle is Gary Miller. He is also pictured below standing just outside the key. The participants are unidentified.

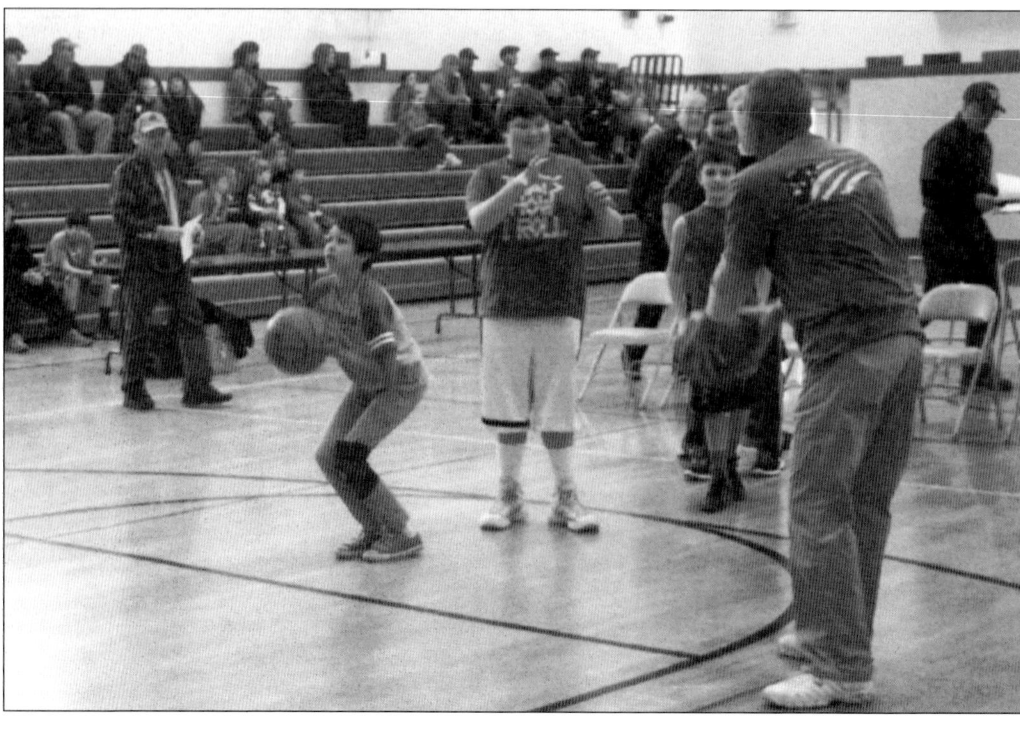

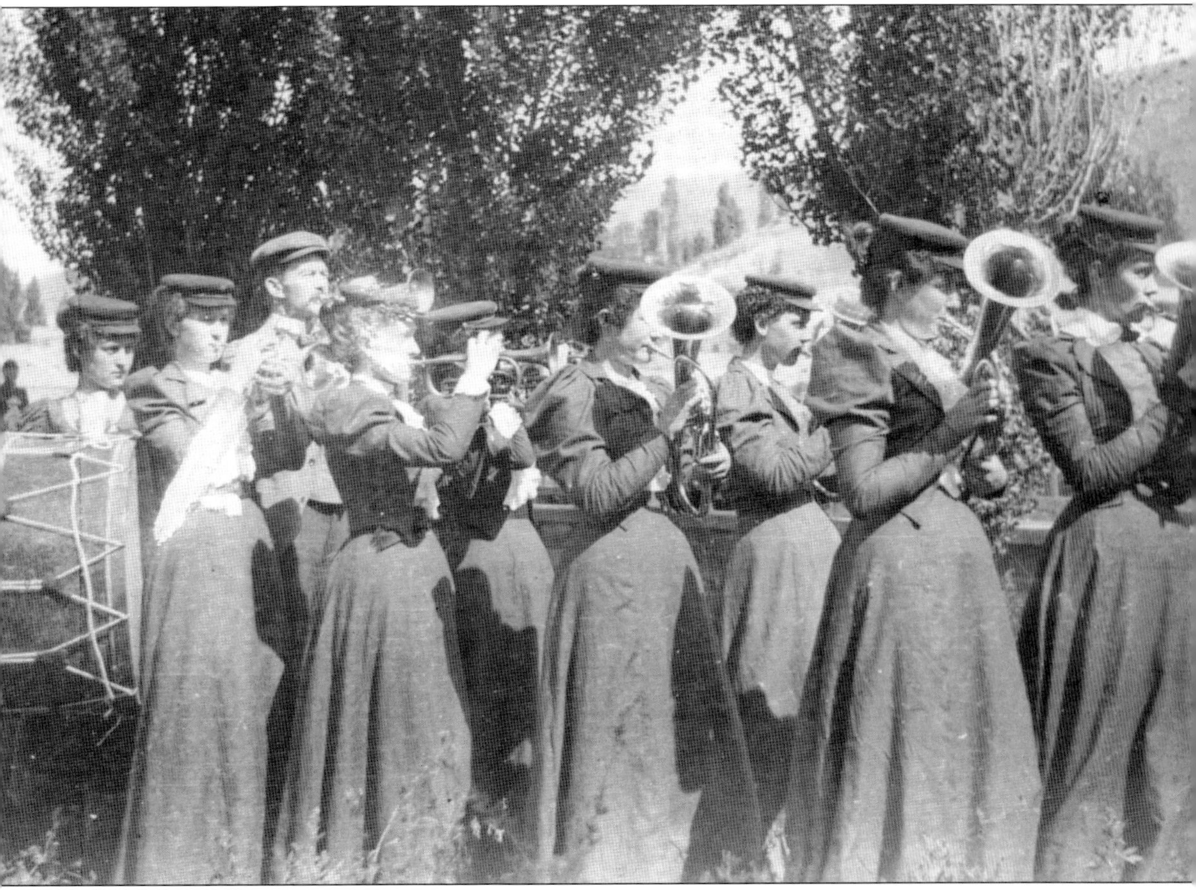

Social organizations take on various identities. Above is the Canyon City Women's Brass Band around 1900. George H. Cattanach was the director. Quite likely he is the gentleman in the back with the hat playing the horn.

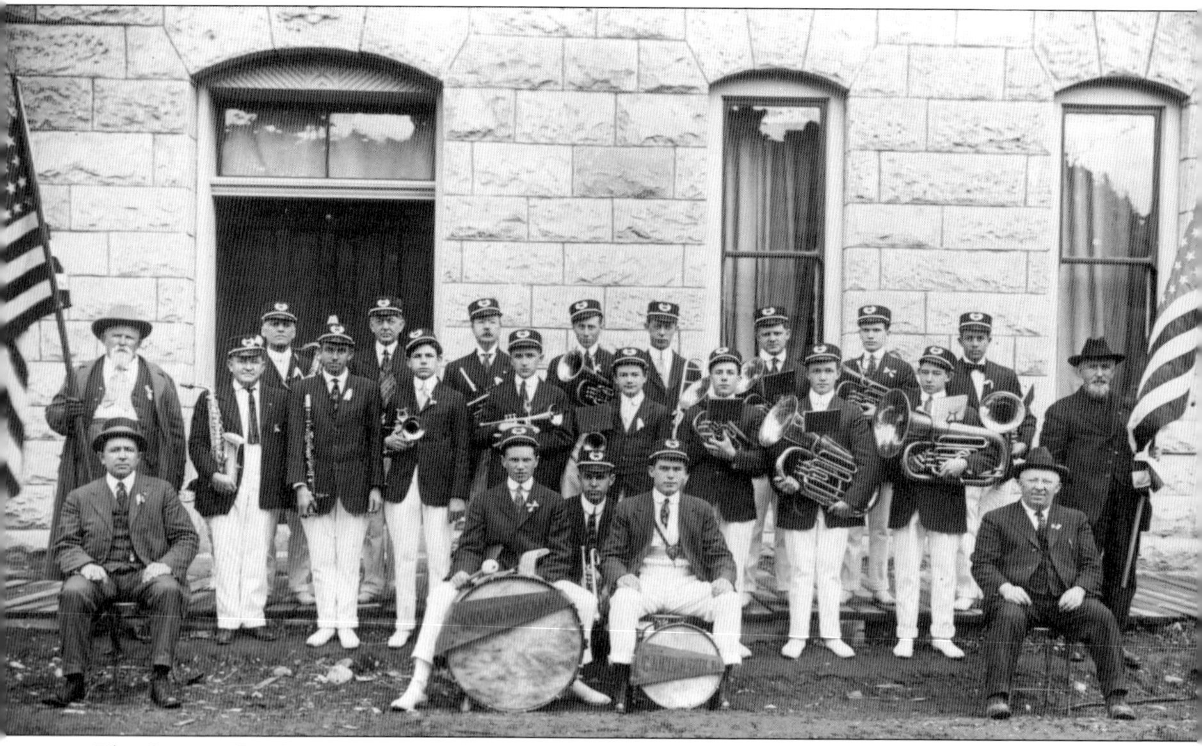

The Canyon City Men's Brass Band is pictured in front of the Masonic hall around 1915. Pictured are (first row) Charles W. Brown (treasurer), J.W. Finlayson, Warren Glaze (leader), Henry Guernsey, and Louis Woldenberg (manager); (second row) Landrum Birge (with flag), Bascom Glaze, Vernon Glaze, Glenn Chandler Sr., Harold H. Brown, Arthur Hicks, David Masson, Harold Patterson, Dale Tracy, and Martin Lucas (with flag); (third row, in no particular order, with one unidentified) Frank Slater, George Cattanach, Neil Niven, Arley Sollinger, Phil Ashford, Dr. Vern Johnson, and Wilbur Carlin.

Five

Recreation and Festivities

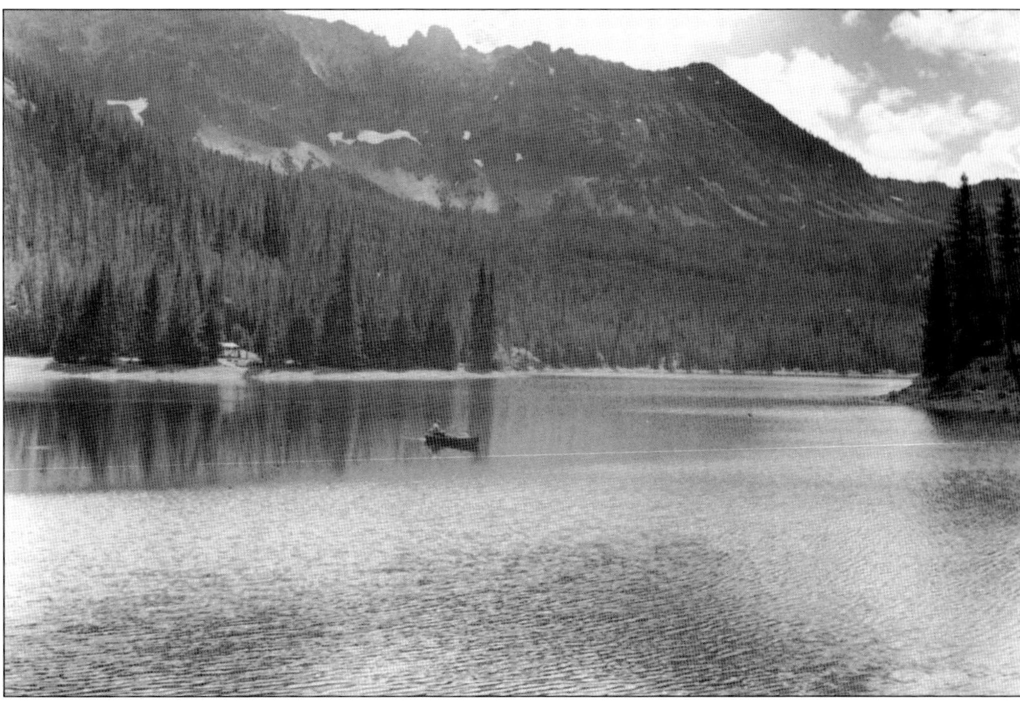

Grant County has always offered a wide range of activities. It has high mountain lakes, such as Strawberry Lake, above, where there is camping and fishing. The John Day River, or one of its tributaries, is less than an hour's drive from most locations, and salmon and steelhead trout abound. Additionally, there are frequent parades, an annual county fair, and sporting events, as well as hunting. These activities attract visitors from miles around and the entire state.

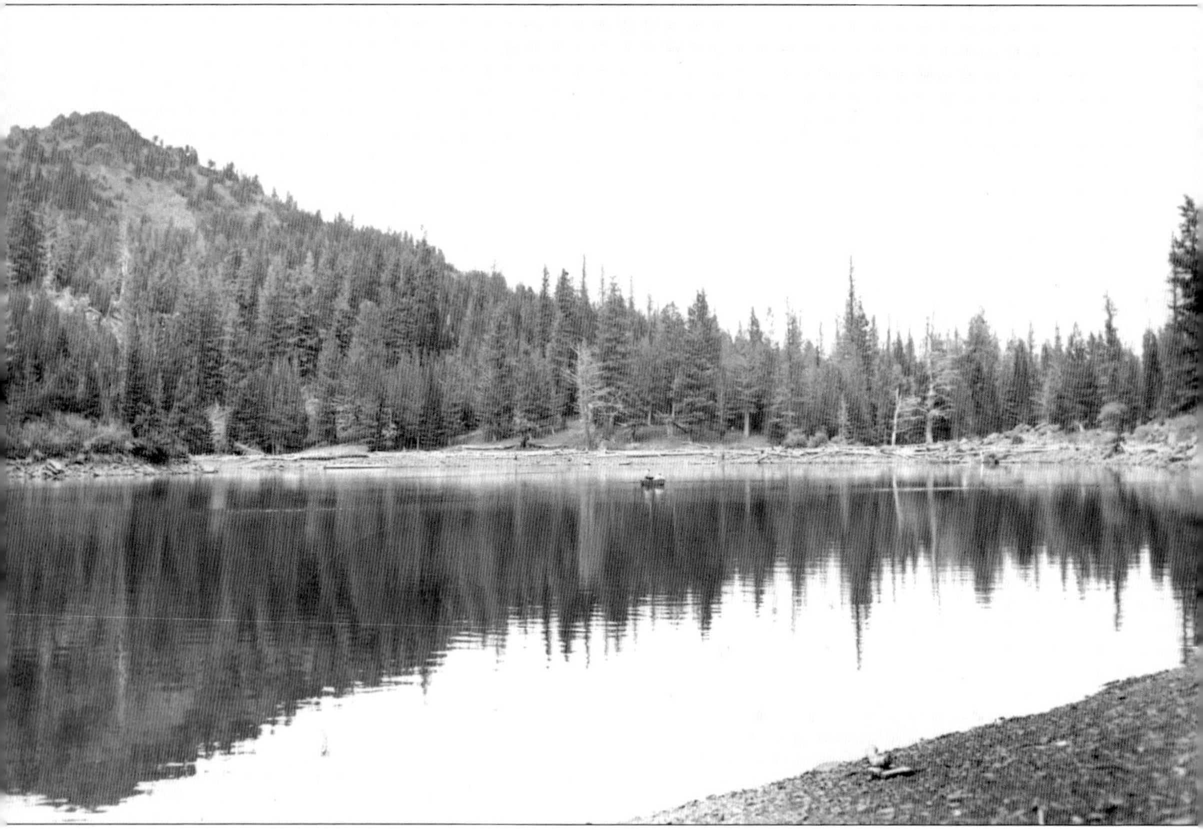

This image offers another view of Strawberry Lake, located about 10 miles south of Prairie City. Strawberry Creek drains Strawberry Lake and enters the John Day River just east of Prairie City. It is a favorite camping spot, and there are several campsites along the creek. It is located in the Strawberry Mountain Wilderness Area. It is a shallow natural lake that covers an area of about 36 acres. It is surrounded by lush forests and offers opportunities for hiking, backpacking, cross country skiing, and fishing.

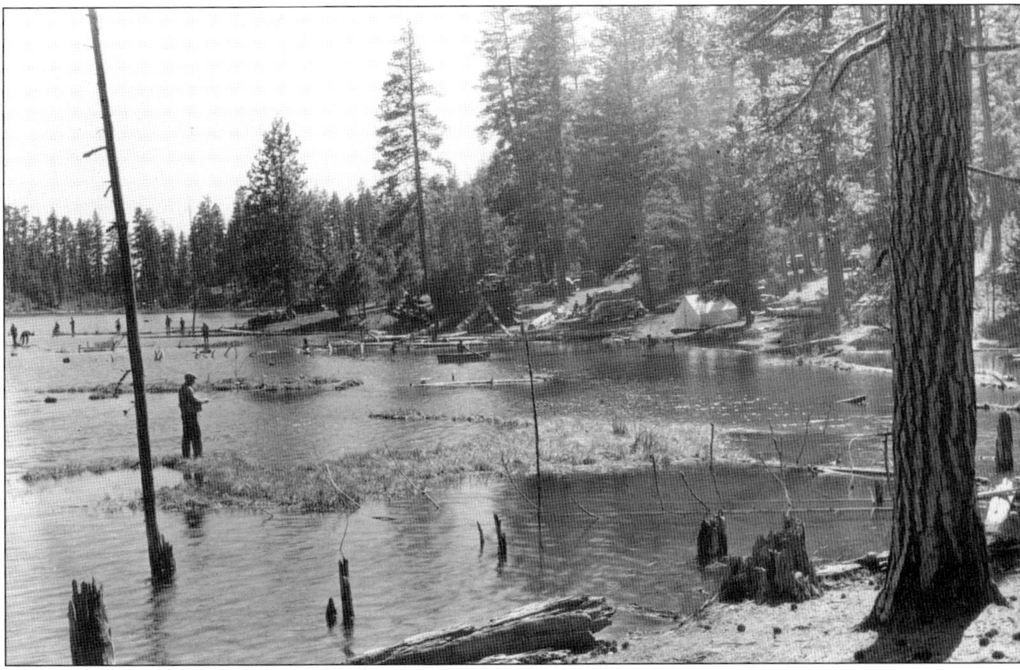

One of the more popular lakes in the high mountain areas throughout Grant County for fishing and camping is Magone Lake, located a short distance north of John Day at the headwaters of Beech Creek. Initially, most high mountain lakes are without fish. Such was the case until Maj. Jos Magone (right) captured several trout from the John Day River, placed them in containers, carried them up to the lake, and released them. Magone was a colorful character who walked from the Canyon City Courthouse to the Chicago World's Fair in 1893, a distance of over 2,100 miles.

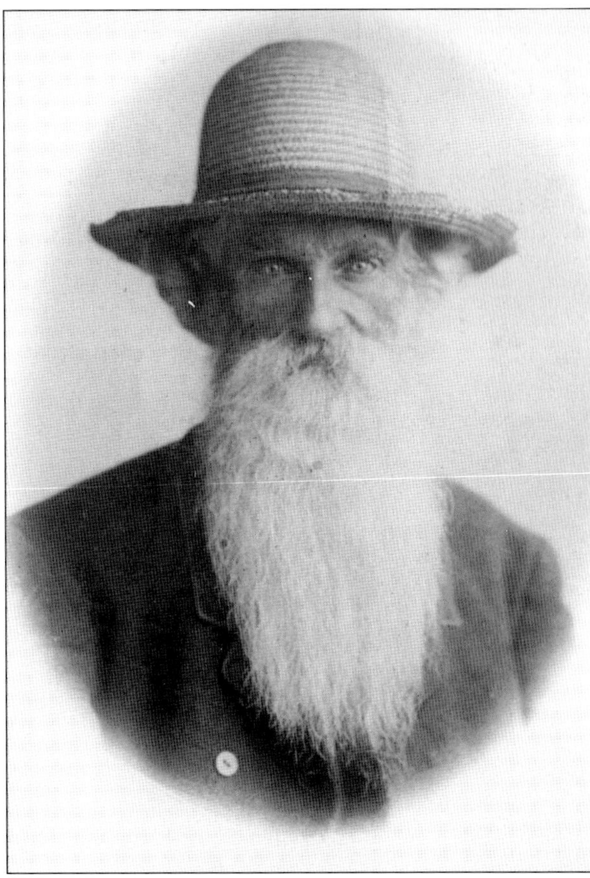

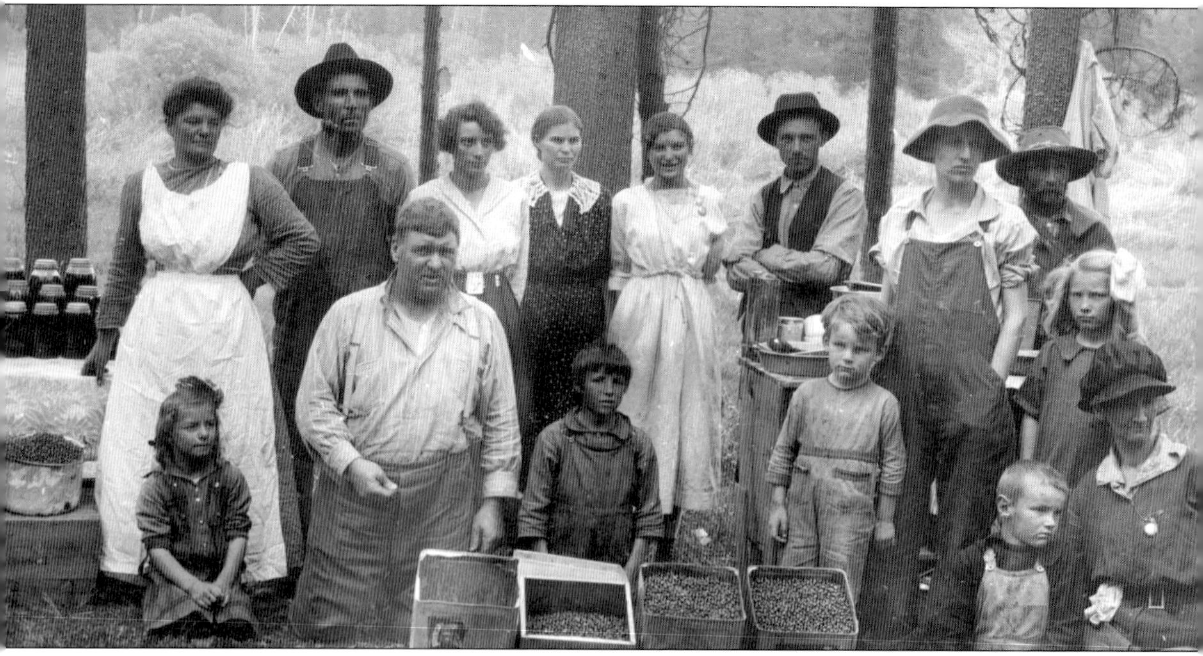

Growing at higher elevations within the Malheur National Forest are wild blueberries, called huckleberries by the local citizens. Generally ripening in late summer or early fall, these luscious, sweet berries were sought after by many. Searching for huckleberries was a family affair that could also involve several neighbors. Note the large buckets full of berries in foreground and jars at left. Those identified include, from left to right, (first row) Anna Lee Mason, Cy Bingham, Stewart Bingham, Harold Gleason, and an unidentified small boy near a woman. The small girl with a large hair ribbon is Frances Bingham Krechel. The woman in the back row wearing bib overalls and a hat is Mrs. Dan Gleason. In the back row, Al Lucas is second from left, and Connie Bingham is fifth from left. Other individuals are unidentified.

It did not take long for America's favorite pastime to reach Grant County. This image shows the Canyon City baseball team of Simpson and Brown, managed by C.W. Brown, in front of the Canyon City Courthouse in 1897. From left to right are (first row) W.W. Wood and Pete Helmer; (second row) unidentified, Elmer Overholt, unidentified, and "Adams" from Sumpter; (third row) Herb Chandler, Earl Dustin, C.J. Guernsey (probably the coach), and A.J. Stephans.

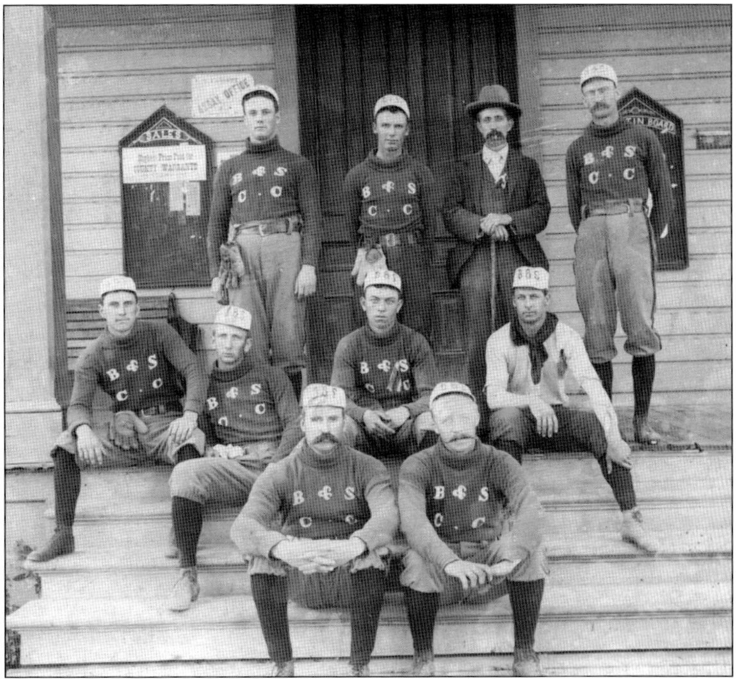

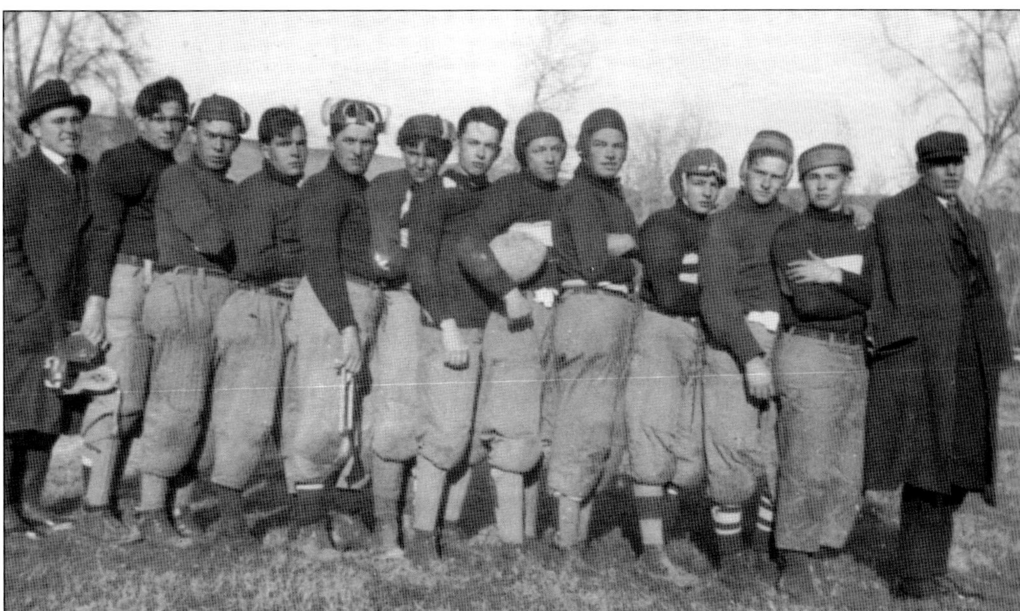

Football teams also came into existence as the area grew and the populations of the towns and cities increased. The Prairie City football team is pictured here in 1916. It is amazing to see just how meager the uniforms and helmets were 100 years ago. The sport either must have been not as rough then as it is today, or injuries were far more common. Helmets appear to be no more than pullover caps, and one wonders what the concussion level was.

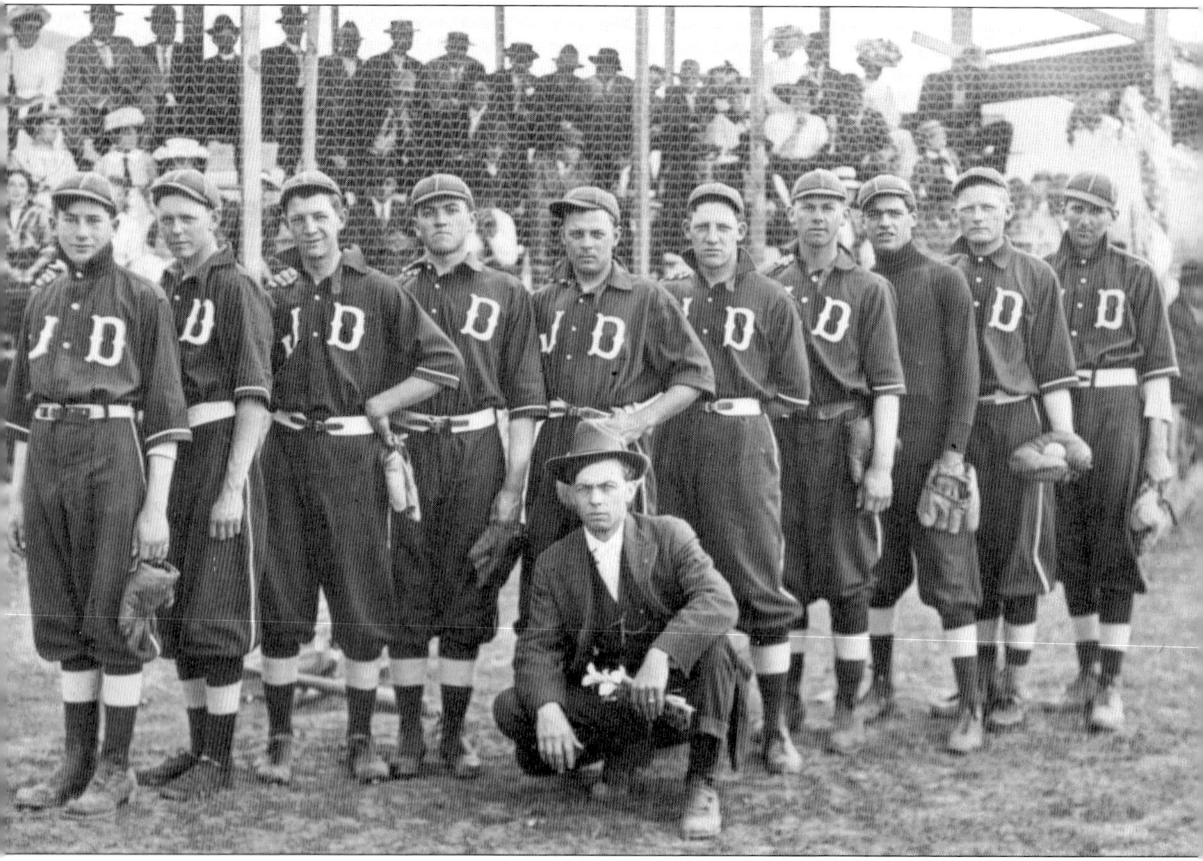

Baseball became very popular in grant County in the early 1900s. The John Day baseball team is pictured around 1920. Uniforms have not changed that much. The attire that the catcher now wears allows that person to be much more protected from foul balls.

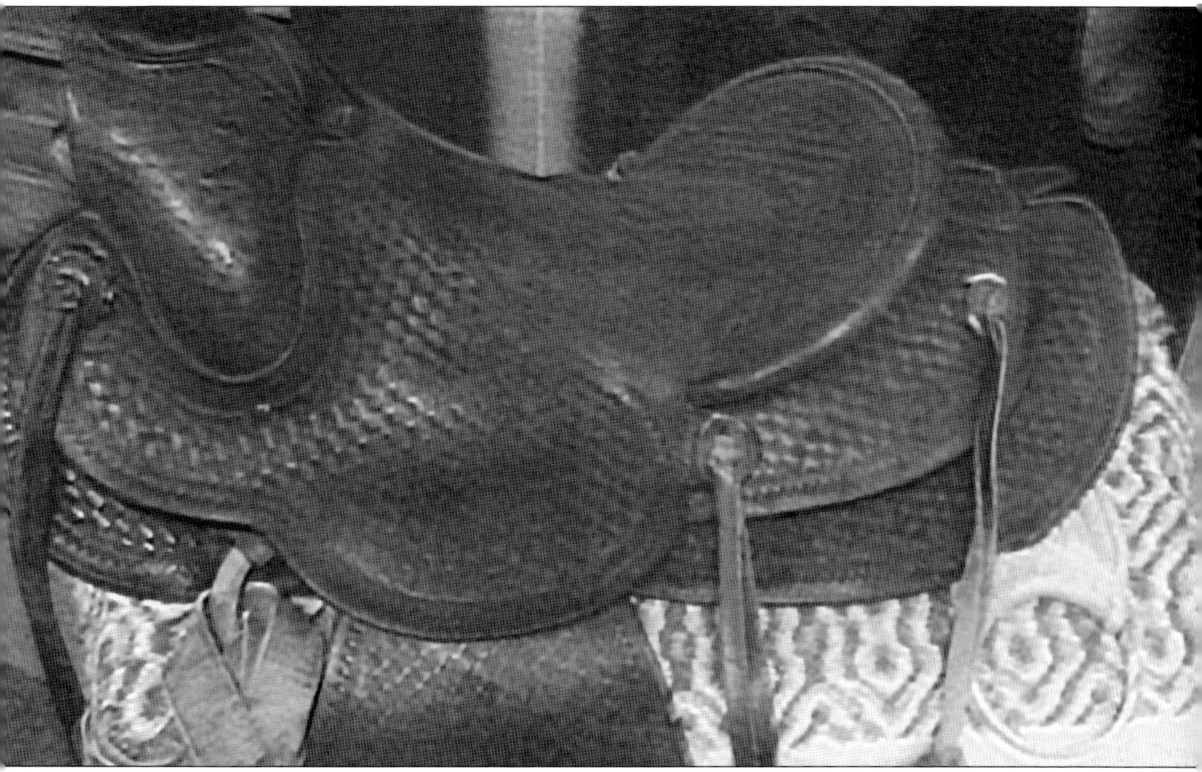

Herman Oliver won this Hamley saddle in a cow bucking contest at Oregon Trail Days in Baker City around 1939. Herman gave the saddle to his wife, Eliza. She, in turn, gave it to her grandson Herman Oliver Keerins for his eighth birthday, right after he broke his first horse. The saddle has a 14-inch tree and was made in Pendleton, Oregon. Hamley made prize saddles for all the local rodeos and the Pendleton Round-Up. No duplicate saddles were ever made unless the original owner signed a permission slip. The saddle is on display at the Grant County Historical Museum.

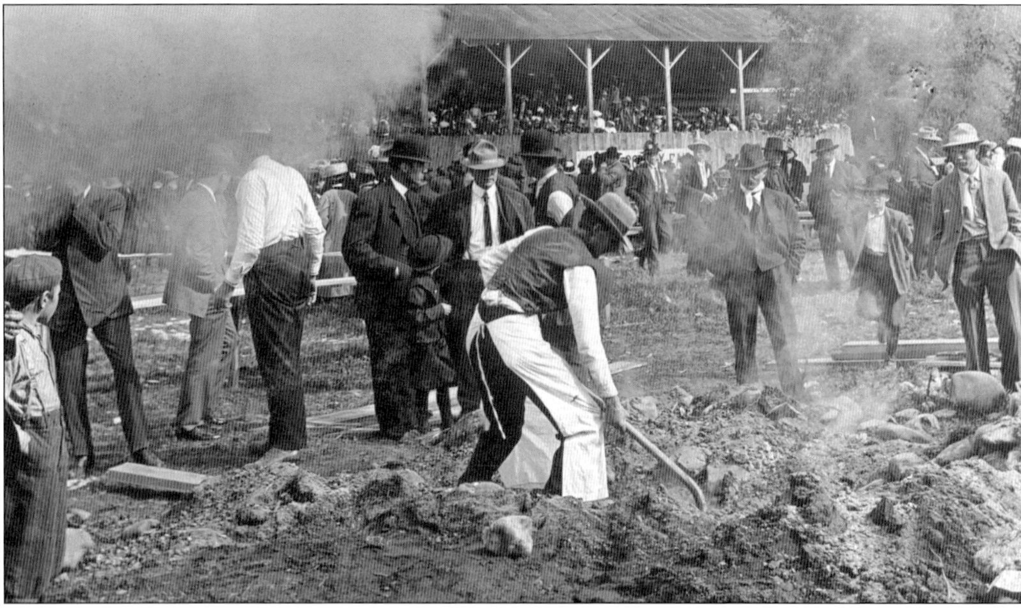

What is a county fair without a barbecue? These 1910 images of the Grant County fair show a large pit being dug. What went into and over the pit is hard to tell. Heated rocks could have been thrown into the pit along with succulent meats or corn. The Grant County Fair, held in August at the fairgrounds in John Day, is now the longest-running annual county fair in Oregon.

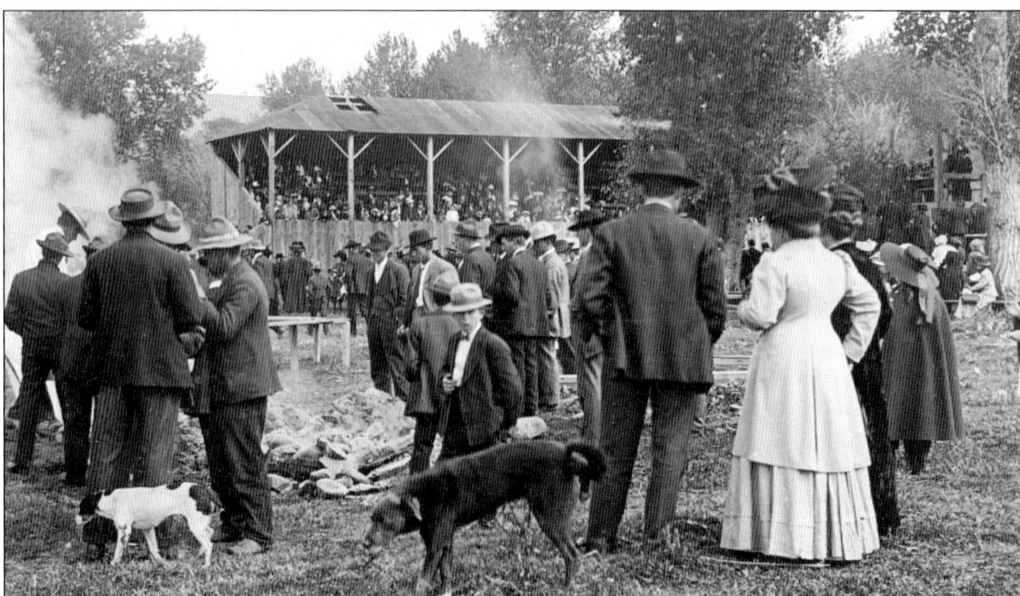

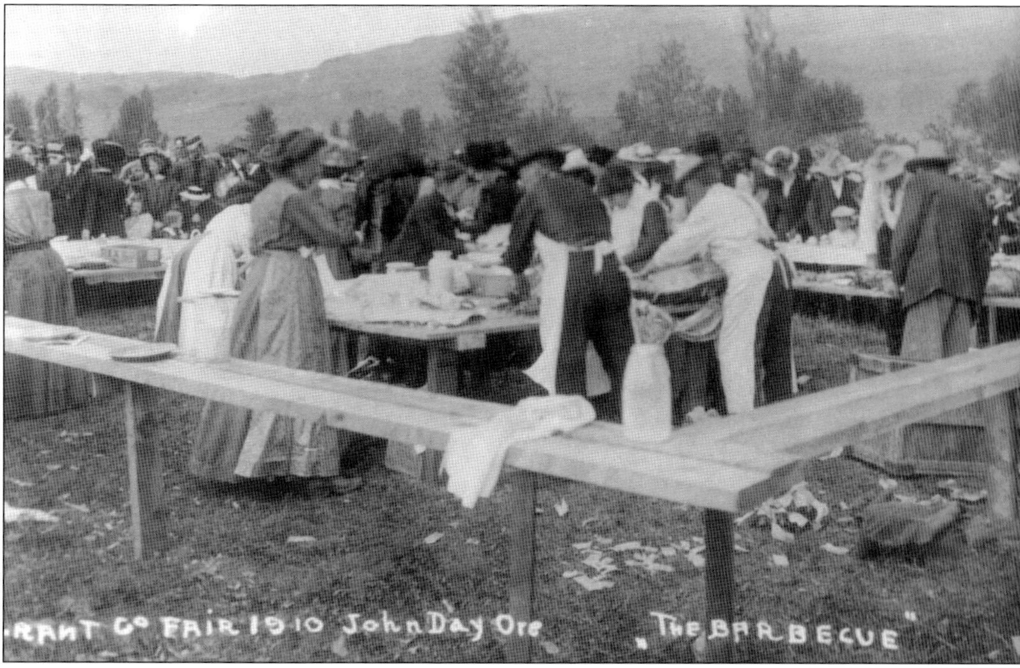

The crowd has gathered in the background above at the 1910 fair. "We're about to eat, folks!"—that was the announcement hungry folks were waiting for. Wrapped in white aprons, the chef and his staff are preparing the dishes for serving.

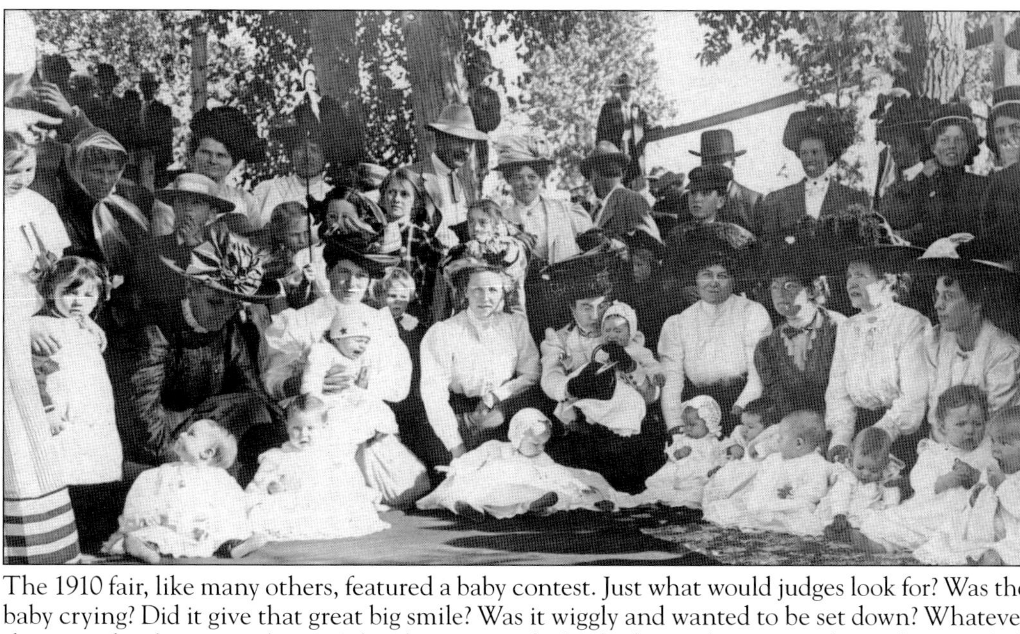

The 1910 fair, like many others, featured a baby contest. Just what would judges look for? Was the baby crying? Did it give that great big smile? Was it wiggly and wanted to be set down? Whatever the case, this feature at the 1910 fair drew a crowd of onlookers. There were obviously a few dads to ensure their son or daughter was given proper review.

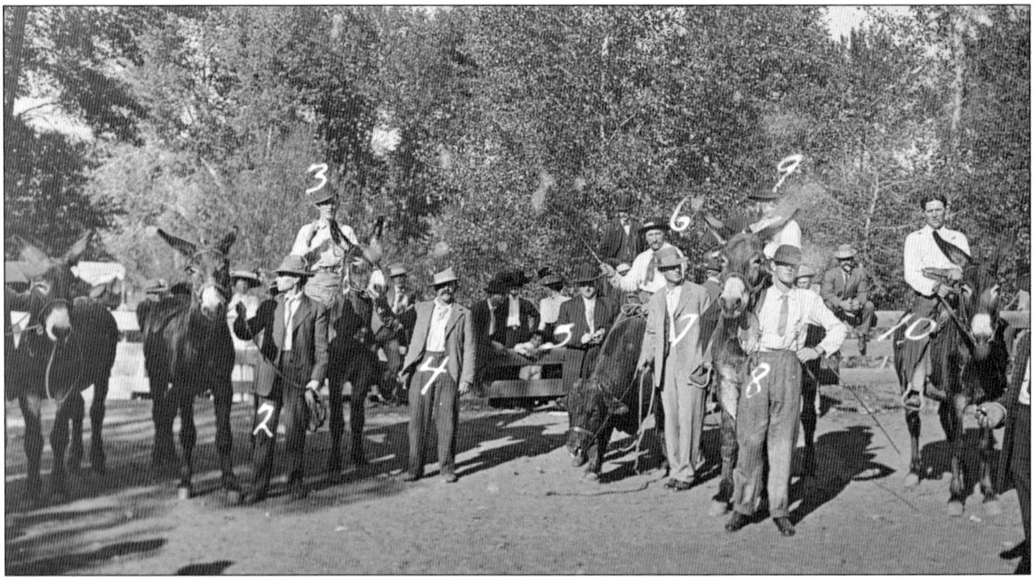

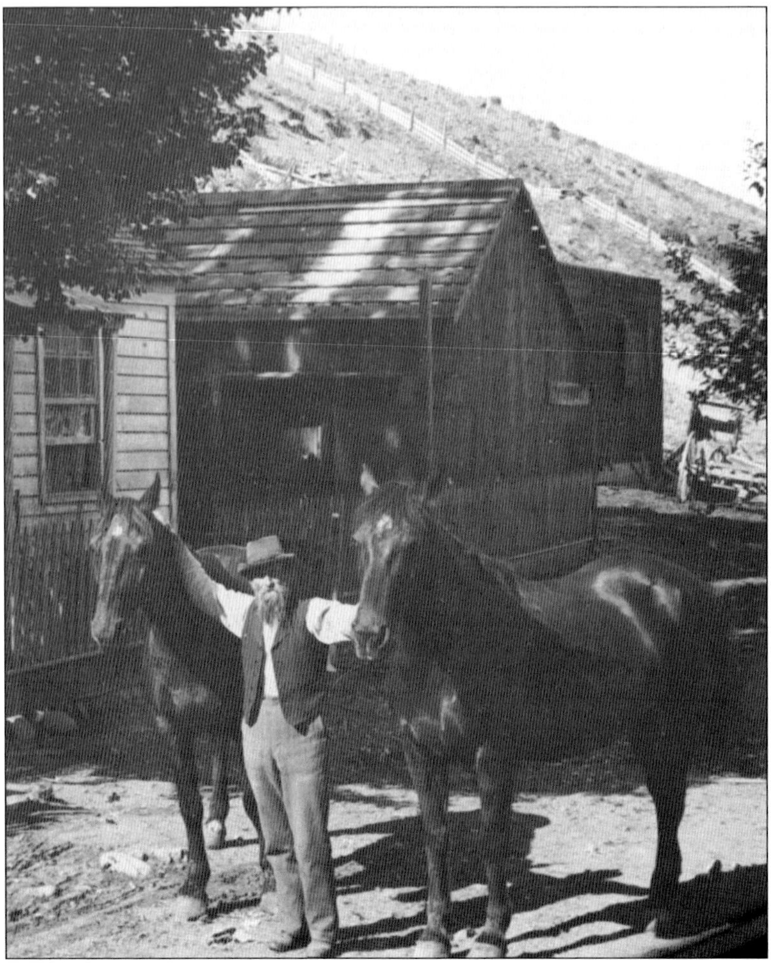

Horse and mule races were not only fair events but also occurred throughout Grant County. These horse races attracted many people especially, at the annual fair. Above, the mules that will be raced are held by their owner, trainer, or handler. The horses at left are Boy Doc and T.J. Cozard. The images are both from around 1890.

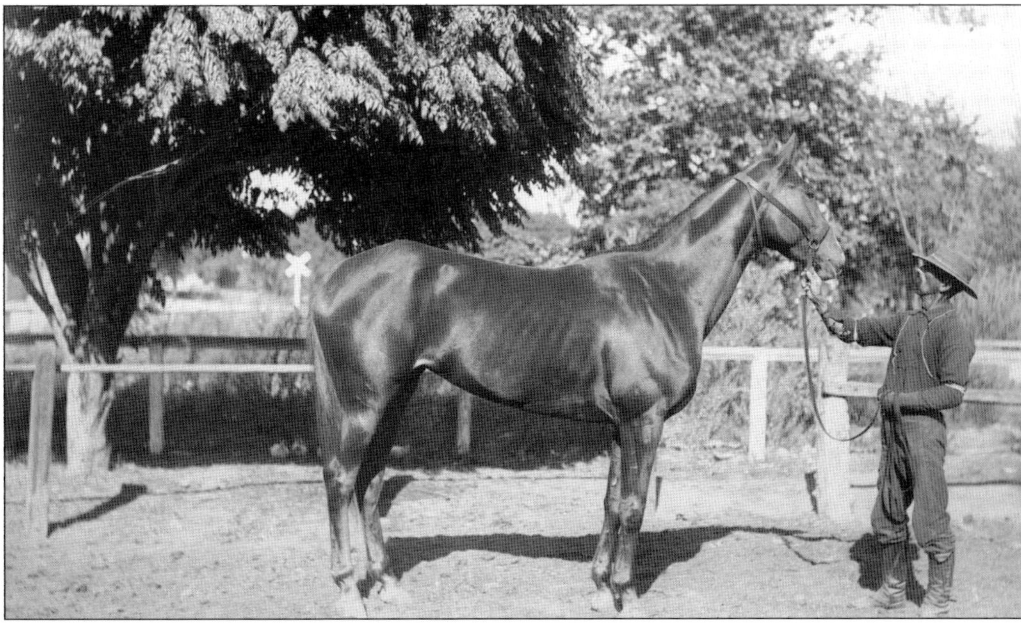

Horse racing was a popular sport in the late 1800s and early 1900s. Almost every town of any size had a race track. Races could be planned weeks and months ahead, but there were most likely occasions when a challenge was made, some wagering was done, and perhaps only two horses competed. Horses were prime possessions, as is shown in the image above where the unidentified owner is admiring his horse. They were protected. Such was the case of David Jenkins, who owned a black stallion by the name of Mount Vernon. During the Bannock War, he built this stone structure to house his horse so it would not be stolen. The structure still stands on the north side of Highway 26 just east of Mount Vernon.

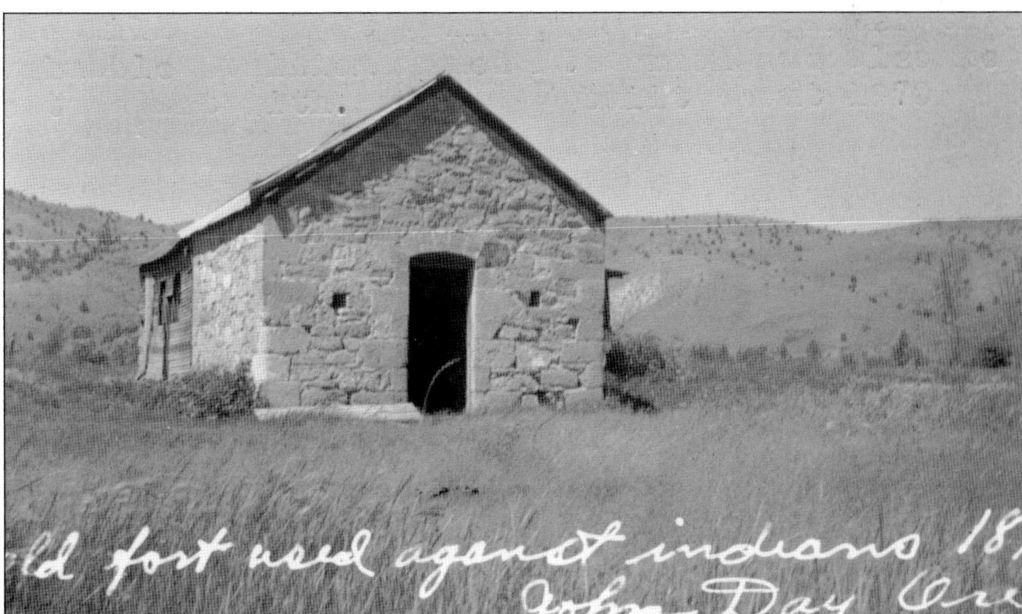

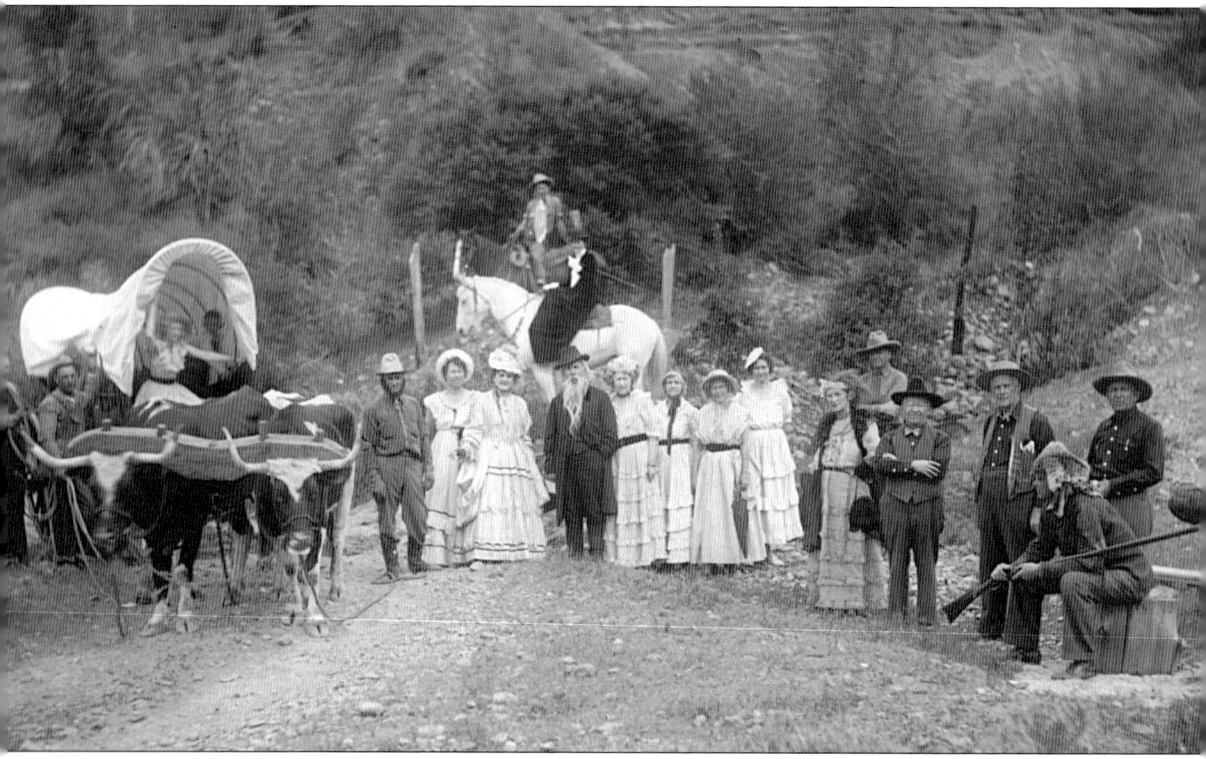

One of the grandest and most anticipated events in Grant County is the 62-Day Parade, held in commemoration of the year gold was discovered in the area in 1862. A terrific amount of preparation is needed for the event to be successful. It is held the second week in June in Canyon City. Pictured above planning for the 1935 parade are Robert Herburger (on horseback, upper center), Ramona Chambers Morris (below him), and, from left to right, E.P. Truesdell, George Dustin, Virginia Truesdell (in wagon), R.W. Cozad, Lillian Cozad, Lulu Chandler, Perry Chandler (as Joaquin Miller), Selma Brown, Mayme Cozad (Mrs. George Hagney), Mrs. Russell Pierpont, Dow Wilson's sister, Florence Woldenberg, Lee Overstreet, Orin L. Patterson, C.W. Brown, Louie Woldenberg, and R.G. Johnson (the trapper).

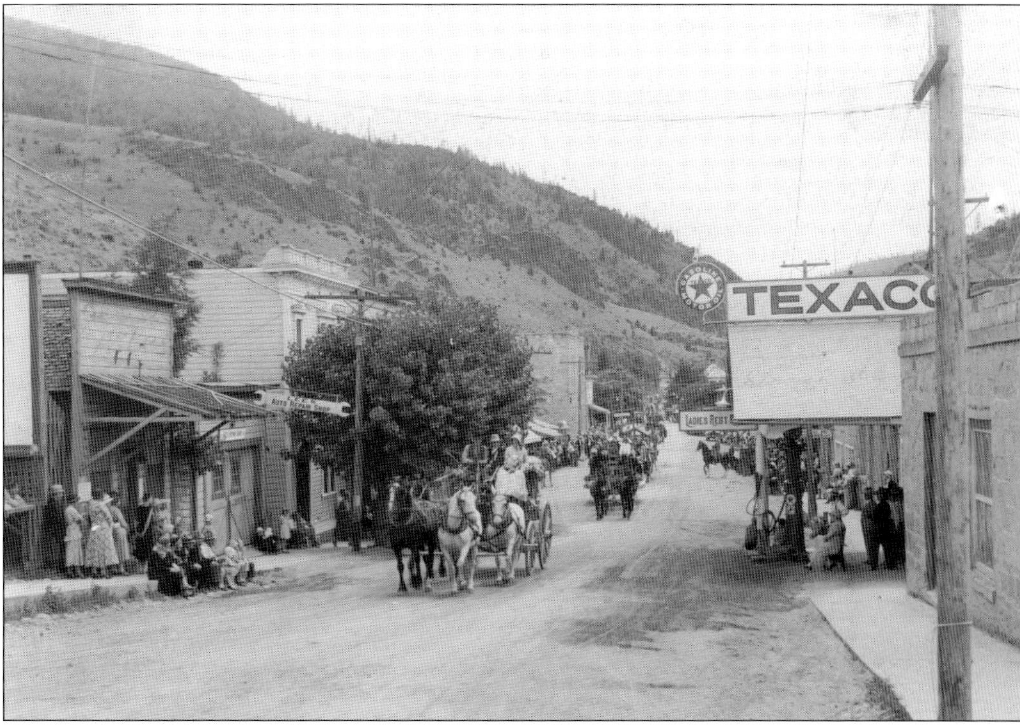

The 62-Day Parade in Canyon City features memories of the 1862 gold rush and the colorful history of Canyon City. It took center stage in 1935 with an array of activities drawing residents and visitors alike from all over Grant County and some areas beyond. It usually offers something for all ages, with a parade, a chili contest, a walk, a run, a magic show, and even a staged hanging. The centerpiece of the 62-Day Celebration—the parade—offers an array of entries, with wagons, horses, ATVs, and dogs on leashes making the trek.

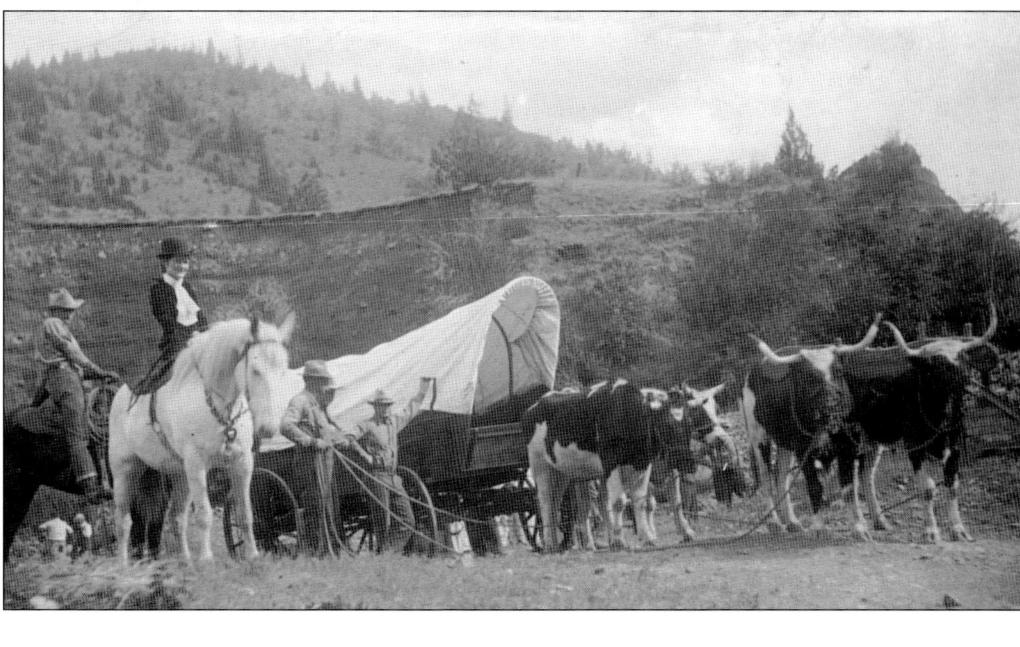

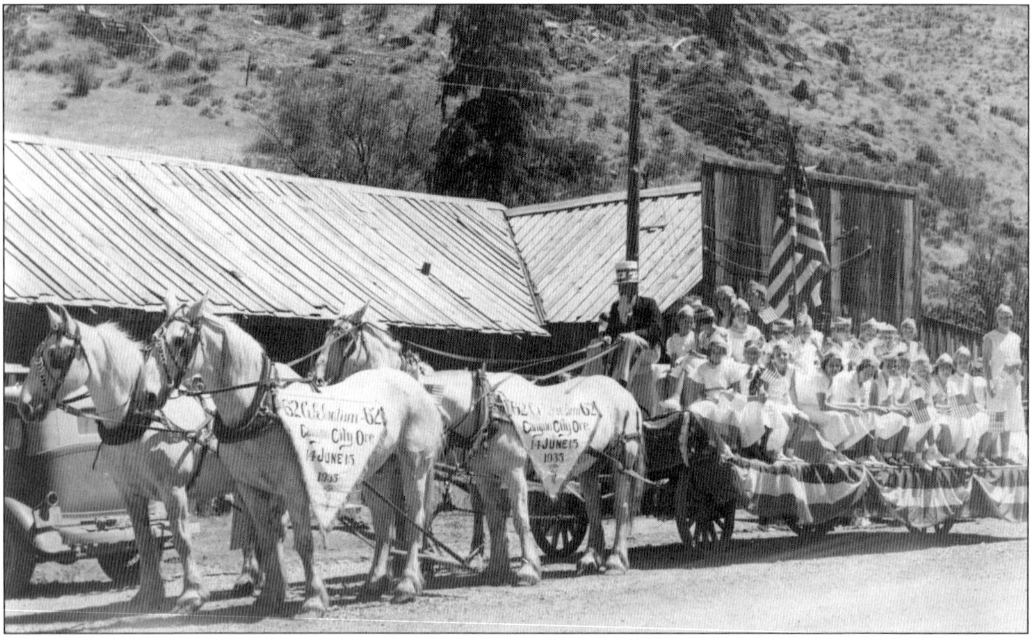

One could find almost anything in the 62-Day Parade in 1935. In this image, four white geldings are pulling a float filled with young ladies all dressed up in their parade dresses. The 62-Day Parade is one of those events that folks circle on their calendars and then count the days until its arrival.

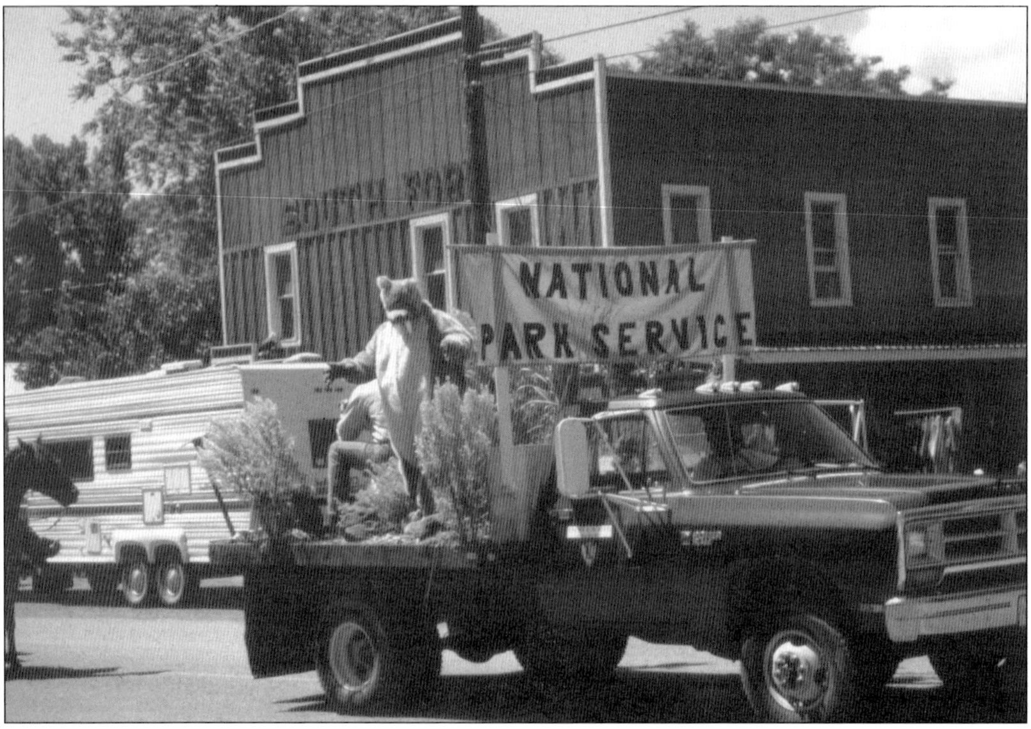

Not only are festivities held in Canyon City and John Day, but other towns also have their celebrations. The above image features the Dayville Parade in 1993. One of the entries was from the John Day Fossil Beds National Monument. The person in the bear suit is unidentified.

Despite inadequate roads on bicycle paths, Ellie (left) and Cora Brown were not discouraged from riding bicycles in 1897. As with most other items, the bicycles were brought into the county via the train to Prairie City or by the long wagon road to The Dalles.

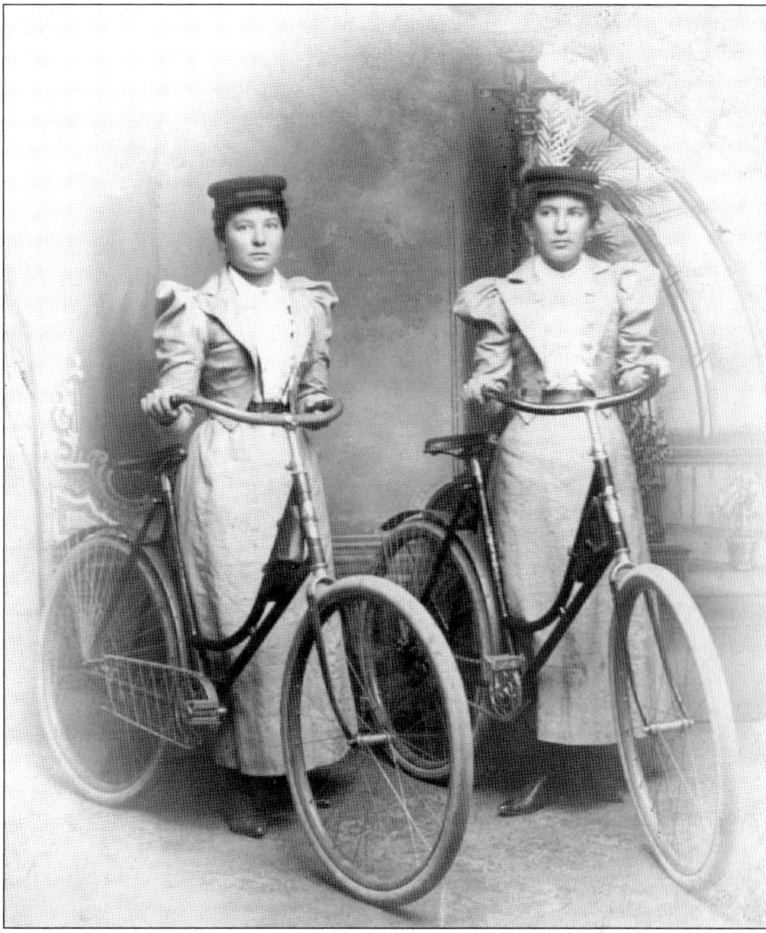

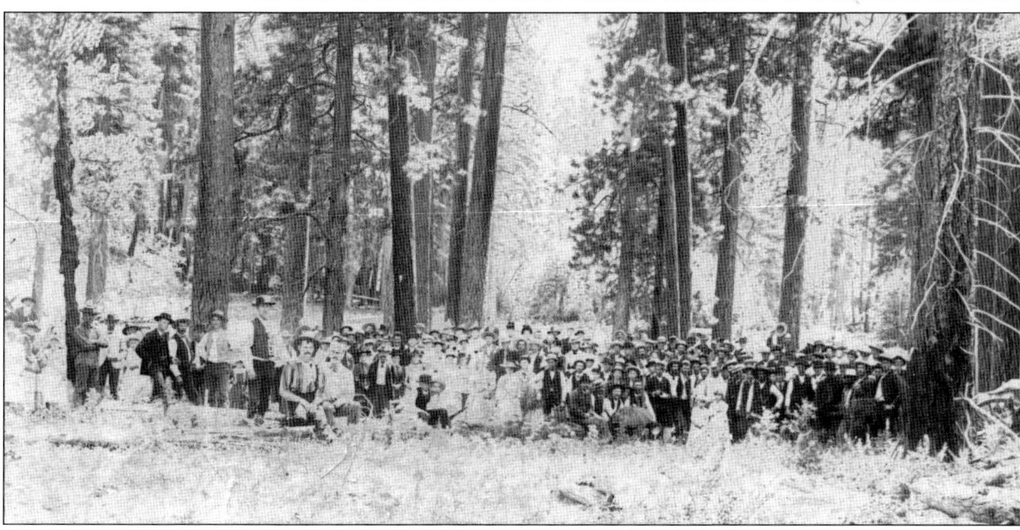

Large crowds would often gather from several towns in Grant County in past years to enjoy the surrounding forests. This image is from the Flat Creek area, between Mount Vernon and Dayville, which drew hundreds of locals.

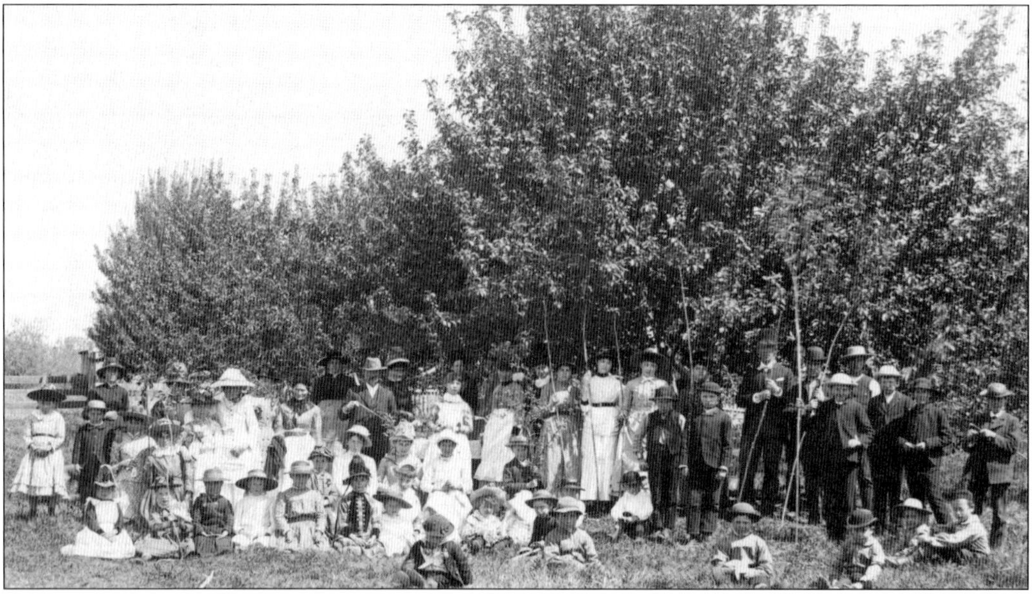

One of the ways to teach schoolchildren about the outdoors was to take them fishing. The above image shows a group of schoolchildren on a fishing trip in 1880. There is no record of the number of fish caught.

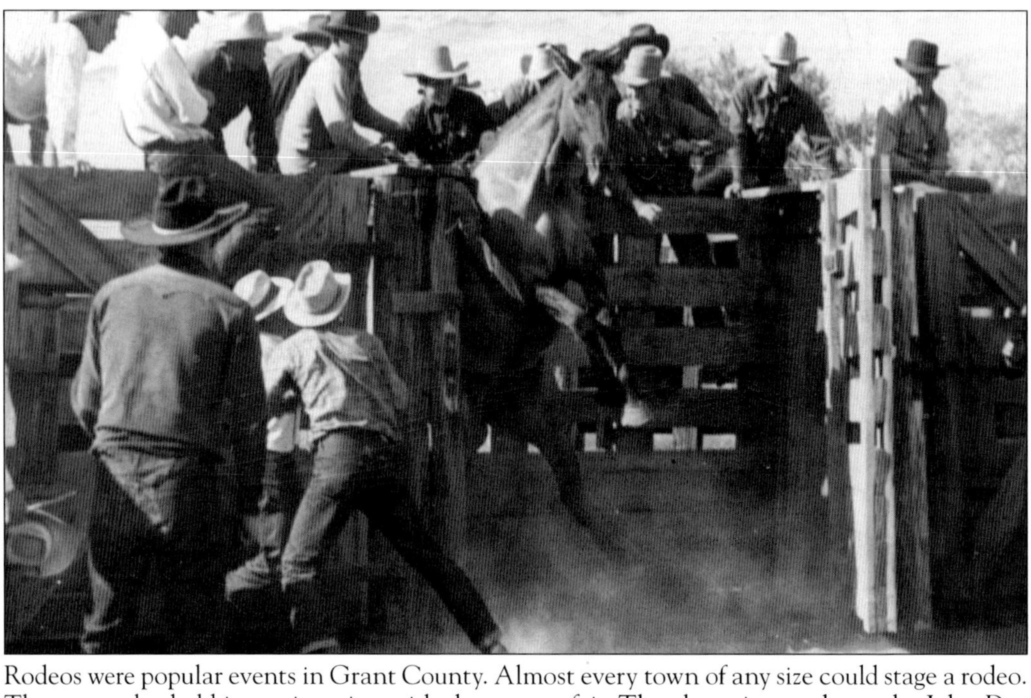

Rodeos were popular events in Grant County. Almost every town of any size could stage a rodeo. They were also held in conjunction with the county fair. The above image shows the John Day rodeo and a cowboy attempting to ride a bucking horse. Riders came from all over the state to compete.

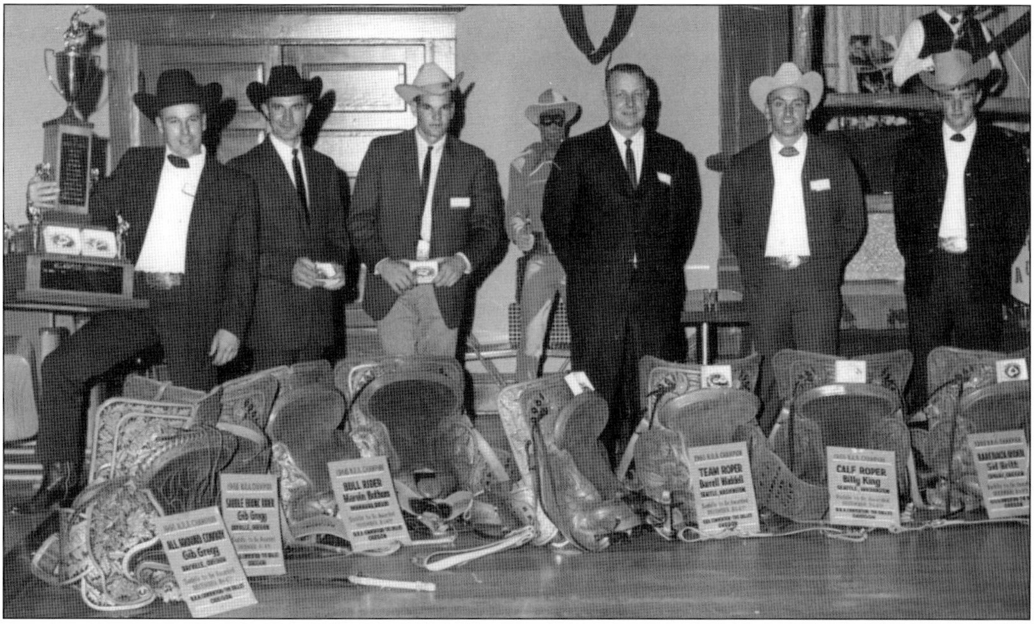

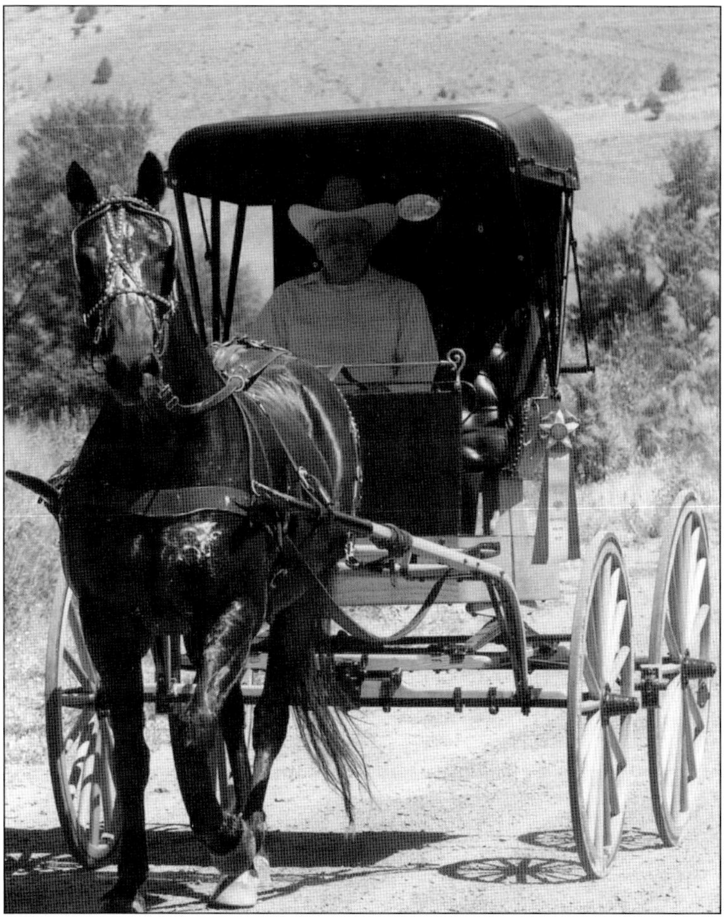

Rodeo competition has continued and indeed expanded. The individuals above participated in the Northwest Rodeo Competition and were quite successful. From left to right are Gib Gregg, All Around Saddle Bronc; Marvin Bothum, Bull Riding; Dick Kelly, Bulldogging; Darrell Waddell, Team Roping; Billy King, Calf Roping; and Sid Britt, Bareback. Gary Gregg, sitting in the carriage at right, was 1959 National Intercollegiate Rodeo Association Saddle Bronc champion. Over the years, he discovered a new vocation: making carriages from parts he mostly scavenged over the years. He is shown in one of the carriages he made. (Both, courtesy of Grant County Ranch and Rodeo Museum.)

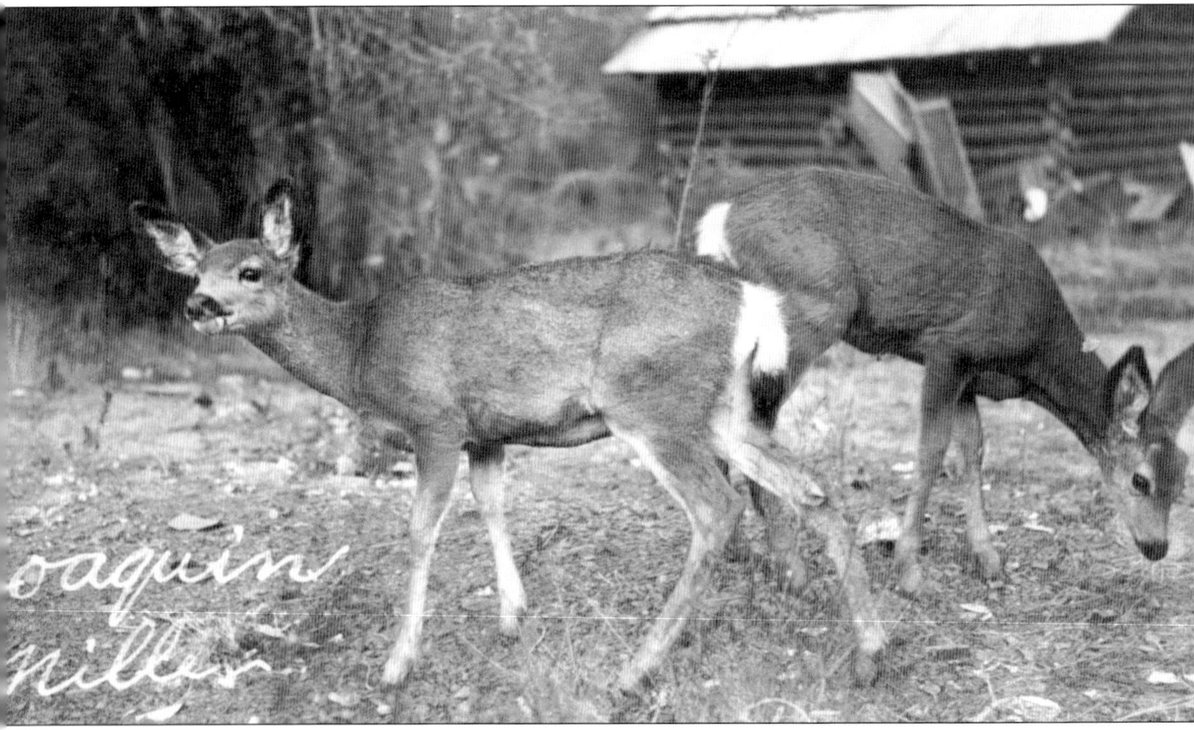

Hunting is a popular pastime in Grant County. A hunter has several opportunities to seek animals such as deer, antelope, elk, and mountain rams. Bears and cougars can also be found. Hunters come from all over Oregon and the Pacific Northwest to seek that trophy set of antlers. At lower elevations, pheasants can be found in the acres of grassland and ducks and geese where there is a body of water. All of this adds income to the local community. Annual events are held, such as the Rocky Mountain Elk Foundation John Day Big Game Banquet in the spring.

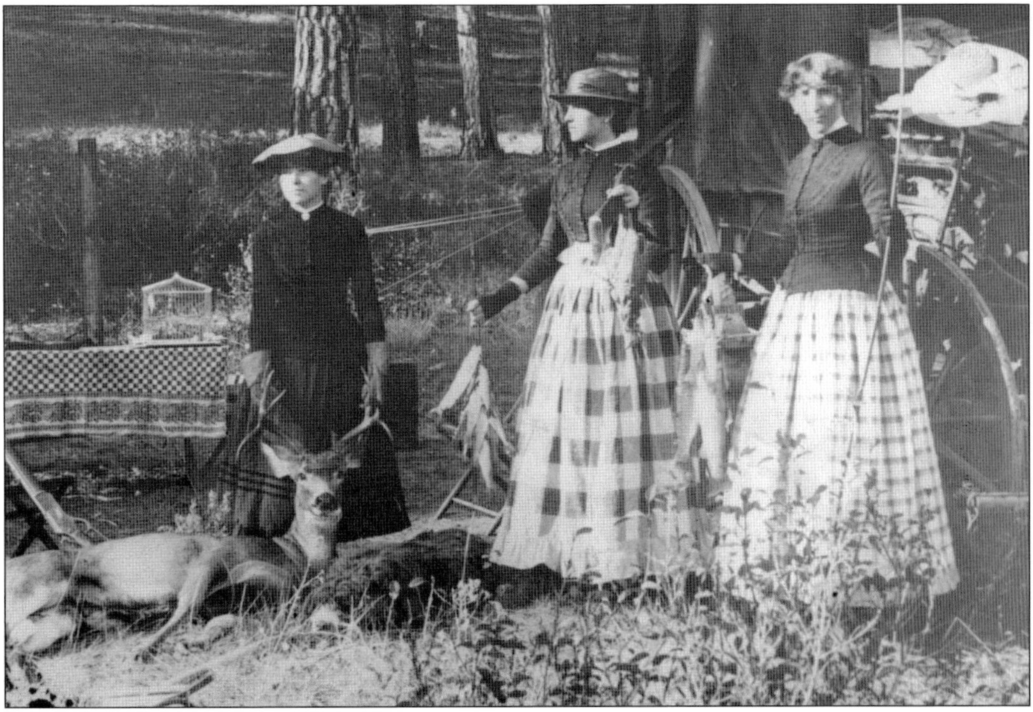

These images show two successful hunting and fishing trips. The John Day River and its tributaries offer excellent fishing opportunities for trout, steelhead, and salmon. From left to right above are Gracia Hazeltine, Nea Small Hazeltine, and Viola Parker Hazeltine, all daughters of Martin Hazeltine of Baker (City), Oregon. Their hunting and fishing trip proved quite successful. Below, John Muldrick is shown near the rear wheel of the Unid automobile with his prize for the day.

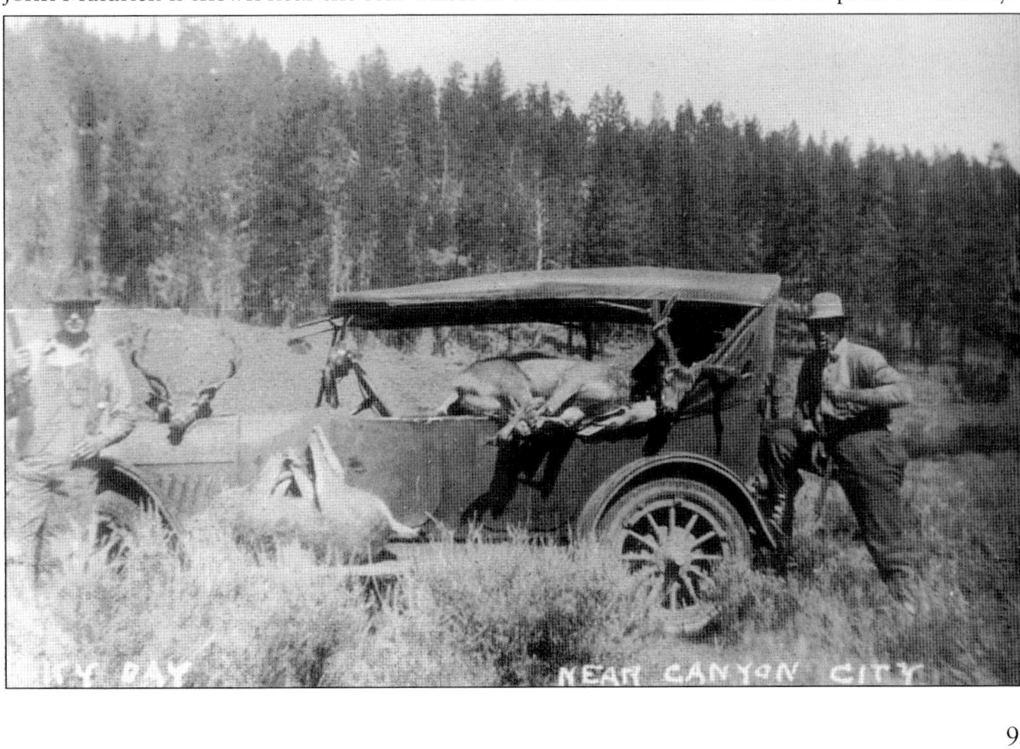

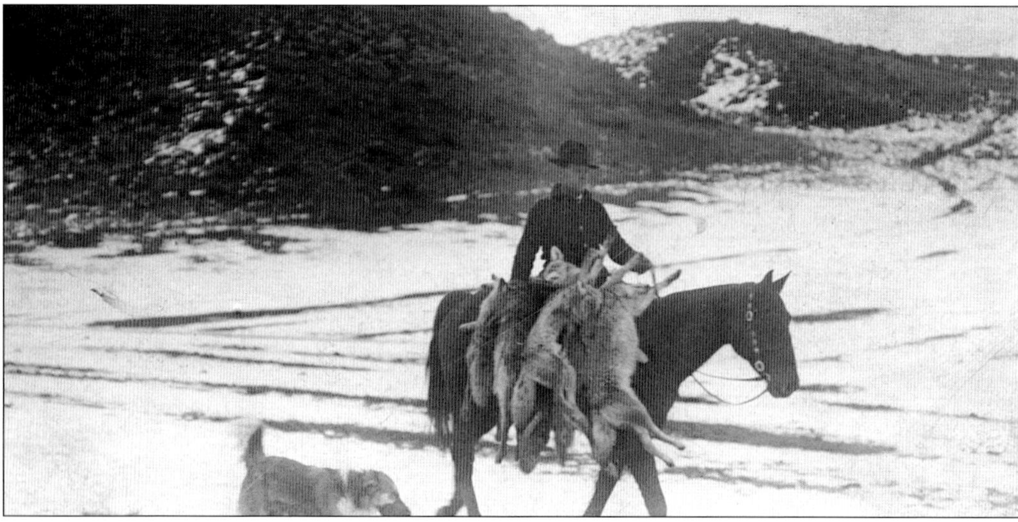

In the late 1800s and early 1900s, after gray wolves were exterminated from the area, coyotes increased in number. They became a threat to cattle and sheep, so ranchers and Forest Service personnel began trapping them. Bert McIntyre (or McEntire) was perhaps one of the most successful. He is shown in both images. He would trap coyotes in the winter months and work for the Forest Service as a forest ranger during the summer months. Coyote pelts could be sold on the Eastern market and were often sewn into rugs.

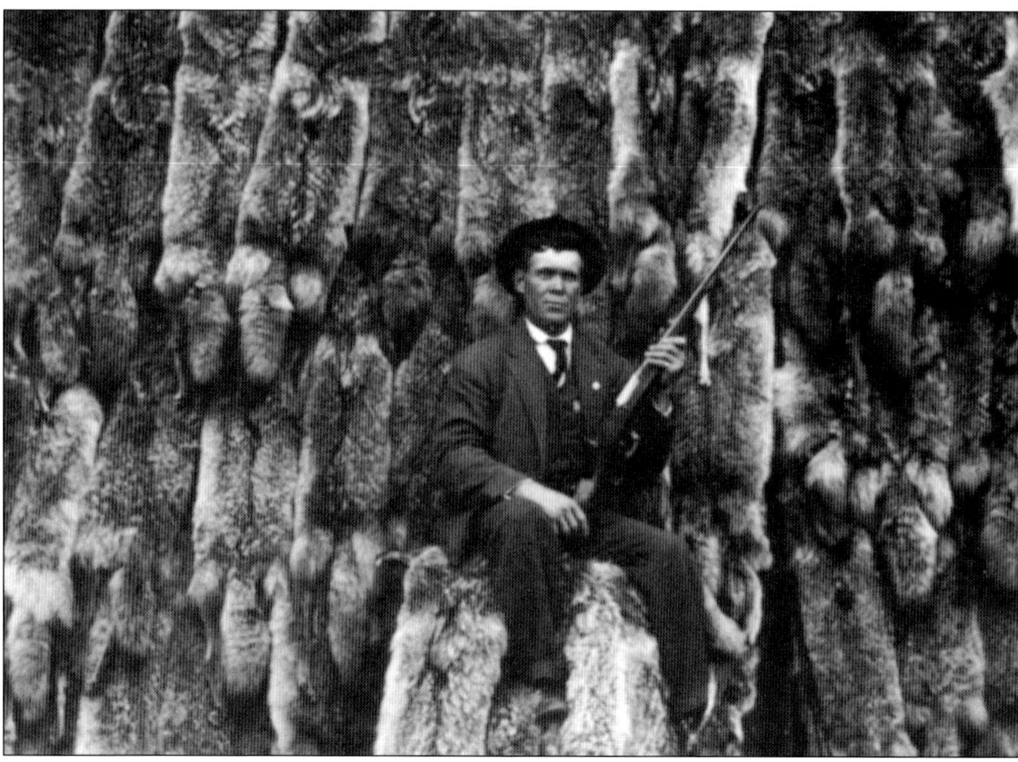

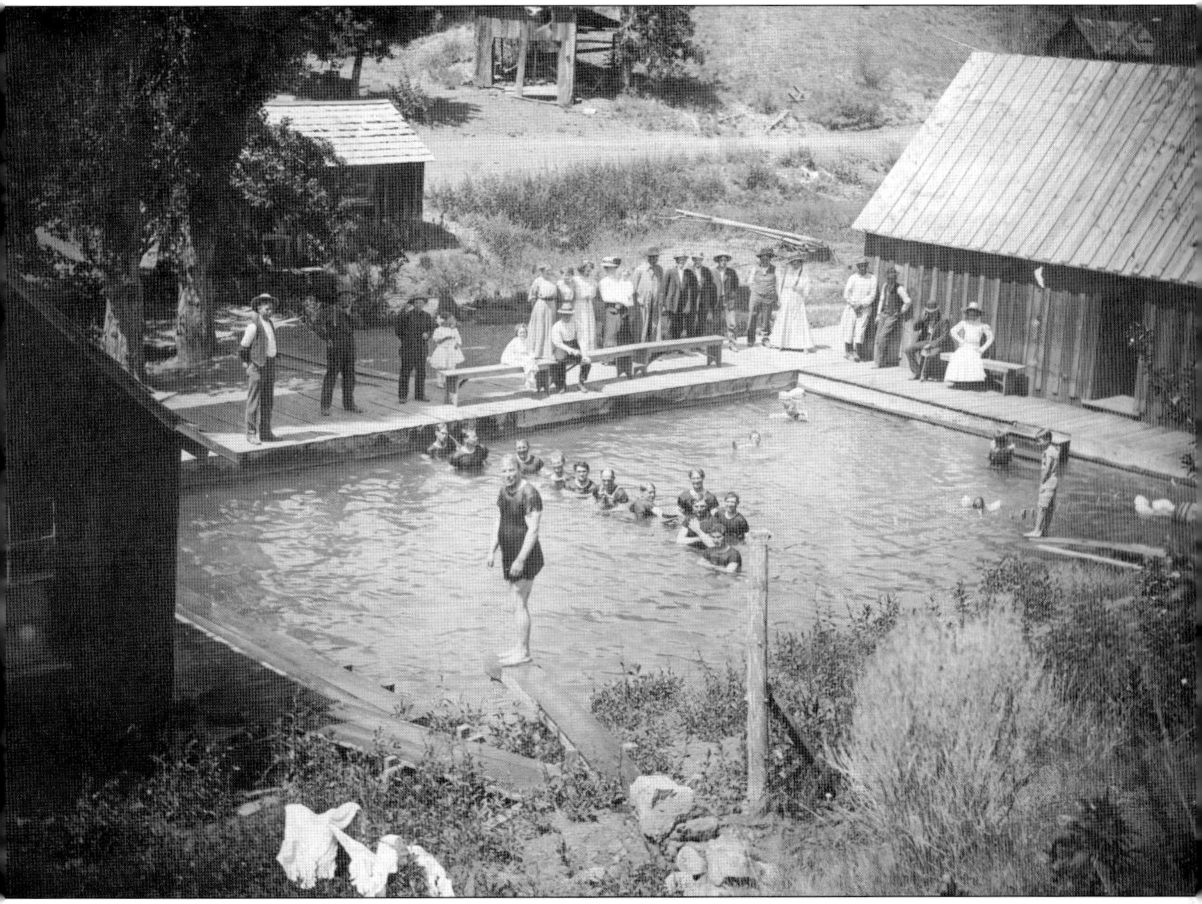

There are several hot springs in eastern Oregon. These are the Mount Vernon Hot Springs, north of Mount Vernon just off Highway 395, around 1930. As with most hot springs, this clinic reportedly offered relief for rheumatism and arthritis, purporting to soothe and remedy the ailments. Johnnie Johnson is on the springboard, and the resort builder, Henry Murphy, is on the left. The site is now closed.

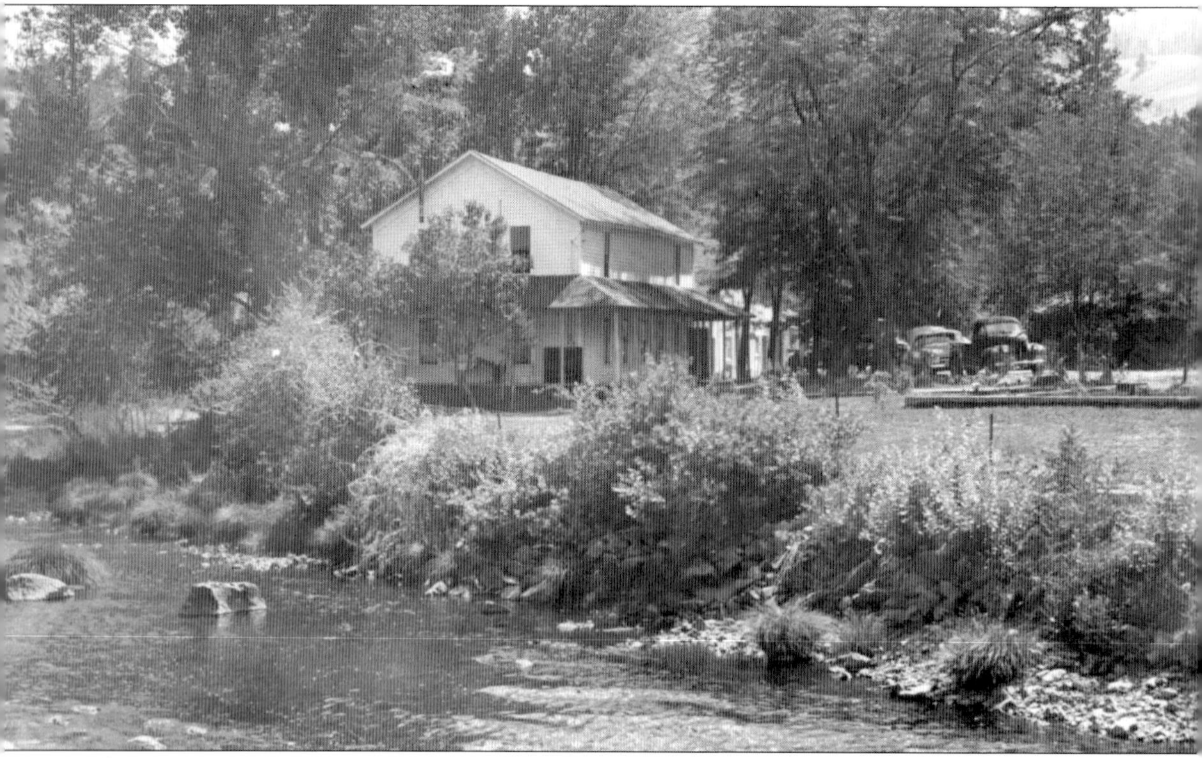

The Ritter Hot Springs are in the northwest corner of Grant County along the Middle Fork of the John Day River. As with most hot springs, after relaxing in the mineral water, some relief from arthritis and other ailments is often realized. The area offers several other attractions, such as hiking, rock hounding, bird watching, fishing, and rafting. There are some ghost towns located in the area.

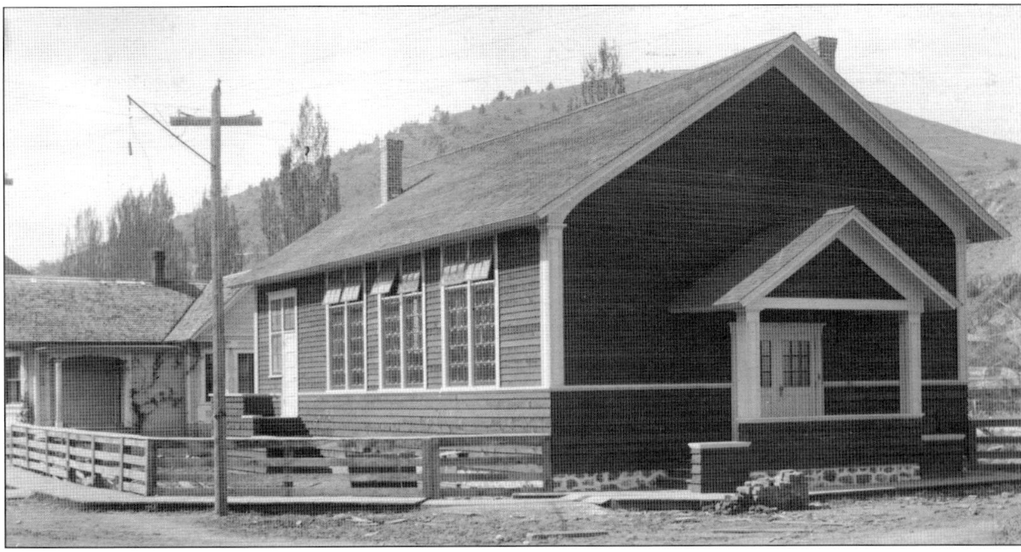

The Guild Hall is located in Canyon City. Although past information is sketchy, it likely served as a dance hall on the weekends and as a meeting location for the various fraternal organizations in the area. It still sits on the corner of Washington Street South and Izee Street. The date of the above image is unknown, but another image of the building refers to 1915.

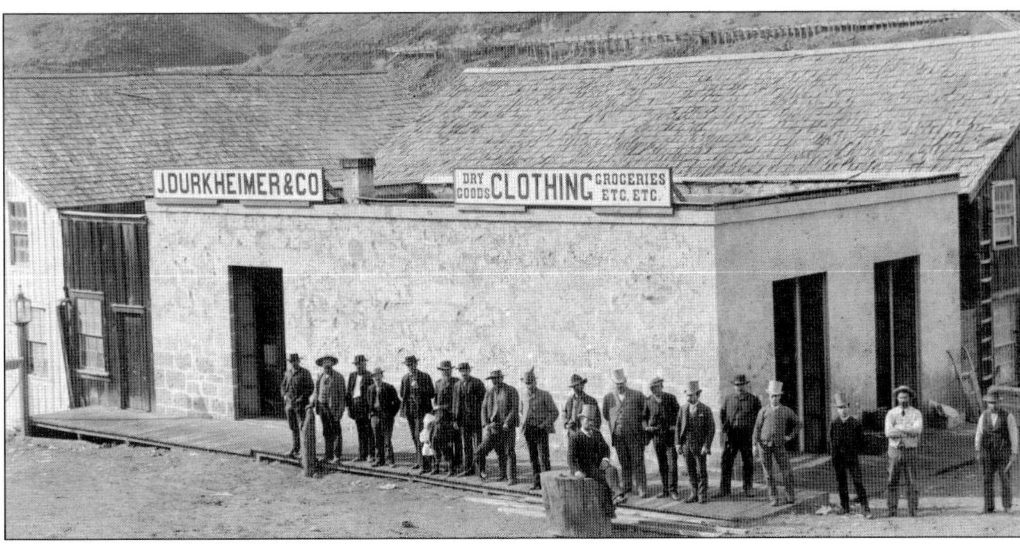

J.D. (Julius) Durkheimer operated a general store in Canyon City around 1885–1890. The stone structure was reportedly built in 1870 at the corner of Washington Street South and Main Street. After it was a general store, it was a doctor's office and pharmacy. The building is still standing and is now a private home across the alley from the museum.

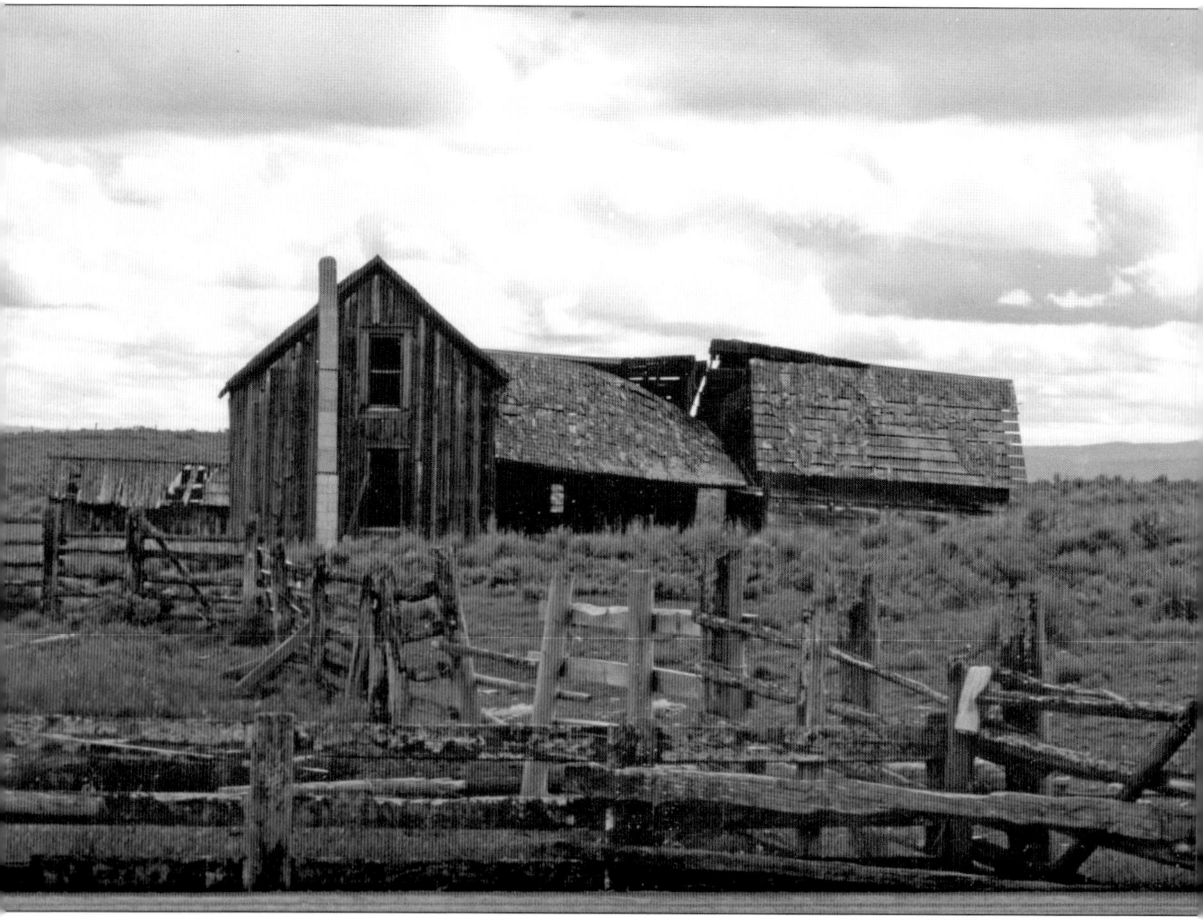

One might be hard-pressed to include the above image in a chapter about recreation. It is the old homestead of John Lowe, sometimes referred to as Low, in Bear Valley. History abounds in the structure. An employee of Lowe, Don Holt, had a dispute with Lowe and beat him to death in 1937. The dispute may have been over bootlegging. An old still was found nearby in the late 1940s or early 1950s, when George Hansen owned the property. (Courtesy of Georgene Hansen-Witmer.)

Six

When Disaster Struck Grant County

At right is the headline in John Day's *Blue Mountain Eagle* on Friday, June 8, 1894. On the previous Sunday, June 3, one of the first recorded tornadoes in Oregon history thoroughly destroyed the eastern portion of this small, beautiful city in the heart of Grant County. The tornado originated in the mountains to the south from a massive thunderstorm and moved north. The number of persons killed by the tornado has never been accurately determined, but the damage was tremendous.

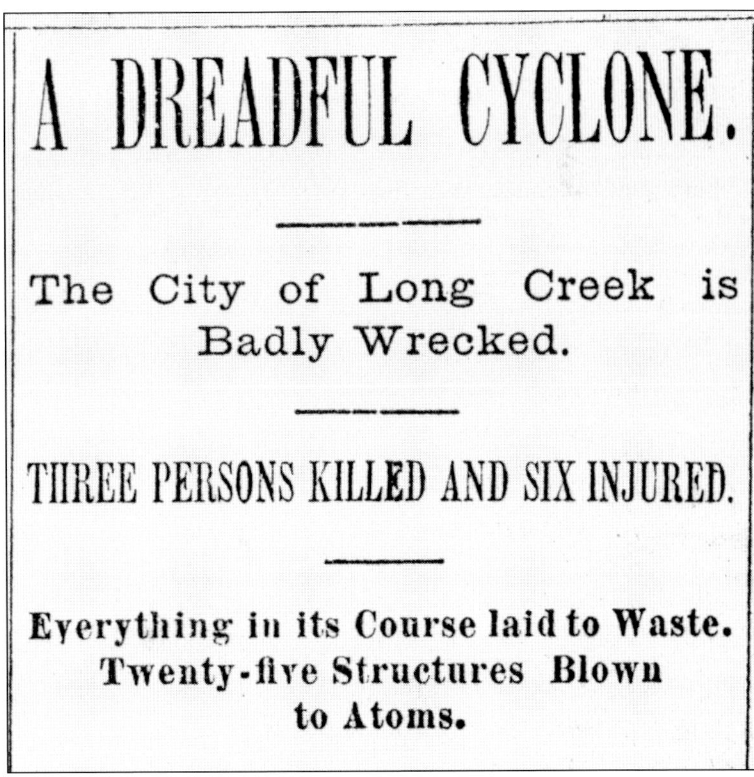

A DREADFUL CYCLONE.

The City of Long Creek is Badly Wrecked.

THREE PERSONS KILLED AND SIX INJURED.

Everything in its Course laid to Waste. Twenty-five Structures Blown to Atoms.

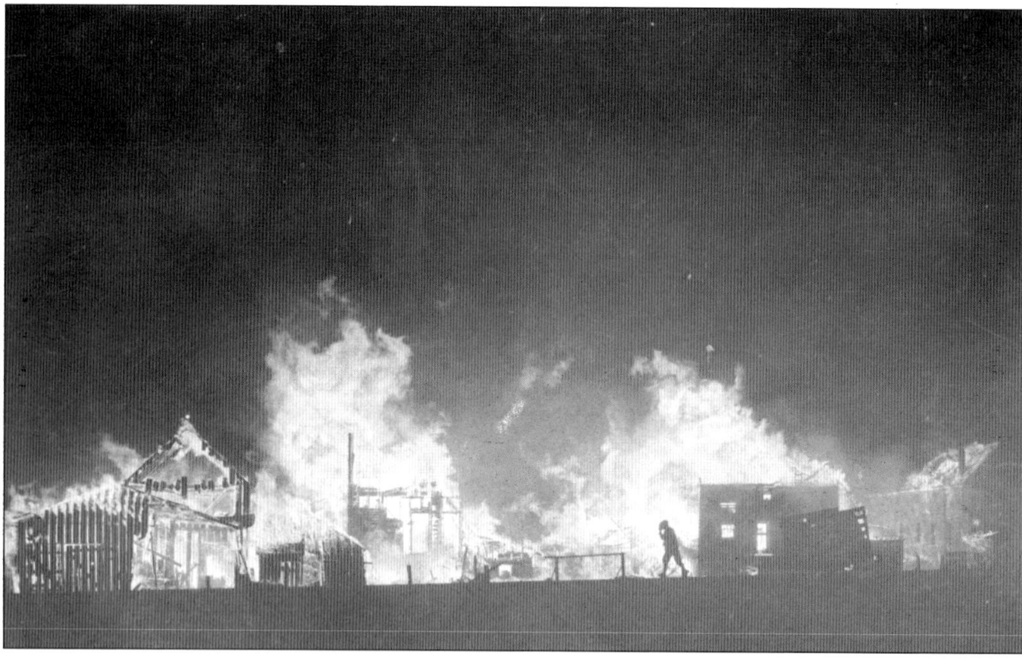

Canyon City has experienced several fires in the downtown area since its beginning in the early 1860s. Because of the vast amount of wooden structures, once a fire started from whatever cause, it would spread rapidly. In the early days, there was not even a volunteer fire department to help in controlling the fires, but after several fires, the citizens saw the need. Above, the 1937 fire burns out of control. Below are the remains of the November 11–12, 1898, fire. It had started in the upper story of the Elkhorn Hotel, and within several minutes, that structure was engulfed in flames. Not to be contained, the fire raced down Washington Street. Actual loss was not determined. The *Grant County News* was spared, and in the early morning, newspapers covering the event were sent to nearby towns that quickly responded with help.

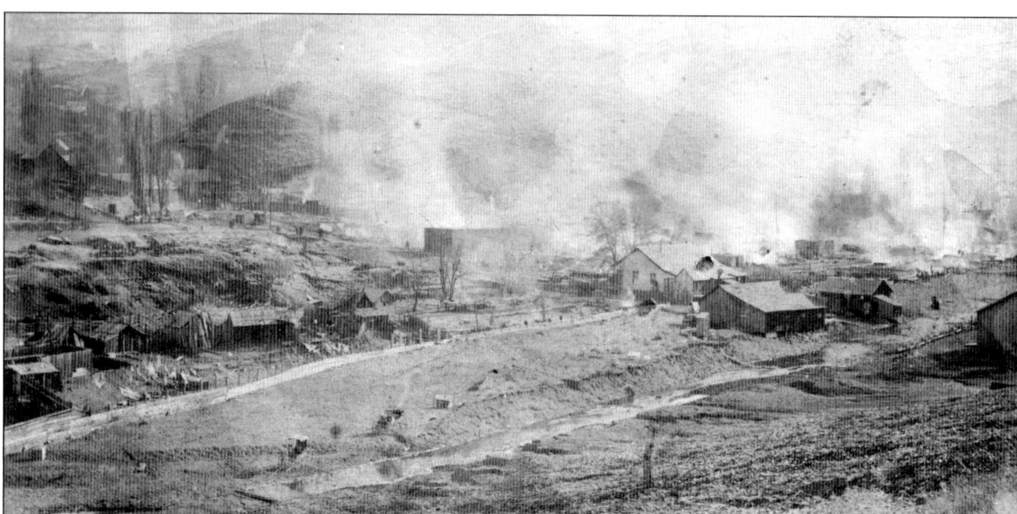

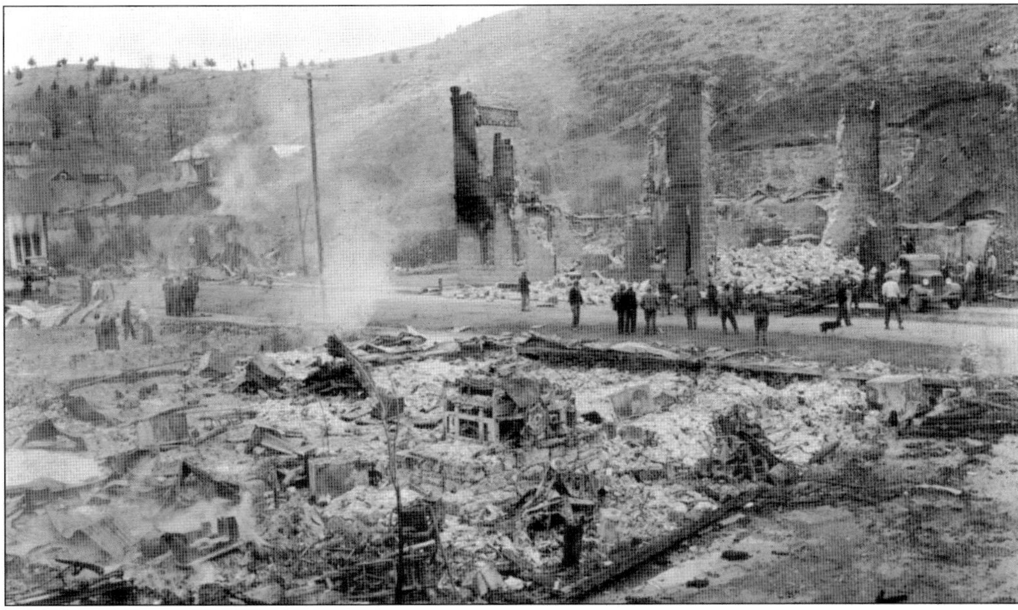

The April 19, 1937, fire in Canyon City destroyed numerous structures in the downtown area. It started in the upper story of the Hotel Canyon and quickly spread to the Canyon Hall Company, where the Interior Drug Store was located. From there, it jumped across the street to the Canyon City Mercantile. Continuing down Washington Street, it virtually destroyed the *Blue Mountain Eagle* newspaper, law offices, and the Blue Mountain Stage Company. Also destroyed were the Canyon City Garage, the Associated Service Station, and the Fraternal Hall.

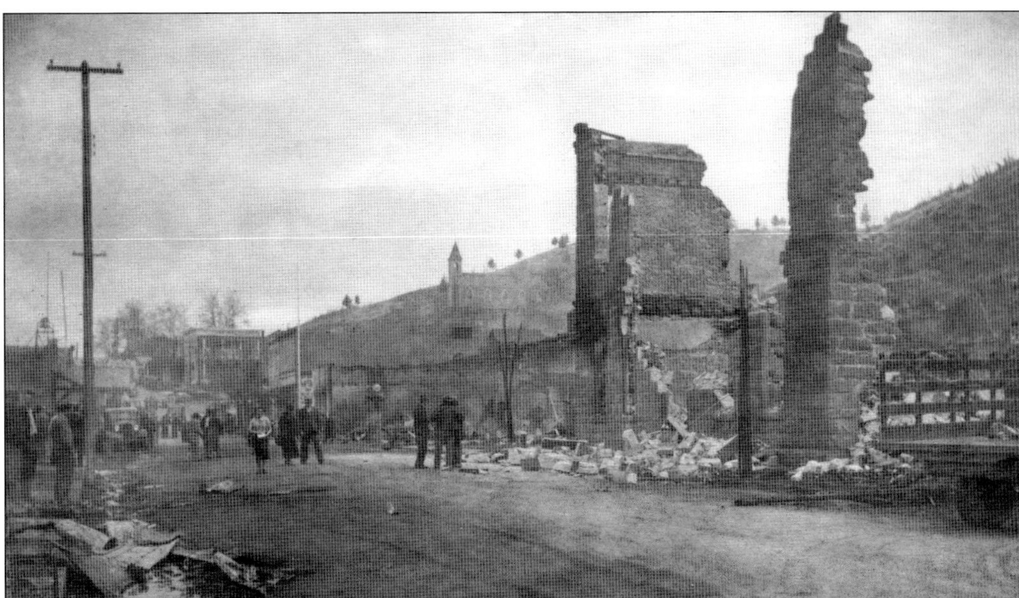

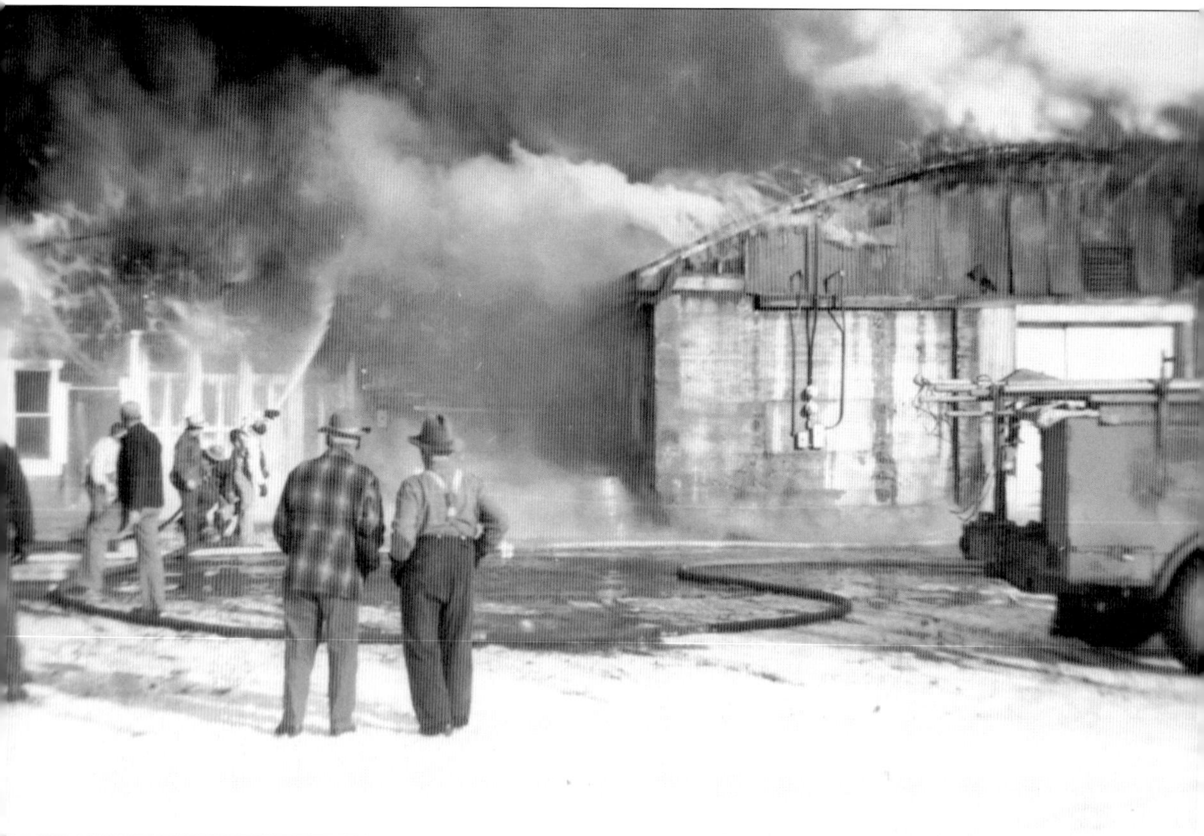

Downtown John Day has not experienced as many fires as Canyon City. The most plausible reason for this was that it looked to its neighbor to the south and passed far stricter building codes. With more buildings of brick and stone, the risk of a fire starting or at least burning out of control as the Canyon City fires had done was reduced. The January 8, 1952, fire (above) was probably one of the most destructive. Even though a strong breeze was occurring during the fire, there was sufficient firefighting equipment to prevent it from becoming a disaster. During the winter of 1921–1922, a fire consumed the Benson Hotel. The fire hoses had frozen, which contributed to the disaster.

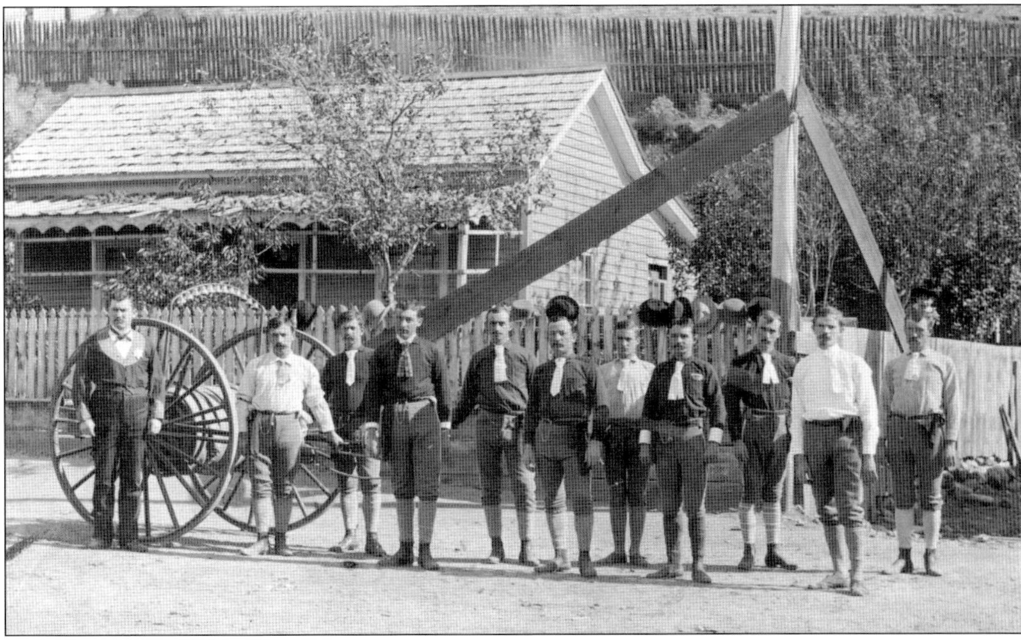

The destructive fires in Canyon City demanded that a volunteer fire department be established. When the fire bell rang, the volunteers would drop whatever they were doing, wherever they were, and scramble to the fire department. They may or may not have been wearing their fancy uniforms. Firefighting equipment was limited in the late 1800s and early 1900s. The hose cart seen above was fed by gravity from a source above the town. The 1885 Canyon City Volunteer Fire Department, pictured above, is, from left to right, Clay Todhunter, Ike Simon, Dick Richards, Frank Metschan, Frank Sels, Hugh Smith, Charles Gray, George Mahon, Vic Cozard, Frank Fleishmann, and Ed Jewett. In the 1920s photograph at right, the participants are unidentified.

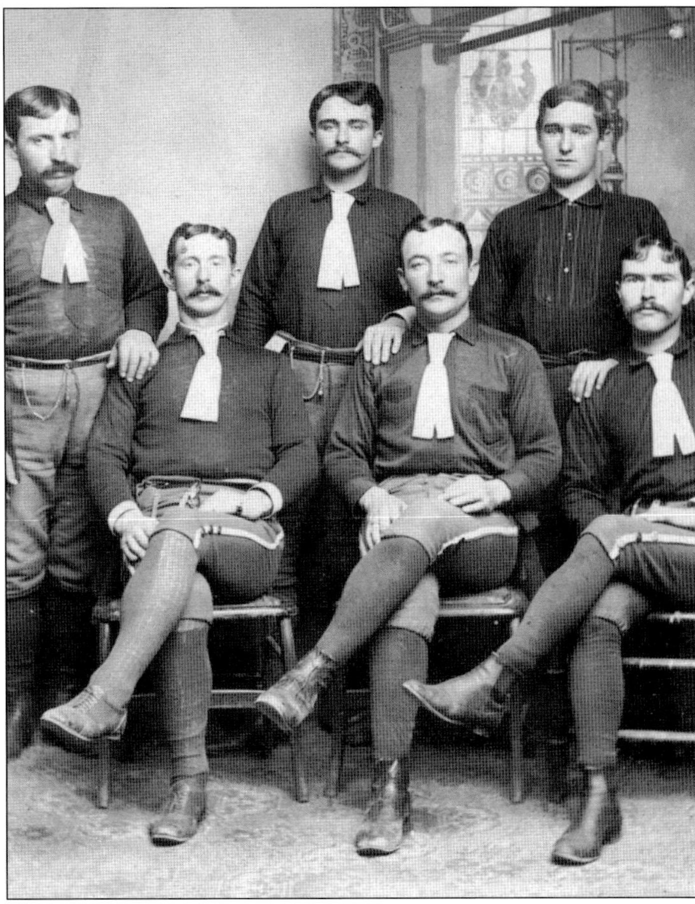

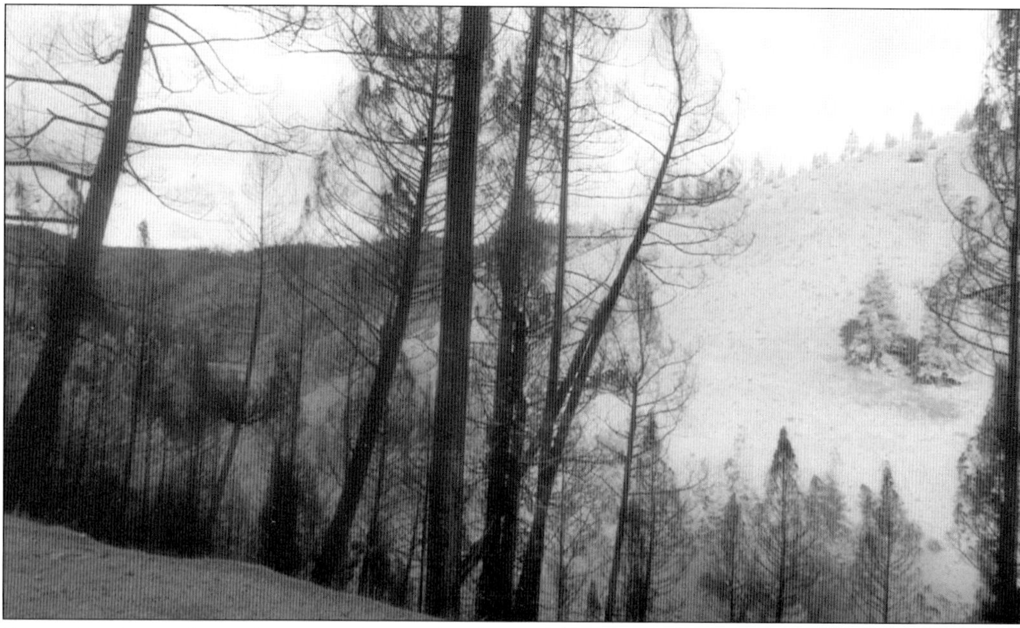

Forest fires have plagued eastern Oregon for thousands of years. Humans and lightning strikes are generally responsible; fires are sometimes set maliciously. When there has been a deficiency of snow fall and rain, the forests become tinder dry. A period of hot, dry weather followed by a lightning strike or thoughtlessly discarded cigarette can quickly spread to hundreds and even thousands of acres. Such was the case in 2015. This fire consumed thousands of acres in the Malheur National Forest. It burned for two months and consumed some private homes and numerous outbuildings. Controversy abounds over whether the fire could have been contained sooner. An answer may never be obtained. Improved spot weather forecasts related directly to these fires have helped. (Both, courtesy of Georgene Hansen-Witmer.)

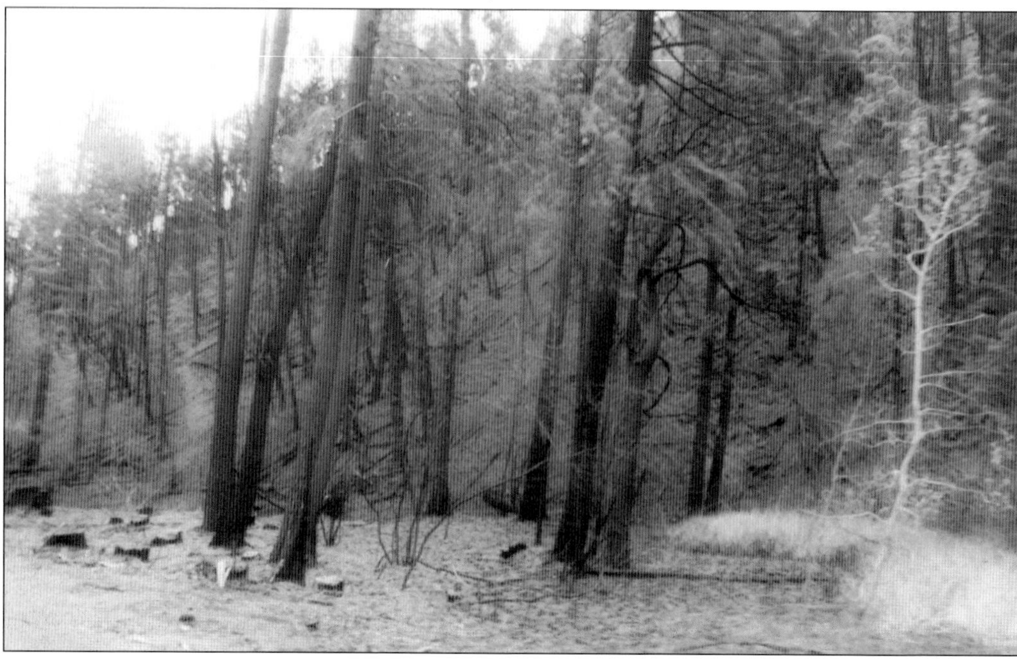

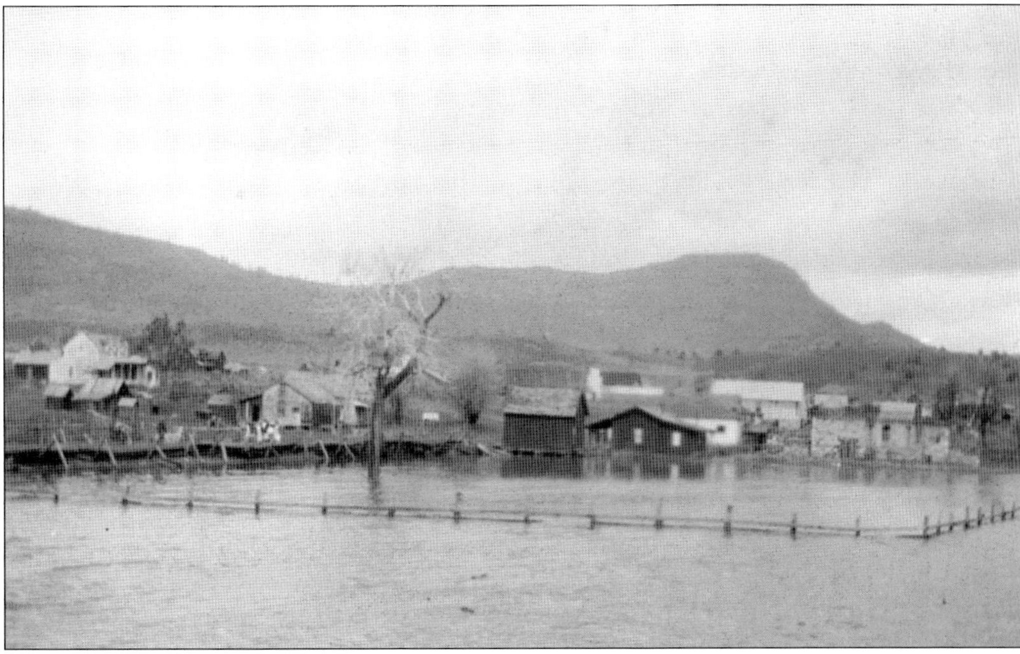

One would think that dry eastern Oregon, where annual precipitation is 15 to 20 inches, would not be susceptible to flooding. Though perhaps not as frequent as locations near the Pacific Ocean, flooding does present a problem. Settlers soon found this out, as lush farmland during the summer could well be under water in the spring. These two images show the spring 1932 flood. Large amounts of snow during the winter can melt rapidly if a very warm period with above-average temperatures occurs. Note the three gentlemen obviously trying to clear away some of the debris that had built up, a very dangerous task. The bridge itself may have already shifted.

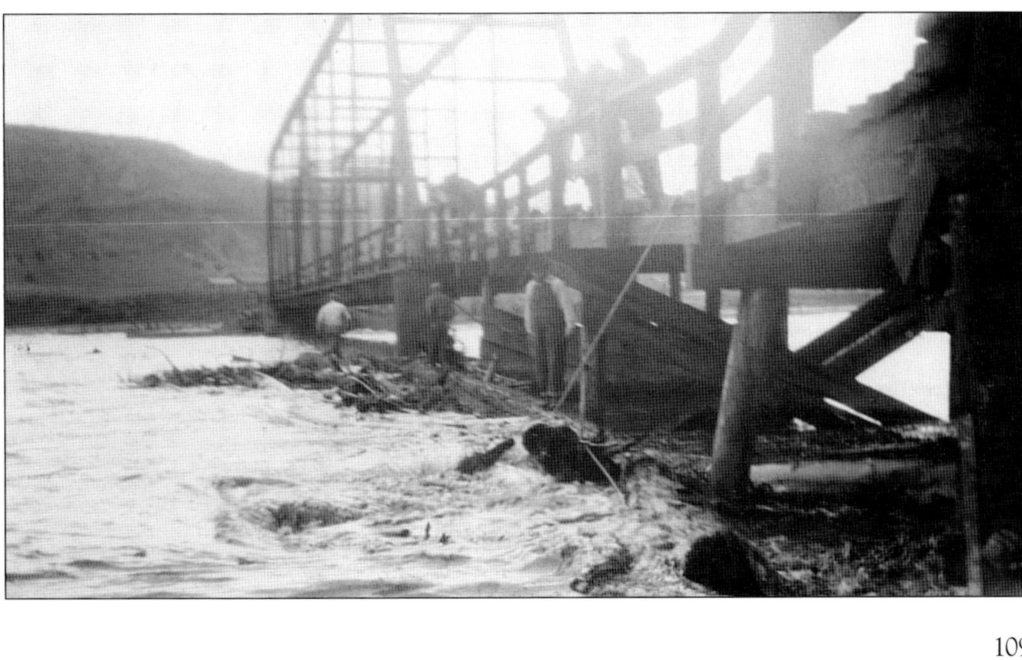

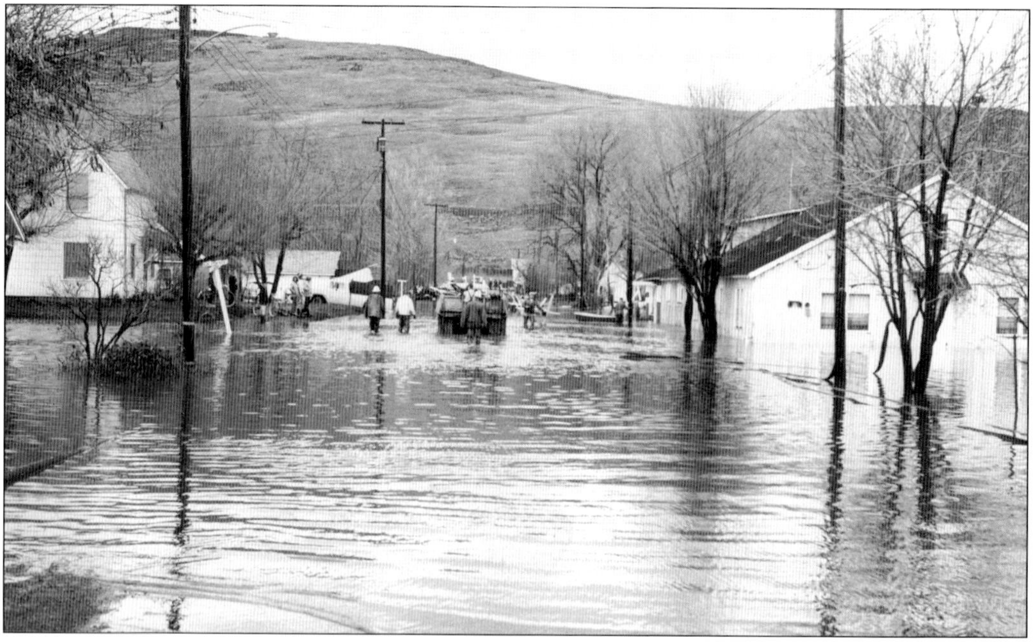

The December 1964 flood was slightly different than the previously shown spring flood. In this case, snow accumulations both in the mountains and at lower elevations had exceeded normal amounts. After the snow had accumulated, a very warm period followed. Snow levels rose far above the mountain elevations, and the southwesterly winds were heavily laden with tropical moisture that had originated at latitudes below even the Hawaiian Islands. This meteorological phenomenon is referred to as the "Pineapple Express." Meteorologists and hydrologists refer to this situation where warm, moist rain falls on a snowpack as a "rain on snow" event. Above is downtown John Day, and below is the John Day River as it overflows its banks.

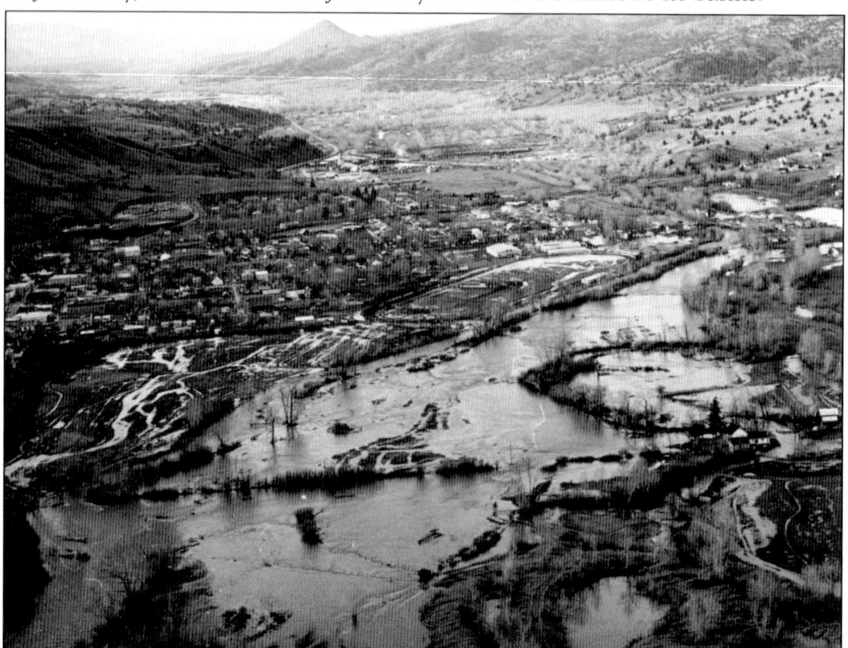

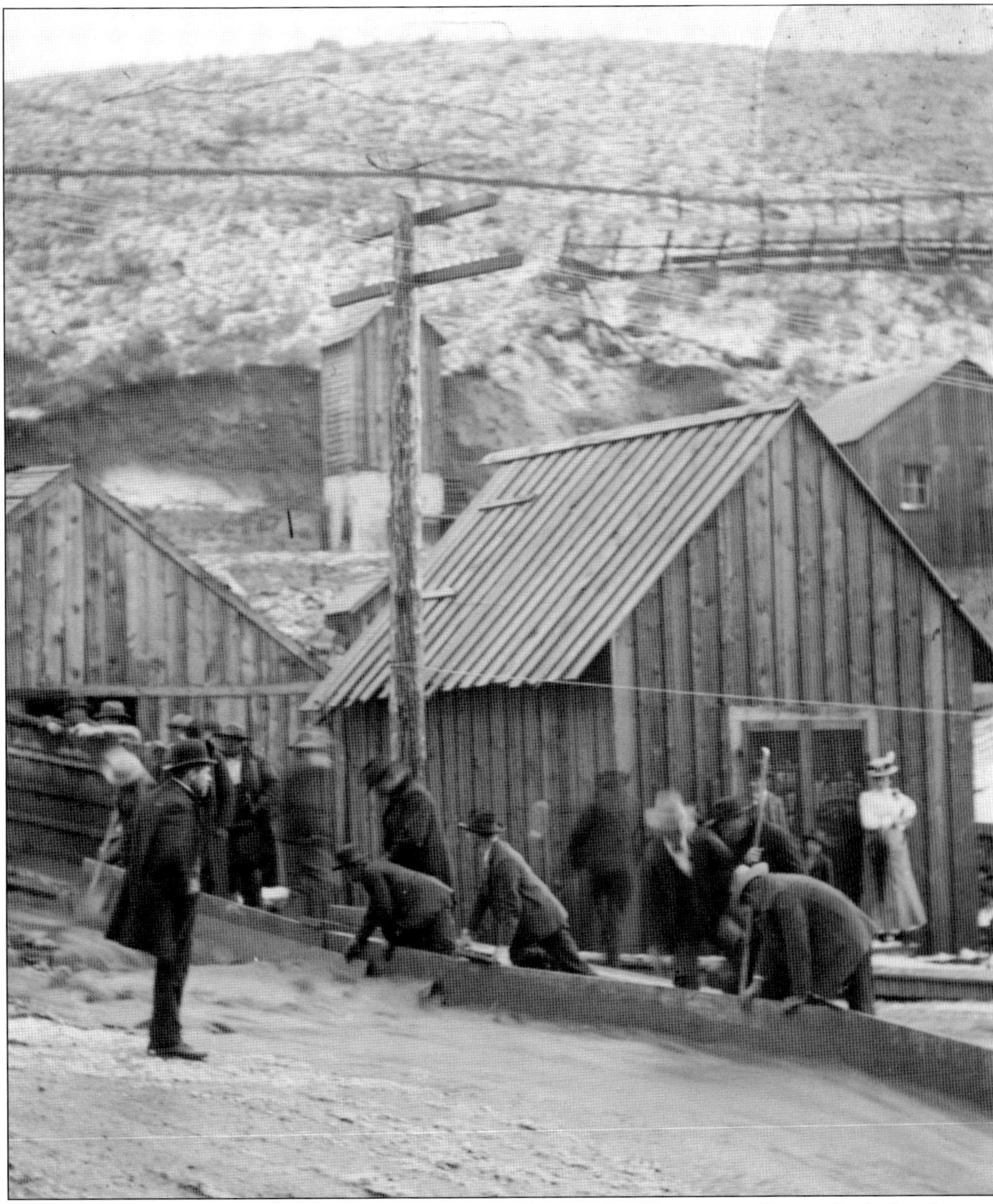

Eastern Oregon, with its many steep hills and valleys, is highly susceptible to flash flooding in the late spring and into the fall season. Rather than copious amounts of rainfall over several days, flash floods result when large amounts of rain fall over a small area over a short period of time. Massive thunderstorms that rise to great heights in the atmosphere can release their moisture suddenly. Rainfall of several inches over a short amount of time can cause dry streambeds to quickly overflow, resulting in massive damage and loss of life. Heppner and Mitchell are two prime examples where there has been destruction of property and loss of life. The above image shows a flash flood in Canyon City around 1896. Canyon Creek, which flows directly through Canyon City, is susceptible to flash flooding. It has steep canyon walls, and the headwaters are in the mountains above the town.

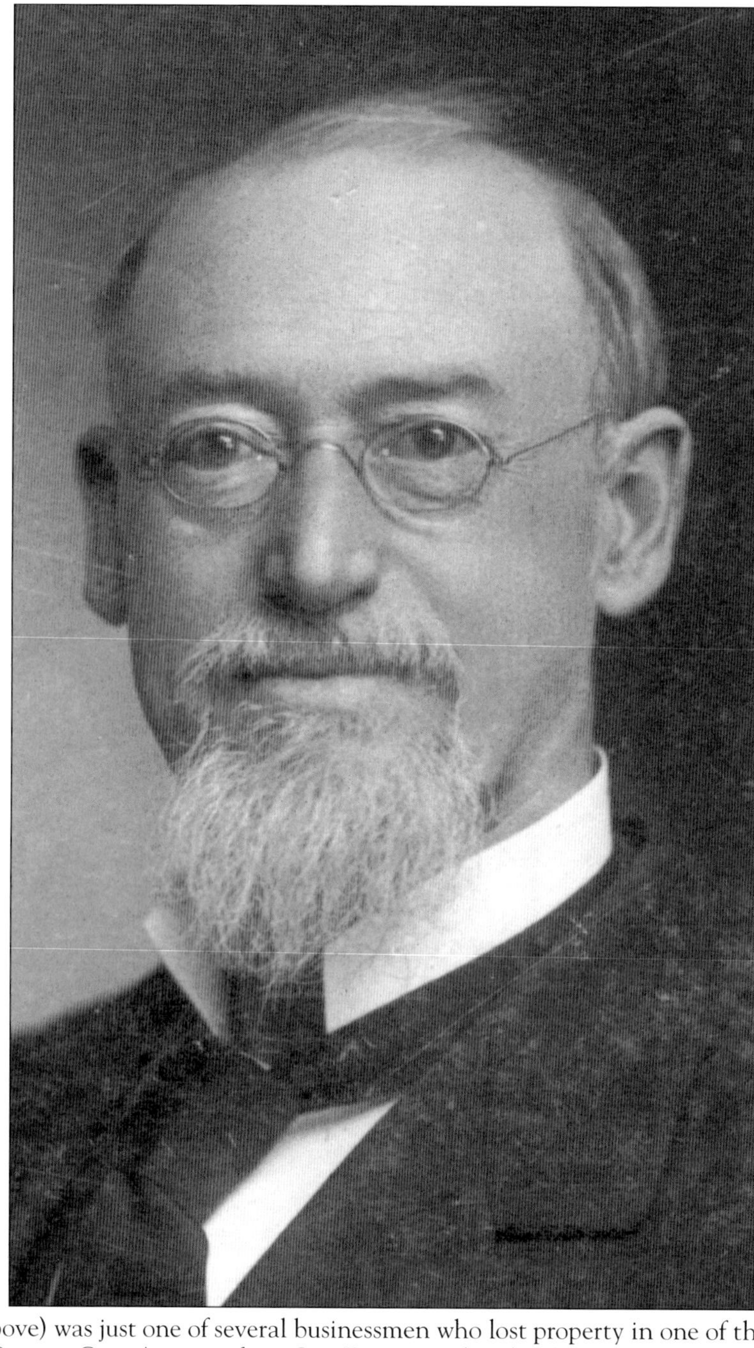

F.C. Sels (above) was just one of several businessmen who lost property in one of the earlier fires to scourge Canyon City. Arriving from San Francisco shortly after gold had been discovered in 1862, he opened a mine (Prairie Diggings) at Marysville, about five miles east of Canyon City. The mine was very successful the first year, and Sels increased his fortune. He purchased the City Brewery on Washington Street in Canyon City but a year later suffered the loss of the building in a fire. Not to be discouraged, he rebuilt the brewery out of rock and stone. Perhaps it was through his beer that he gained fame. It was recognized at the Chicago World's Fair. He was very well liked in the community and even once ran for office but was not elected.

Seven

FEDERAL AND PROTECTIVE ORGANIZATIONS

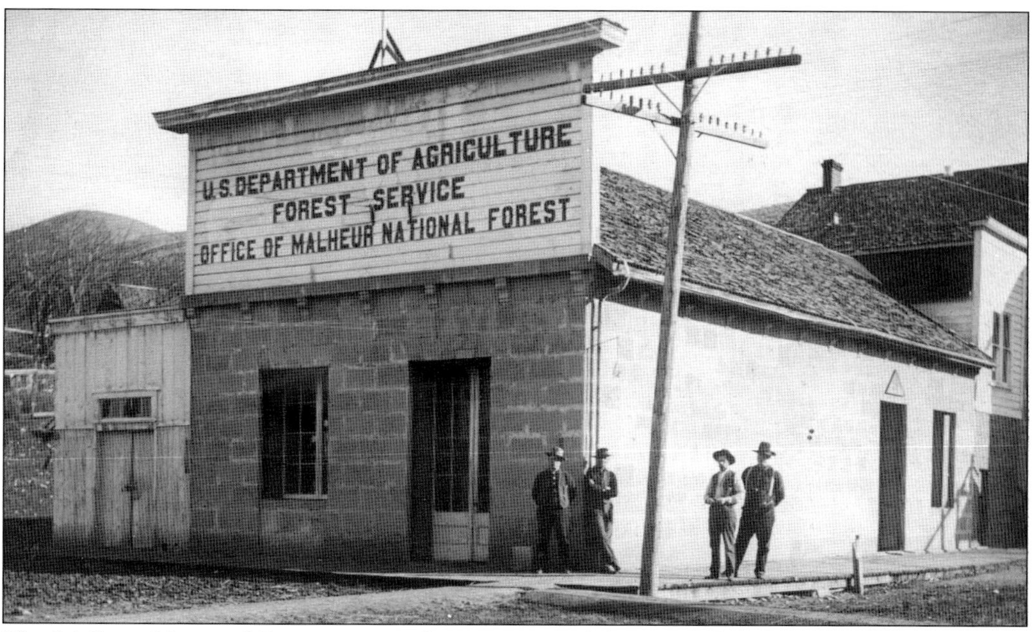

The Malheur National Forest is one of many national forests in the United States. Located in eastern Oregon, it was established by Pres. Theodore Roosevelt on June 13, 1908. Part of the Department of Agriculture, it contains more than 1.4 million acres in the Blue Mountains of eastern Oregon. Not all the forest is in Grant County. It is named after the Malheur River. The forest consists of high desert grasslands, sage, juniper, pine, fir, and other tree species. Elevations vary from about 4,000 feet to the 9,038-foot peak in the Strawberry Mountains. This photograph shows the early forest headquarters around 1910.

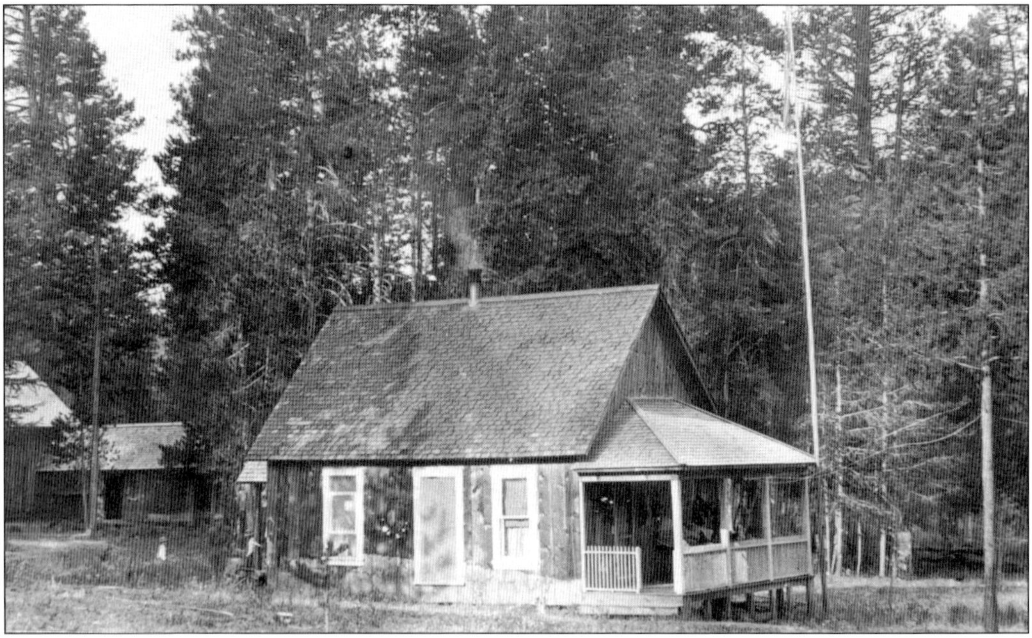

Today, national forests are subdivided into ranger districts, each responsible for a certain portion of the forest. These are modern buildings with up-to-date facilities. That was not the case after the Malheur National Forest was designated in 1908. This is the Deer Valley Ranger Station shortly after the conception of the Malheur National Forest.

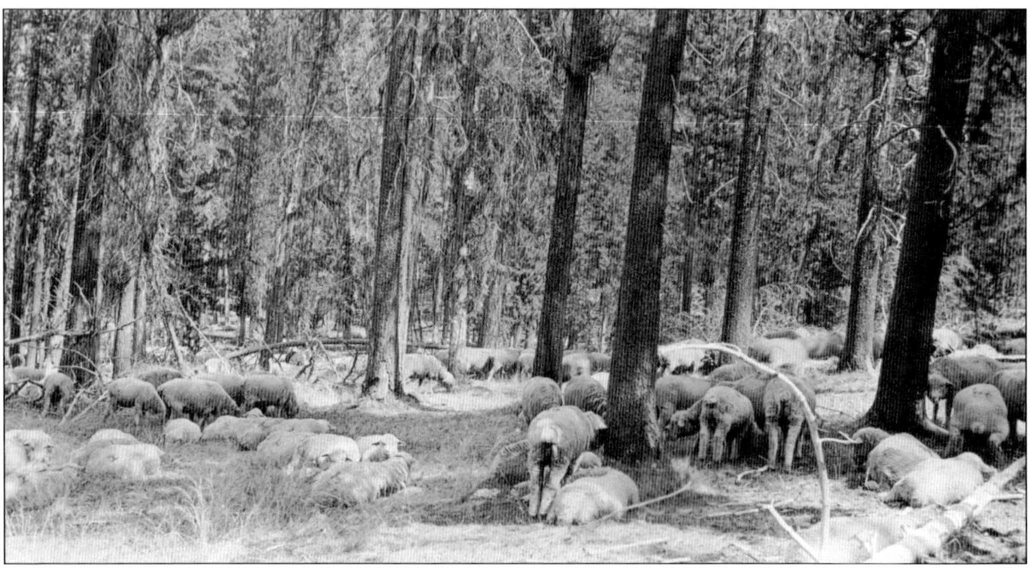

Soon after its conception, the Malheur National Forest began issuing permits for the livestock grazing on land belonging to the national forest. Here, merino sheep are seen grazing among lodgepole and ponderosa pine on the MaCrae allotment in the Scott Creek area. Over the years, these allotments have become a very controversial issue between the cattle and sheep men and the US government.

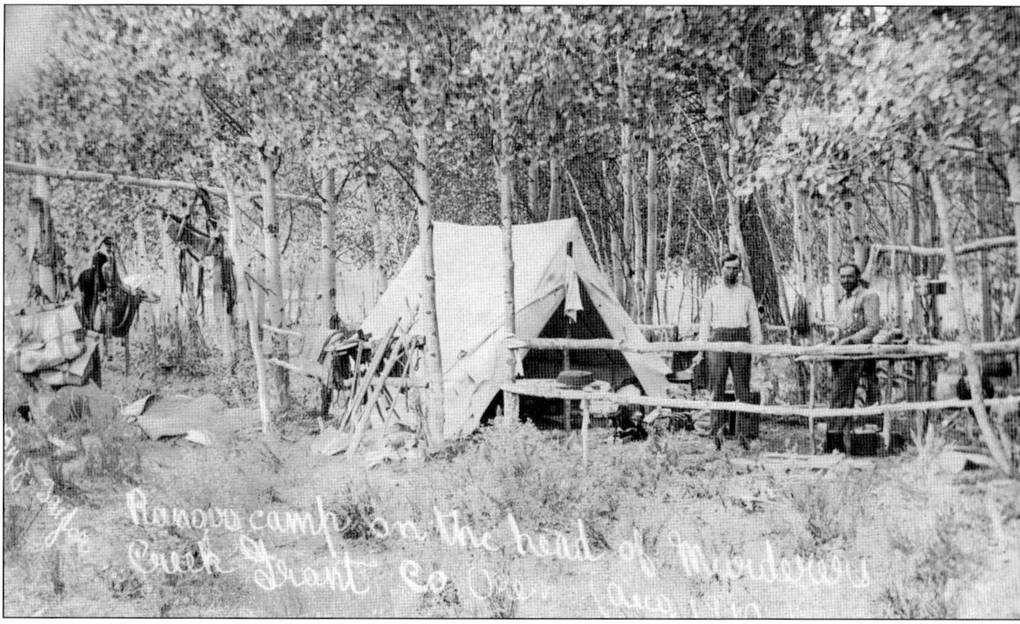

These facilities were popularly known in the early 1900s as work stations. They could be far removed from civilization. The images show them as glorified camp-outs where meals were cooked and the participants slept. Work stations were popular during the summer months in the early stages of the national forest. Above is the Murderer's Creek work station, so named because some Indians killed eight prospectors who were exploring the creek looking for gold in the early 1860s. Below is another, larger early work station.

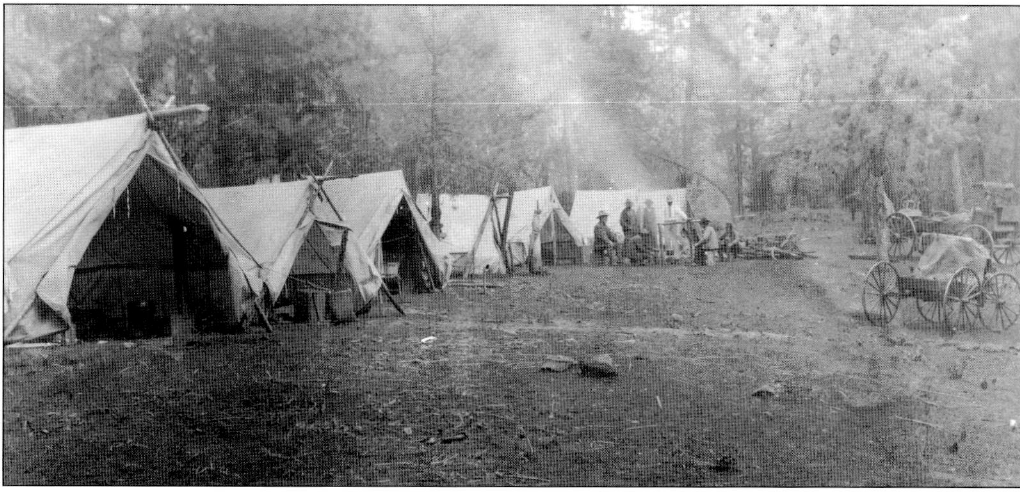

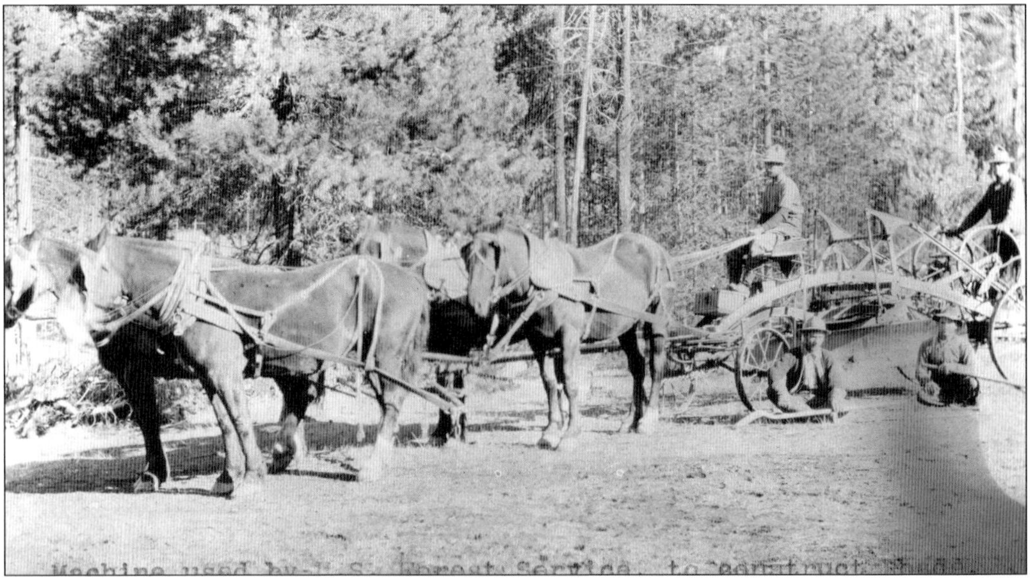

Building roads soon became one of the more important tasks of the newly formed Forest Service. These were needed to open the forest's vast stands of ponderosa pine to logging. It was a long and difficult task using horses to pull plows. Crews generally consisted of 8 to 10 men. The Forest Service also undertook the task of building telegraph lines that connected the ranger stations to the forest headquarters and other places around the county.

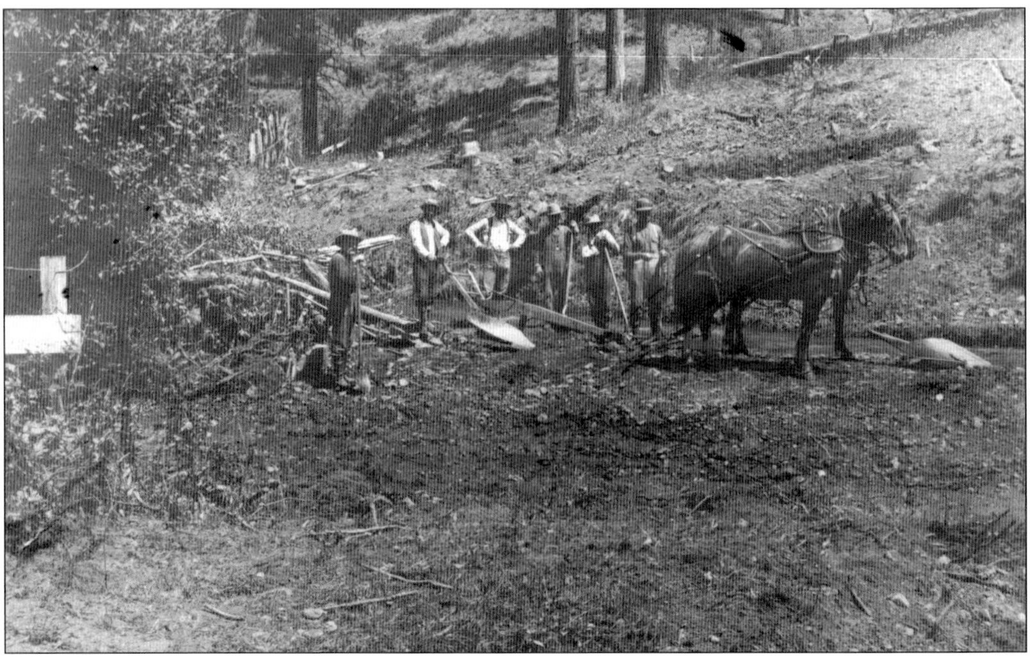

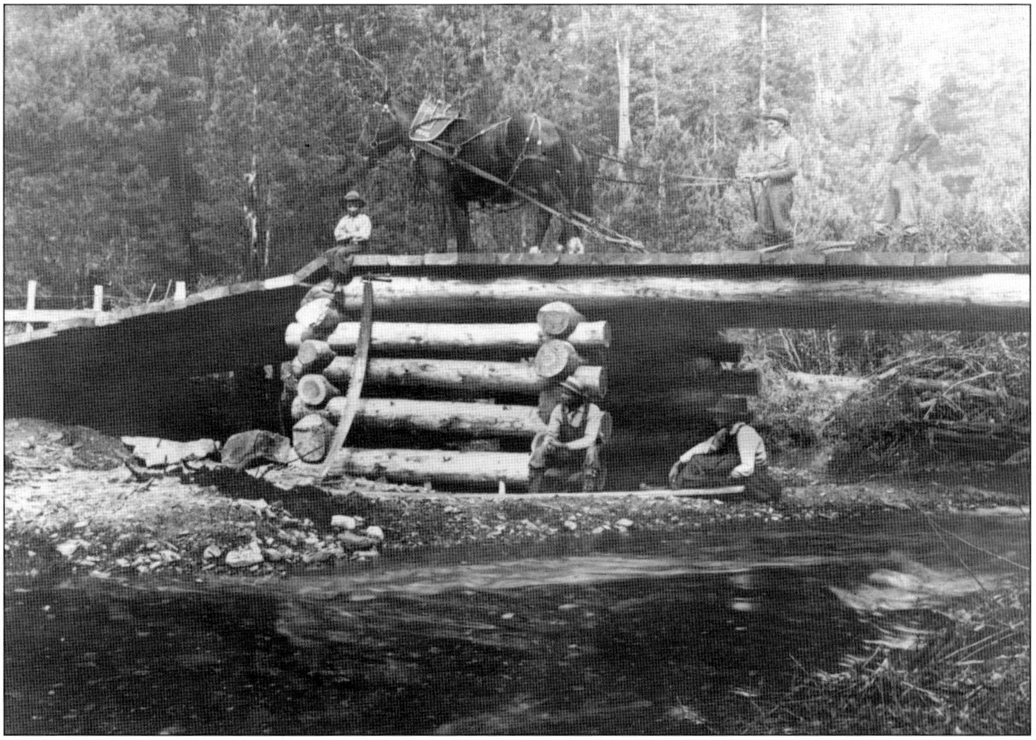

When the proposed road encountered a stream, a bridge had to be built sturdy enough to withstand the spring runoff when the stream filled its banks. Trees had to be cut and sawed into desired lengths and hauled by horses or oxen to the location. Below, in no particular order, Luke McKern, Sid Green, and an unidentified man are shown building a road up Beech Creek.

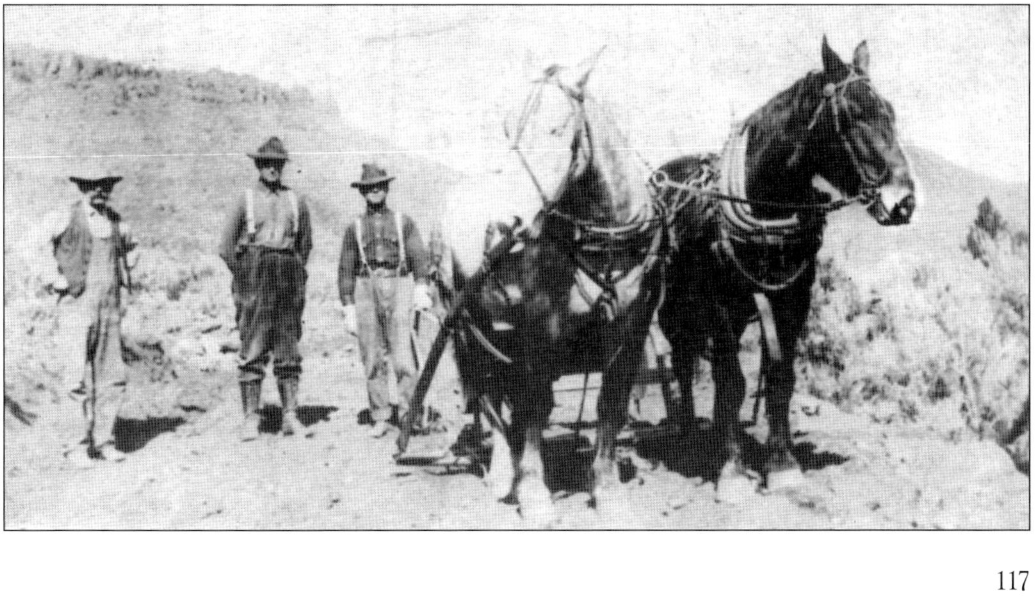

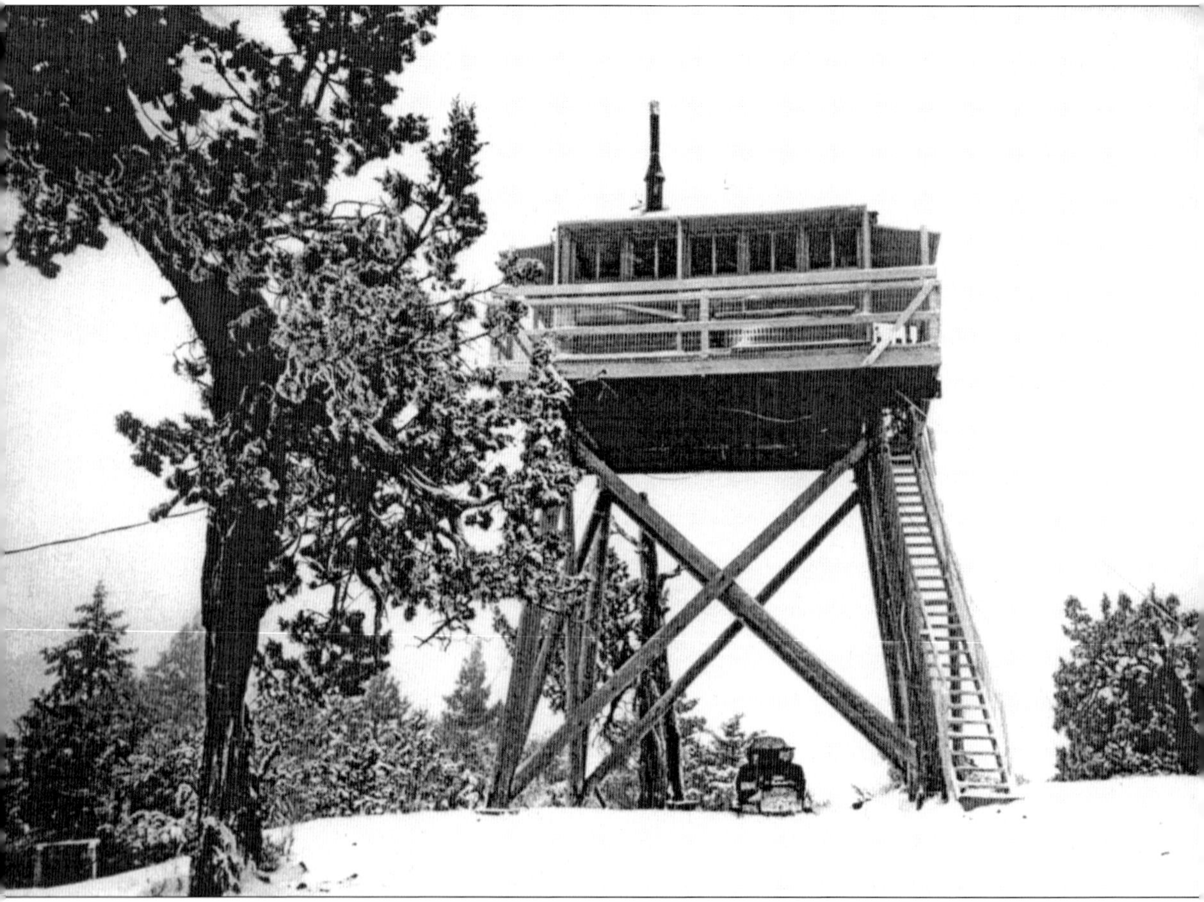

The Forest Service soon established lookout towers at the top of some of the higher peaks in the Malheur National Forest. They were used to watch for fires that may have been started by lightning or by humans. They were normally staffed during the fire season, usually June through September. Once smoke was detected from a small blaze, its coordinates were relayed to the headquarters of the forest. Crews could then be dispatched to put out the fire. Staffing a lookout was a lonely job, but it could be done by either a man or a woman. Food supplies would be periodically brought to the lookout, usually by horse or mule if there was no road. Many lookout towers have been abandoned, as fire detection has been done via airplane or satellite. But many remain throughout forests in the western United States. (Courtesy of USDA Forest Service.)

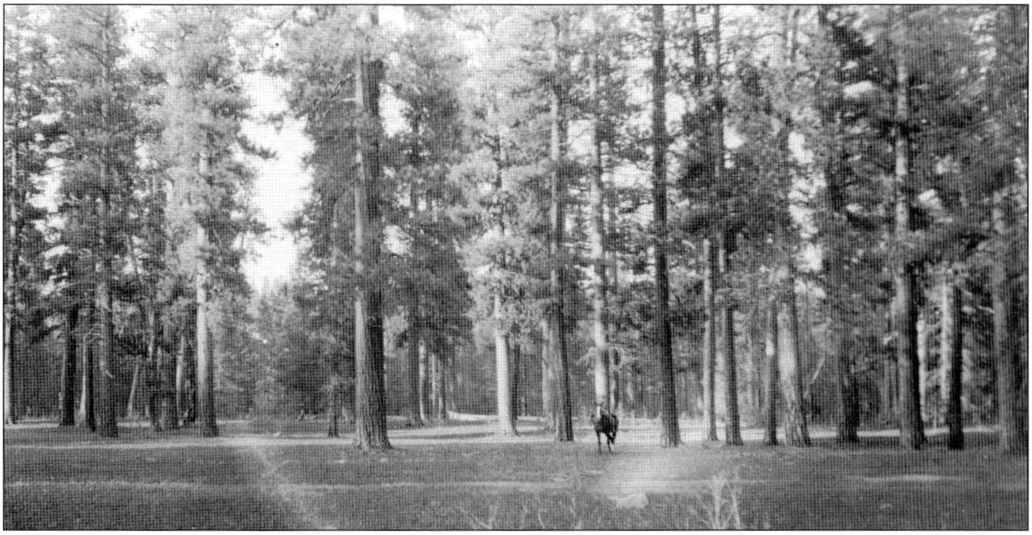

The vast stands of ponderosa pine trees with their thick bark are somewhat resistant to fire. Above is a prime example of what a forest should look like. However, when undergrowth is allowed to get established, fire can easily spread, increasing the threat of larger fires. Some forest researchers contend that the massive effort toward fire suppression over the years has allowed this undergrowth to become a real fire threat. Years of below-normal precipitation exacerbate this condition. A warmer climate could also be a factor. (Below, courtesy of USDA Forest Service, Fire and Aviation Management Program Aid 1572.)

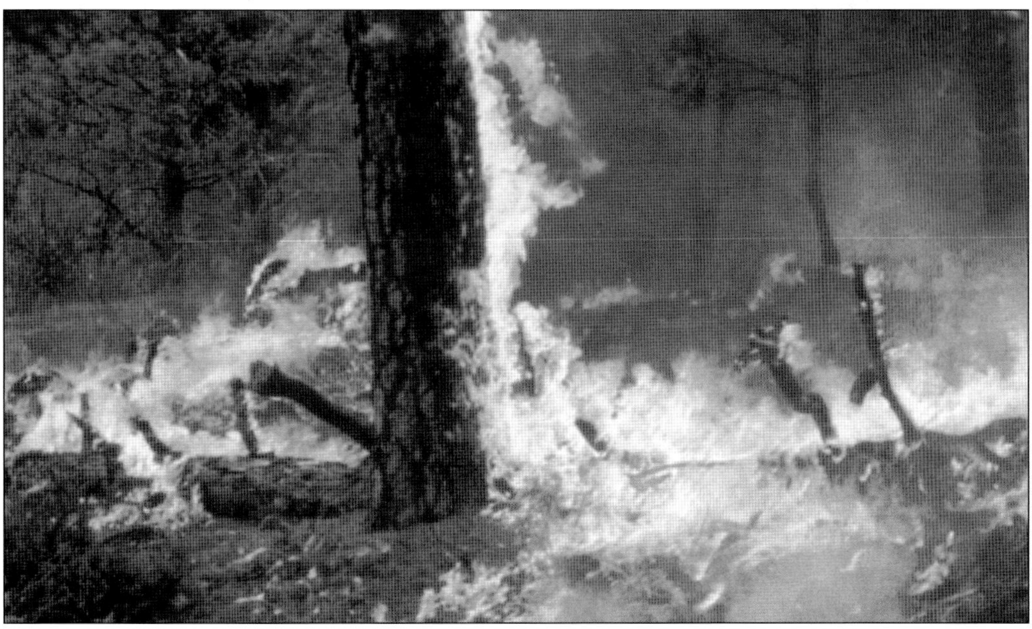

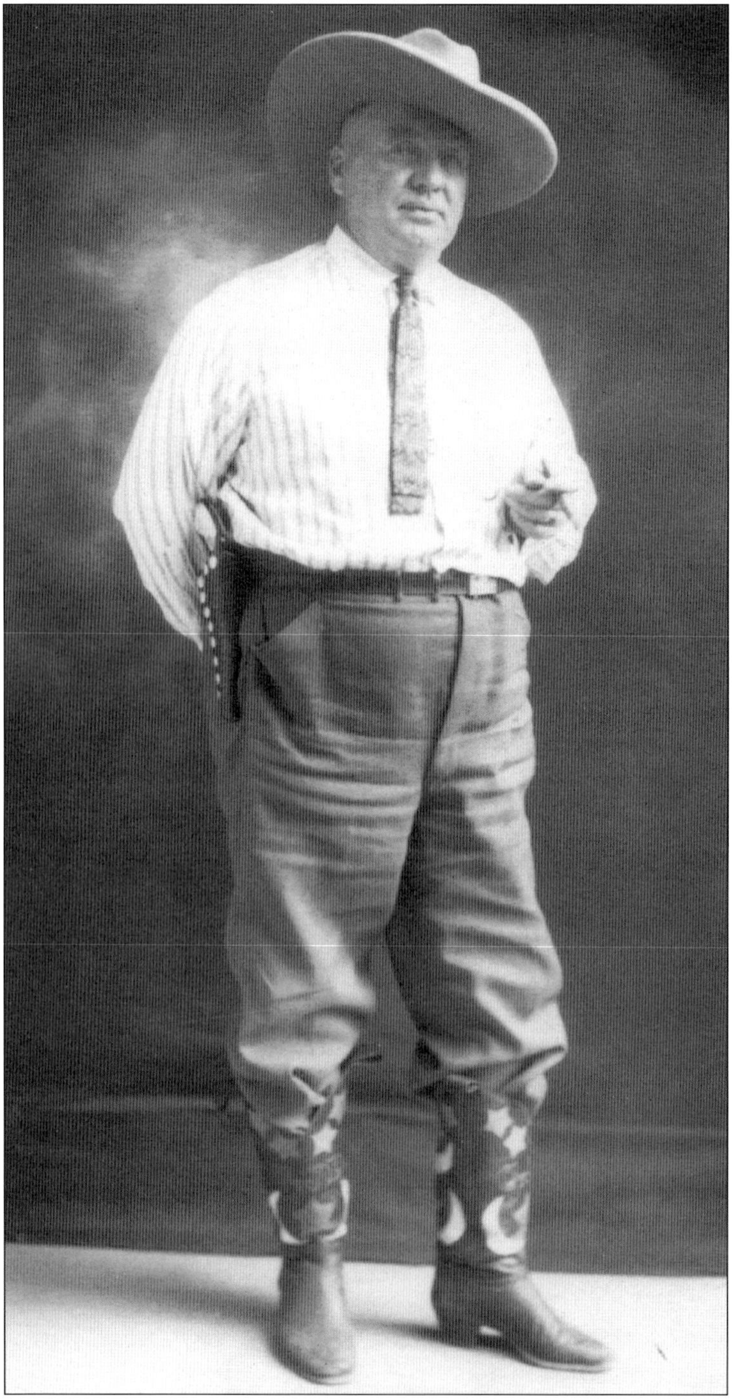

Cy J. Bingham served as the first supervisor of the Malheur National Forest beginning in 1908. His pay was $1,500 per year. He retired from the Forest Service in 1920. After that, he was Grant County's sheriff for 12 years. As the image shows, he was a large man, standing well over six feet tall. He was reported to have a strong personality that combined with the gun he wore on his hip. His career began with the Deschutes National Forest, and he moved to John Day in 1908.

Joaquin Miller has been mentioned earlier in the book. His cabin is in Canyon City next to the Grant County Historical Museum.

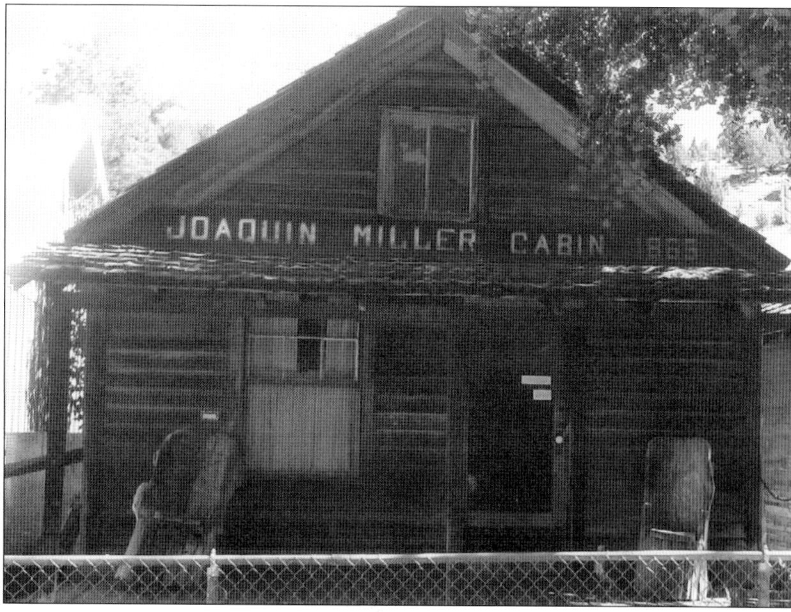

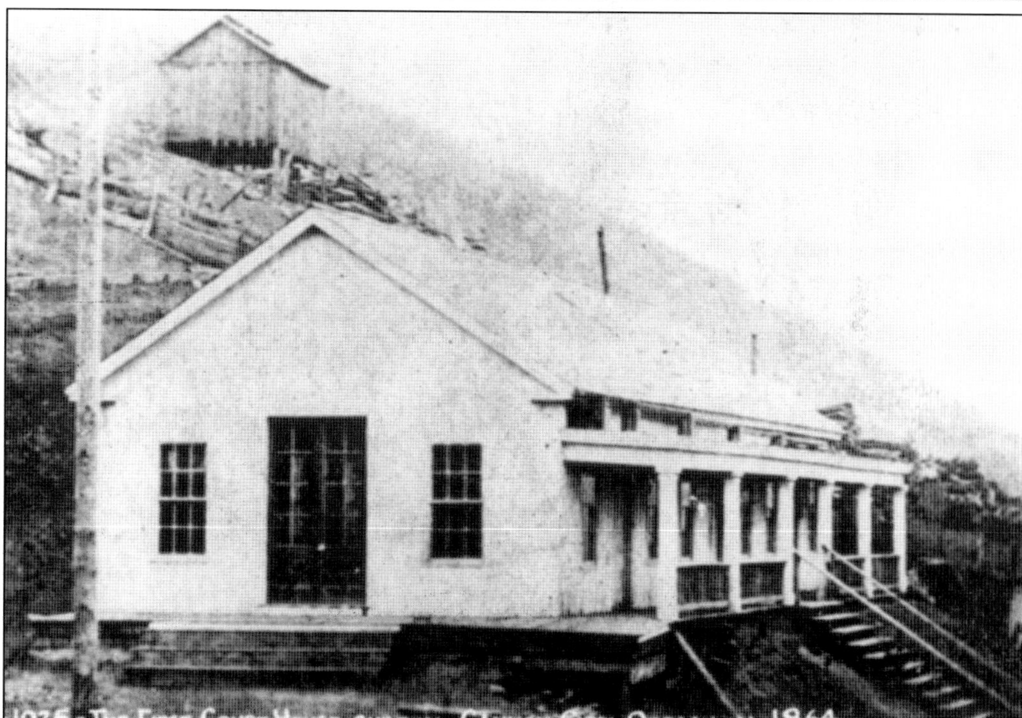

After gold was discovered in the area in 1862, the area grew rapidly as 1,000 miners flocked into the area. As a result, a county government was needed. In 1864, the county seat was established in Canyon City, along Canyon Creek, formerly known as Whiskey Gulch. Due to the miners and Chinese who accompanied them, the city boasted the largest population of any community in Oregon at that time. It remains the county seat today in virtually the same location. The infamous Joaquin Miller was the third person to serve as county judge. The image shows the first county courthouse built in 1864.

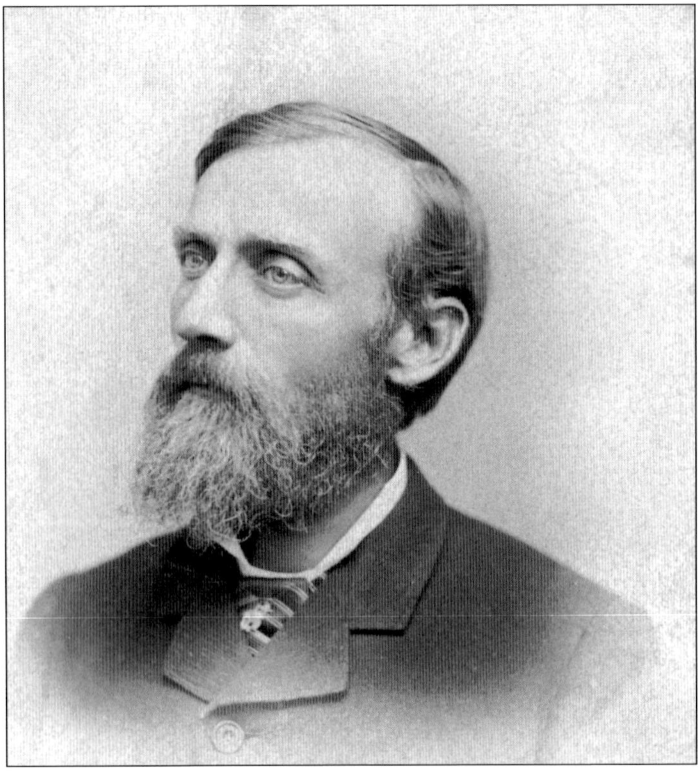

One could say that Grant County was still the Wild, Wild West in the late 1800s. Robert Lockwood (left) was a deputy sheriff in Grant County in 1888. Deputy Lockwood was shot and killed in the line of duty by Pat McGinnis on July 5, 1888. McGinnis was later captured and eventually hanged at the Canyon City Courthouse on April 26, 1889, for killing Lockwood. William P. Gray (below) served as sheriff from 1872 to 1877, for a short period in 1882, and from 1888 to 1889.

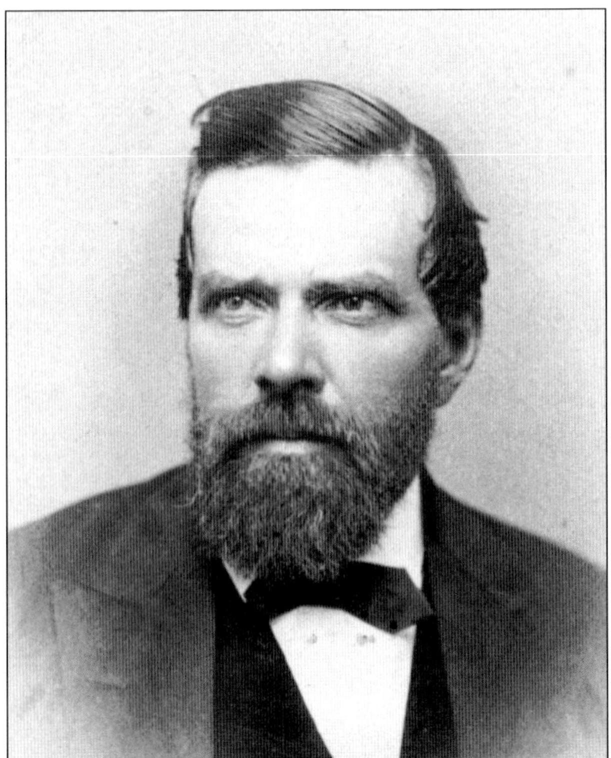

Other sheriffs to have served Grant County over the years prior to 1900 include Newt Livingston from 1896 to 1899. He is shown with his wife. In 1886, he moved from Roseburg to Grant County and settled near Granite Creek. He was recruited by the Populist Party to run for sheriff and was elected. He proved to be a capable and efficient officer and was re-elected.

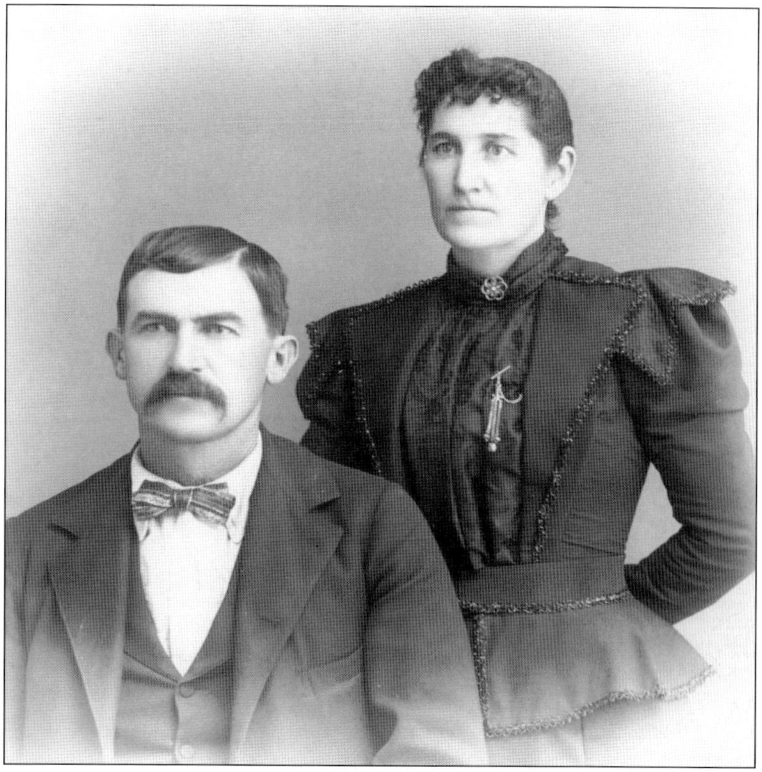

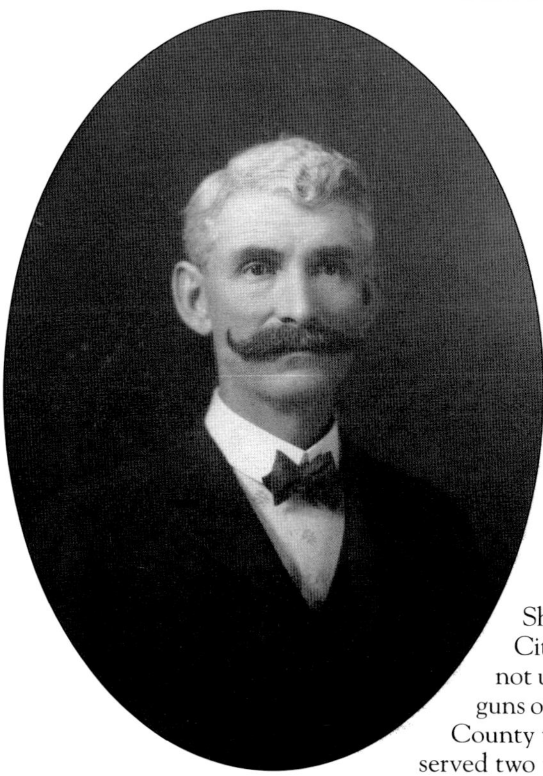

Shortly after gold was discovered in 1862, Canyon City was a town on the western frontier. It was not uncommon to see people walking around with guns on their hips. Things had quieted down in Grant County when Sheriff Ambrose took over in 1904 and served two terms, including 1908.

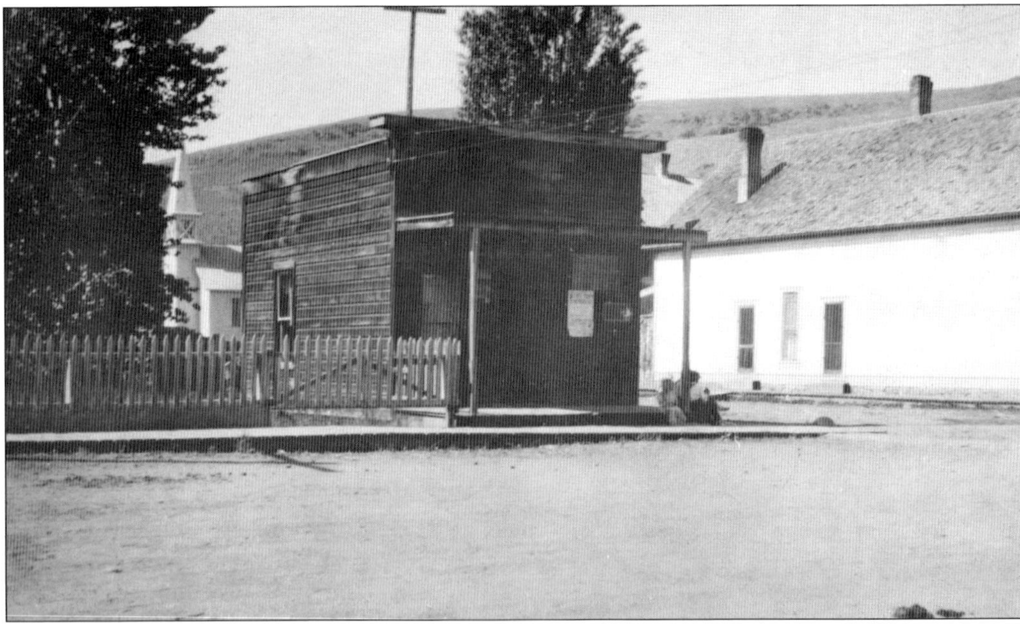

Above is the John Day Post Office around 1900. Charles Brown (below) served as postmaster for Canyon City from at least 1906 to around 1916. He was a colorful character. In the 50 years he lived in Canyon City, he also mined, ran a general store, and operated a filling store. In 1925, while pumping gasoline, someone asked if he would buy an old saddle. Then a week later, someone sold him an old Colt pistol, one of the first in the West. It did not stop there. He kept purchasing other old items. His remark was, "By the end of the month I was spending more money on relics than I was takin' in." The relics, however, were soon to gain some prominence. In 1953, he and Herman Oliver teamed together to spearhead the building of the Grant County Historical Museum, where his relics went.

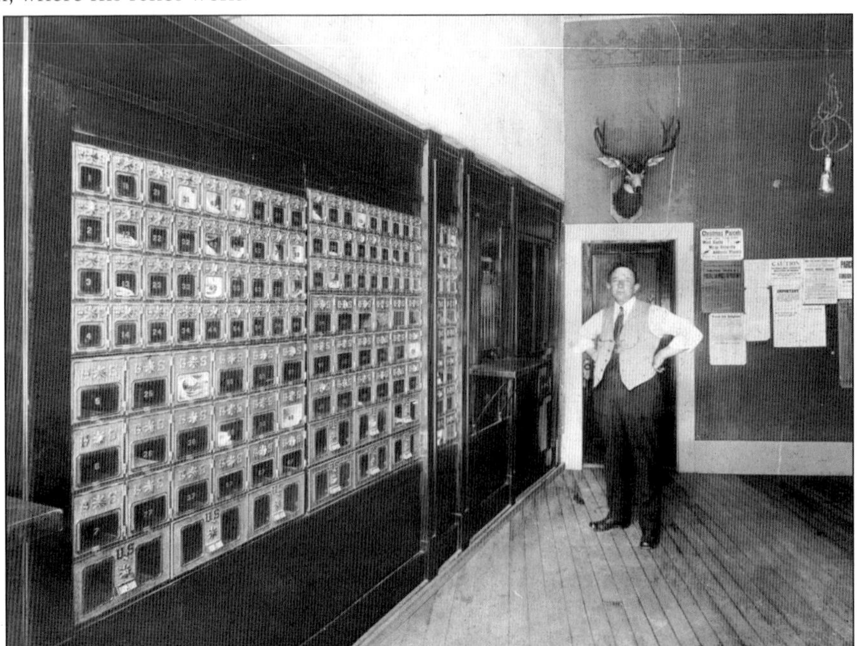

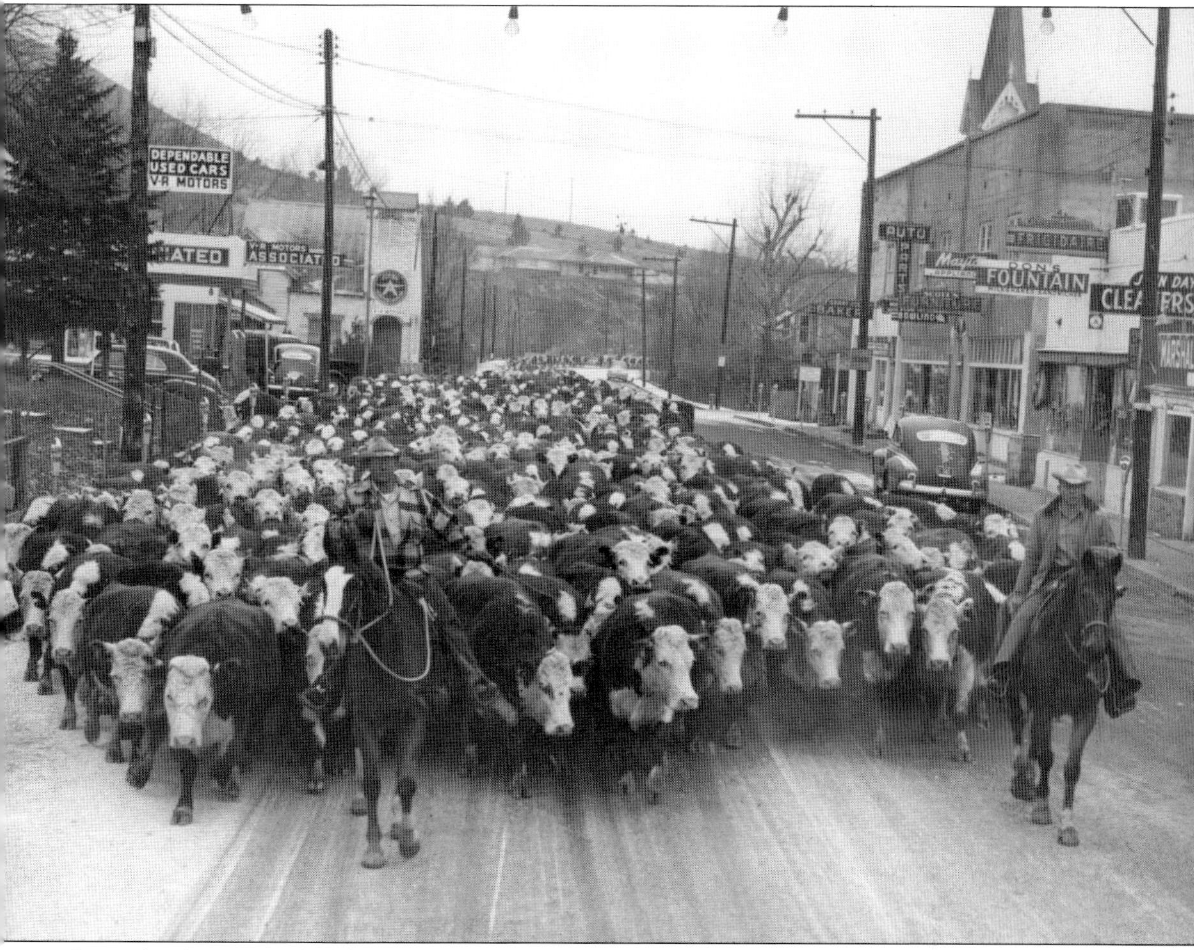

Since the discovery of gold in 1862, there have been many changes in Grant County. This image, similar to the one on the front cover, shows a Herman Oliver herd of cattle moving from its winter quarters to the valley ranch down the Main Street in John Day, an event that is not practiced today. Grant County was not the only town in which cattle were herded down the main street. The author, on a trip to the Grand Tetons in the mid-1970s, encountered a similar scene in Big Piney, Wyoming. Safe inside a restaurant, he observed the cattle lumbering along the sidewalks and down Main Street. Oliver's cowboys seem to have this herd well under control. The cowboy in front with his lasso is ready to rope a wayward steer.

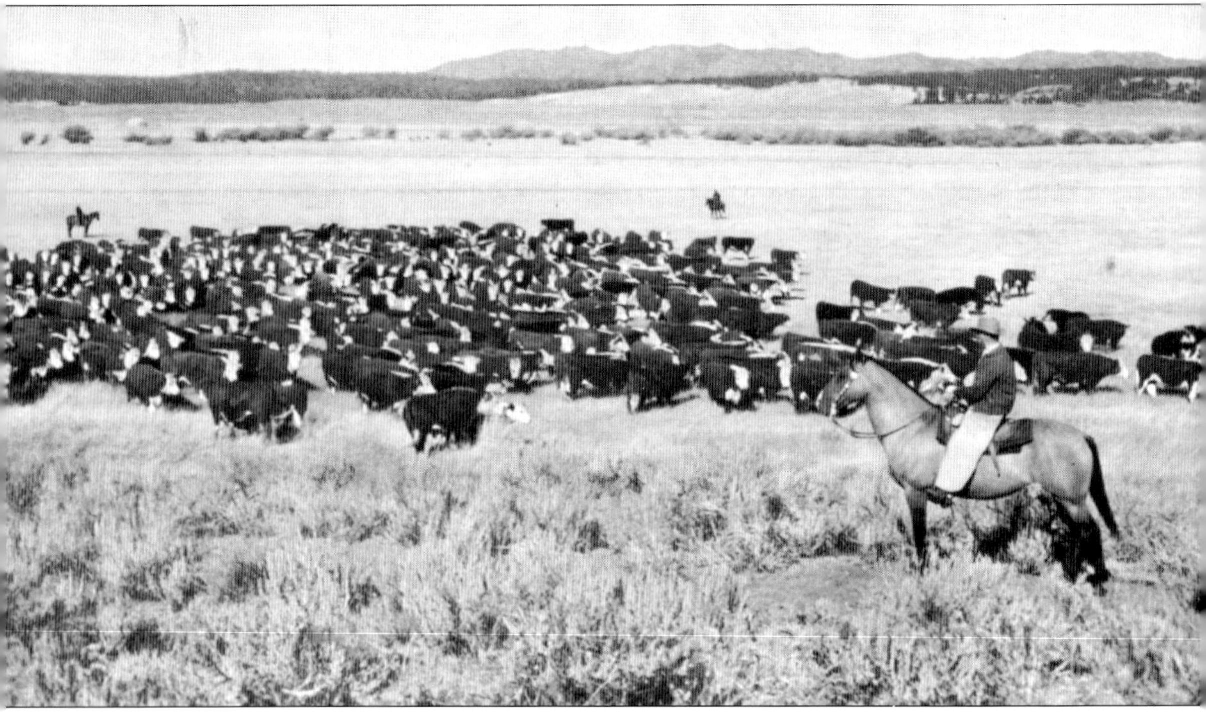

The landscape surrounding the Herman Oliver ranch is typical of the land throughout Grant County. There are lush fields surrounded by magnificent stands of forests, drained by creeks and rivers, all supporting a wide range of activities. The cattle and sheep men, the farmers, and the timber operators all have a stake in the land. The recreationists, hunters, and fishermen all own a part of the county. Herman Oliver would not let dredge mining destroy his land. Nor do the recreationists, hunters, and fishermen want clear cutting to destroy their part of the forests. Where restrictions are imposed, they must be enforced with moderation for the benefit of all. If unrealistic, then mutual ground must be sought. That means working together. Grant County is treasured by those who live here, especially people like Sharon Livingston of Long Creek, who received the 2016 Agriculturist of the Year award. There are others who are working to preserve the land for everyone's use. It is cherished by everyone in this great land of America.

Bibliography

Barlow, Jeffery, and Christine Richardson. *China Doctor of John Day*. Portland, OR: Binford & Mort, 1979.

Grant County Oliver Museum. *The History of Grant County Oregon, 1862–1983*. Dallas: Taylor Publishing Co., 1983.

McArthur, Lewis A. *Oregon Geographic Names and Places*. 5th ed. Oregon Historical Society Press, 1982. Printed in the United States of America.

Oliver, Herman. *Gold and Cattle Country*. Portland, OR: Binfords & Mort Publishers, 1961. Portland, OR.

Phillips, Stanley, Loyce Phillips, and Lorene Allen. *John Day: A Brief History*. John Day, OR: Hutch's Printing Co., 2004.

Smith, Reiba Carter, and Louetta Zumwalt Shaw. *In the Land of Gold, Bunch Grass and Trees*. CA: self-published, 1980s. Long Creek, OR.

Blue Mountain Eagle (John Day, OR), Friday, June 8, 1894.

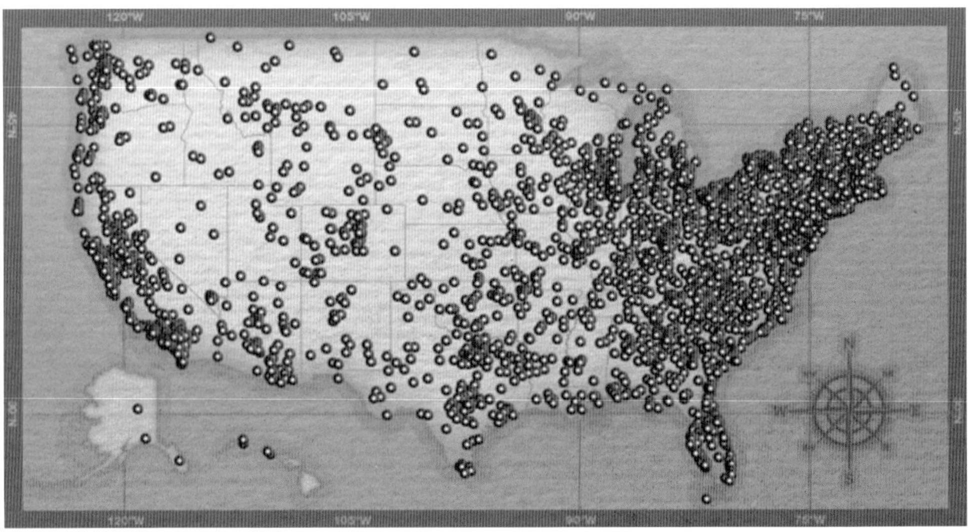